CAUCASUS MTS.

CASPIAN
SEA

MT. ARARAT

LAKE VAN

LAKE URMIA

A S S Y R I A

JERABLUS
(CARCHEMISH)

DUR SHARRUKIN (KHORSABAD)

HARRAN

ARBELA

MEMBIDJ
(HIERAPOLIS)

NINEVEH
CALAH
(NIMRUD)

ASHUR

MARI

PALMYRA
(TADMOR)

EUPHRATES RIVER

TIGRIS RIVER

SIPPAR

B A B Y L O N I A

BABYLON   KISH

BORSIPPA

SUSA

NIPPUR

E
INGDOM
F ISRAEL

ERECH
LARSA

INGDOM
F JUDAH

UR
ERIDU

TIGRIS RIVER

A   R   A   B   I   A   N

D   E   S   E   R   T

PERSIAN

GULF

Miles

0   50   100   200   300

map by palacios

Peoples of the Sea

Books by Immanuel Velikovsky

WORLDS IN COLLISION (1950)

AGES IN CHAOS (1952)

EARTH IN UPHEAVAL (1955)

OEDIPUS AND AKHNATON (1960)

PEOPLES OF THE SEA (1977)

Immanuel Velikovsky

PEOPLES OF THE SEA

THE CONCLUDING VOLUME OF THE *AGES IN CHAOS* SERIES

1977

Doubleday & Company, Inc.

GARDEN CITY, NEW YORK

Library of Congress Cataloging in Publication Data

Velikovsky, Immanuel, 1895–
Ages in chaos.

Bibliographical footnotes.
CONTENTS: v. 1. From the Exodus to King Akhnaton. Peoples of the sea.
Concluding Volume.
1. Jews—History—1200–953 B. C.   2. Bible. O. T.—
History of contemporary events, etc.   3. Tell el-Amarna.
4. Egypt—History—To 332 B. C.   I. Title.
DS121.55.V44   932

ISBN: 0-385-03389-3
Library of Congress Catalog Card Number 52-5224
Copyright © 1977 by Immanuel Velikovsky
All Rights Reserved
Printed in the United States of America
First Edition

ACKNOWLEDGMENTS

In the early stages of my work I incurred a debt to the late Egyptologist Dr. Walter Federn, for information, mostly of a bibliographical nature, given in a spirit of scholarly co-operation. After many years of exchanging views and information, toward the end of his life he became strongly inclined in favor of my reconstructed chronology.

The work was read in proofs by Dr. N. B. Millet, curator of the Egyptian Department of the Royal Ontario Museum in Toronto, who supplied a list of useful suggestions. Dr. Martin Dickson, professor of Oriental studies at Princeton University, with a special interest in Persian studies, and Professor R. J. Schork, at that time chairman of the Department of Classical Studies at Brooklyn College, also read the proofs and offered strong encouragement to this most revolutionary reconstruction of the history of the period covered in this volume; both of them brought additional proofs from their particular fields. Eddie Schorr, Ph.D. candidate in classical archaeology, dedicated much time to reading the galleys, checking many of the sources, and suggesting a number of changes. Dr. Lynn E. Rose, professor of philosophy at the State University of New York at Buffalo, gave very generously of his time to the final version of the proofs before they were returned to the publisher, showing unusual dedication. And the list is still not complete. I express my debt to all of them, but only I assume responsibility for my work in all its details.

Neither I nor those mentioned here put emphasis on incorporating later studies unless they form a break with established views. It appears that most of the new publications follow the main track cut a generation earlier.

This volume, like the entire series entitled *Ages in Chaos*, is dedicated to the memory of my late father, Simon, a pioneer of the Hebrew Renaissance.

CONTENTS

SUPPLEMENT: ASTRONOMY AND CHRONOLOGY

ILLUSTRATIONS

INTRODUCTION

THIS VOLUME, which is part of the *Ages in Chaos* series dealing with the reconstruction of ancient history, can be read independently of the other volumes in that series. The entire period of reconstruction covers a span of twelve centuries, from the end of the Middle Kingdom in Egypt, which I claim was synchronous with the Exodus of the Israelites from Egypt, down to the advent of Alexander the Great of Macedon, and even beyond, namely, to the earlier Ptolemies, Hellenistic rulers of Egypt. The present volume deals with the more than two hundred years at the end of that span.

Ages in Chaos, Volume I, *From the Exodus to King Akhnaton*, published in 1952, carried the reconstruction through the six centuries ending with the kings Jehoshaphat of Jerusalem and Ahab of Samaria and with the el-Amarna period in Egypt, near the end of the Eighteenth Dynasty, which I place in the ninth century. The promise to supply the reader with the rest of the reconstruction in a short space of time was made in good faith—the second and final volume of *Ages in Chaos* was already in page proofs. But the subsequent decision, to extend the second volume into three or even four volumes, by itself delayed the execution of the plan. (The concluding events of the Eighteenth Dynasty became the subject of my *Oedipus and Akhnaton*, published in 1960.)

Peoples of the Sea, as just said, covers the nearly two centuries of Persian domination of Egypt and continues, through the conquest of Egypt by Alexander the Great, down to the time of the earlier Ptolemies. Within this time span I locate both the Twentieth Dynasty (the dynasty of Ramses III) and the Twenty-first Dynasty, which are conventionally placed up to eight centuries earlier; in no other part of the reconstruction has there been such a great rift with the accepted structure for the chronology of events.

With the Eighteenth Dynasty moved down the scale of time by more than five centuries, the first volume of *Ages in Chaos* took away one abutment from orthodox history and erected instead an abutment for the reconstruction. With the removal of the Twentieth and Twenty-first Dynasties to the age of Persian domination over Egypt, anchoring them centuries away from their usual places, the present volume erects a second such abutment. On these two abutments now rests the span of ancient history. Conventional ancient history, shown to be misplaced and distorted at both ends, cannot plead for the salvaging of the mid-part intact.

Intermediate volumes of the *Ages in Chaos* series (one of which, *Ramses II and His Time*, is in printer's proofs even now) deal with that mid-part, the ninth through sixth centuries.

The extension of the originally planned Volume II of *Ages in Chaos* into four volumes, namely *The Dark Age of Greece*, *The Assyrian Conquest*, *Ramses II and His Time*, and *Peoples of the Sea*, could explain why no book by me appeared between 1961 and 1977. In apology I could draw attention to the new version of the *Cambridge Ancient History*, which took many years to produce, occupied a great number of scholars, each writing a separate chapter, an undertaking well funded and supplied with editors and secretariat, whereas I worked alone and had to fund my own work in research and writing; and the armada of scholars rewriting the *Cambridge Ancient History* did not innovate and radically change the history whereas it fell to my task to do exactly this. Such a comparison might vindicate me for my tardiness. But if this is part of the excuse, the truth lies also in the fact that the Space Age inaugurated in October 1957 with the first Sputnik and the years that followed with Mariner and Apollo flights deflected my interest toward astronomical problems. In cosmology the views began to gain ascendancy that the members of the solar system are not on primeval paths, always peacefully repeated since the beginning of time; or that earth's axis has changed its position or the day its length; in celestial mechanics the view became unavoidable that, besides gravitation and inertia, electromagnetic fields and forces, too, play a calculable role. These changes in the understanding of natural phenomena gave to my concepts, derided in previous decades, great support and to me some satisfaction. It is not hard to understand that the discovery of Venus' near incandescent state, its massive cloud envelope and its atmosphere creating 90 atmospheric pressures near the ground, or the travels to the moon and excursions on it, with the discoveries of strong remanent magnetism in its rocks, strong radioactivity in certain areas, like the Aristarchus crater, a steep thermal gradient under the surface, traces of hydrocarbons, and rich enclosures of neon and argon in the rocks, or the richness in radioactive elements of Martian and lunar soils—all phenomena claimed in my works and memoranda—alienated me for long stretches of time from the pharaohs and Assyrian and Persian kings.

Possibly also there were some psychological motives in my long procrastination. Should not more and more archaeologists have the opportunity of reading the first volume of *Ages in Chaos* before the sequel appeared? Should not those who refused this mental effort enmesh themselves in more and more contradictions and meet more and more impasses and print more and more volumes they would need to retract? Or, possibly, after some bitter experiences, I enjoyed being the only possessor of the knowledge—in later years shared with just a few of my close associates—of how history took its way?

If this self-accusation is not borne out, then my interest in the problem of the reactions of the human community to the traumatic experiences in the past certainly kept me vigilant during the time when my readers claimed I had not fulfilled my promise to issue the second volume of *Ages in Chaos*.

But one thing I certainly wished to happen before the balance of *Ages in Chaos* was published—confirmation from radiocarbon research. The problem of Carbon 14 and its applicability to the chronology of ancient history is most involved because of the fact that, when cosmic cataclysmic events took place, the imbalancing of the C_{14}–C_{12} ratio in hydrosphere and biosphere must have taken place.

I have discussed the problem elsewhere.[1] But I can disclose here that for twelve years after the publication of Libby's *Radiocarbon Dating,* which appeared in the same year as *Ages in Chaos,* Volume I (1952), I tried vainly in every way possible to have the New Kingdom of Egypt, especially the Eighteenth Dynasty, submitted to carbon testing on suitable specimens.[2] Not until 1963 did I succeed in having the Cairo Museum release three small pieces of wood from the funerary equipment of Tutankhamen for testing in the laboratory of the Museum of the University of Pennsylvania. Whereas in accepted chronology the young king died in −1350,[3] and in my reconstruction about −835, the carbon analysis pointed to −1030 (or, by Libby's, −1120); next (on March 2, 1964) I wrote to Dr. Elizabeth K. Ralph of the University Museum in Philadelphia inquiring whether the carbon age of the wood reflects the time formation of the rings and asserting that, if this is the case, the larger of the three pieces, all tested together (30 grams are needed for one test), being of the very long-lived cedar of Lebanon, could cause the divergence and if only short-lived material like reed, seed, or papyrus was used the result would point to ca. −840. Dr. Ralph confirmed that radiocarbon age is a reflection of the time the rings were formed, not when the tree was felled.

But it took seven more years. In the spring of 1971 the British Museum Laboratory processed reed and seed from the tomb of Tutankhamen—namely, the reed of a mat and kernels of a palm. The latter showed the age of −899 and the former of −846. I learned these figures from a letter by Dr. Edwards, curator of Egyptology in the British Museum, to Dr. Michael of the University of Pennsylvania Museum, dated April 6, 1971.[4] The British Museum did not publish the results it obtained, as originally assured, presumably on

[1] Immanuel Velikovsky, "The Pitfalls of Radiocarbon Dating," *Pensée,* IVR IV, Spring–Summer, 1973, pp. 12ff.

[2] See the collection of letters called "ASH," *Pensée,* IVR VI, Winter, 1973–1974, pp. 5ff.

[3] According to W. Christopher Hayes of the Metropolitan Museum of Art.

[4] A copy of the letter was given by Dr. Edwards to Mr. Bruce A. Mainwaring of Collegetown, Pennsylvania, on the occasion of his visit to London with the purpose of influencing the British Museum to make tests to check on my work of reconstruction.

the ground of a later suspicion that, in view of such disagreement with accepted dates, the seeds and reeds must have been contaminated, though the funerary cave of Tutankhamen had remained sealed since soon after his entombment until it was discovered by Howard Carter in 1922 and its objects had been stored since then in the Cairo Museum; nor had water percolated into the tomb.

It would have been natural, in view of such results, predicted by me long in advance, to repeat the test on some other objects from Tutankhamen's funerary equipment; but if such tests were made, their results have not been announced.

It would have been important to compare the carbon age of ivory from the tomb of Tutankhamen with the age of ivory from the fort of Shalmaneser III near Nimrud. If cataclysmic events of the eighth century and of the beginning of the seventh could affect the results of carbon datings, the two hoards of ivory, considered by me nearly (within two or three decades) contemporary, must yield similar results. It will not surprise me if in the bottom of the huge hoard of objects of art in ivory in the military fort of Shalmaneser one or more originals of the el-Amarna letters could be found.

Not that the work of reconstruction is in need of confirmation from the carbon method—I feel it is strong enough to serve as a control of the efficiency of the method and not vice versa; but for many occupied in the domains of history and archaeology such corroboration, repeated a number of times, may arouse the desire to investigate my reconstruction, first of all, by reading *Ages in Chaos;* and possibly this will provide the impetus for the release of many carbon datings that have never appeared in print because these results diverged by half a millennium or more from accepted dates.

As time goes on, other methods of age determination (such as thermoluminescence of inorganic material—tiles, glass, pottery) may bear witness in the contest of a reconstructed history with the enshrined version of history. Thus the tiles from the palace of Ramses III (discussed in Chapter I) could provide excellent material for the thermoluminescence testing of their age.

The readers of this volume will find a number of surprises. The "Peoples of the Sea" who fought in Egypt were not twelfth-century wanderers but fourth-century mercenaries, mostly from Asia Minor and Greece, of the days of Plato. Alexander the Great visited the sacrarium of the oracle of Ammon in the Libyan desert, and historians say that we will never know what transpired there, since Alexander never told. But the reader of this volume will indeed know what transpired, since the Egyptian record of what happened, written by the priest of the oracle, is presented in this volume. And another priest-prince, Si-Amon, who has usually been put in the tenth century, and has sometimes been mentioned as a possible father-in-law of King Solomon, turns out to have lived under Ptolemy II in the third century.

Peoples of the Sea

Part I

Chapter I

TWELFTH OR FOURTH CENTURY?

The Scheme of Things

THE SCHEME OF THINGS as offered in every book on ancient history presents the beginning of the twelfth century before the current era as a time of great convulsions in the life of nations around the eastern Mediterranean, the region usually known as the Ancient East. This scheme has it that out of the gloom of the north hordes of peoples swept over the lands of ancient civilization and in each of them left in ruins everything that had been rich and glorious; order was changed to chaos, abundance turned to want, and destitute populations, leaving behind them the glory of their own past, followed the crest of migration and transgressed frontiers of other nations. The Mycenaean culture, which was centered around Mycenae in Greece and which embraced the Aegean isles, came to an end; the Trojan War is regarded by many scholars as one of the terminal effects of the vast dislocation caused by the migratory waves that uprooted populations of whole lands.

This scheme also has it that soon after the Trojan War, in a matter of only a few years, armed hordes, sufficiently organized to be called armies, reached Egypt, which was ruled at that time by Ramses III.

Ramses III is generally regarded as the last great pharaoh of the imperial age in Egypt. The three great dynasties of the New Kingdom, the Eighteenth, the Nineteenth, and the Twentieth, lived through apogees and declines; and as Thutmose III was the greatest conqueror on the throne of the Eighteenth Dynasty and Amenhotep III its most opulent occupant, and Seti I and Ramses II were

the great warriors of the Nineteenth Dynasty, so Ramses III, and
he alone, was the heroic king of the Twentieth Dynasty. With the
end of that dynasty comes the age that is termed Late Period or
Late Kingdom, to differentiate it from the New Kingdom. In the
accepted scheme, the Late Kingdom spans the time between the
end of the Twentieth Dynasty in the final years of the twelfth century and the extinction of the last dynasty of native kings, the
Thirtieth, ten years before the conquest of Egypt by Alexander of
Macedon.

According to the reckoning of modern historians, Ramses III
started to reign in the year −1200 before the present era, or only a
short time later.[1] The major event of his reign was the successful
opposition to the armies coming from the north. In their sweep of
conquest, the northern hordes came to the very gates of Egypt, the
greatest and most glorious of kingdoms. In all ages conquerors have
made Egypt their goal—Esarhaddon and Assurbanipal the Assyrians, Cambyses the Persian, Alexander the Macedonian, Pompey
the Roman, Omar the Arab, Selim the Turk, and Napoleon; and
some unidentified leader or group of leaders, before any of these,
led armed troops to drink water from the Nile. But Ramses III rose
to the occasion. He battled the invaders on land and sea and turned
back the tide that threatened to envelop Egypt.

This war is known as the war against the Peoples of the Sea, or
the Peoples of the Isles, by which names Ramses III referred to
them.[2] Historical texts and extensive illustrations cut in stone, which
illuminate this war and the pharaoh's ultimate victory, are preserved
in Egypt. But of the sweep of the invading troops across the lands
of the Near East before their arrival at the frontier of Egypt nothing
is known from any historical source, literary or archaeological. It is
only by inference that the conclusion is made: Mycenaean Greece,
the Hittite Empire, and many lesser kingdoms were swept out of

[1] Ed. Meyer places the beginning of Ramses III's reign in −1200; Alan
H. Gardiner (*Egypt of the Pharaohs,* 1961) in −1182; Rowton (*Journal of
Egyptian Archaeology,* Vol. XXXIV) in −1170.

[2] When Ramses III speaks of "Peoples of the Sea" he specifies the Tjeker, the
Shekelesh, the Teresh, the Weshesh, and the Sherden (or Sardan); he specifies
the Denien as "Peoples of the Isles."

existence by the wandering and conquering Peoples of the Sea. This inference is made on the basis of the fact that all these kingdoms and empires were found to have been terminated in about −1200. For the next four or five centuries there is no record and no relic of their existence and scarcely any vestige of the surviving population in these lands.

What can Greece and the isles, Crete included, show for the period between −1200 and −750 or even −700? After the end of the Mycenaean Age and the fall of Troy darkness envelops the history of these places and the first rays of light penetrate into the area with the beginning of the Greek, or Ionic, Age about −700. Suddenly, as if out of nothing, comes the Homeric poetry, and the intimate familiarity displayed by the poet with the smallest details of the life of the Mycenaean Age, five to ten centuries earlier, is a persistent cause for wonder among scholars, a theme for incessant debate.

The centuries from −1200 to −750 are called Dark Ages. They were not dark in the sense in which this term is applied to the period of European history between the end of the Roman Empire in +475 and the end of the Crusaders' wars in the East: these centuries from the end of the fifth to the middle of the thirteenth of the current era represent a regression in learning, in commerce, in administration and law, when compared with the time of the Roman Empire, but they abound in historical relics and literary testimonies; whereas the Dark Ages between −1200 and −750 before the present era are dark because no document survived from that time in Greece, in Crete, in the Aegean world, or in Asia Minor.

This scheme of things is never questioned; however, its acceptance raises a great many difficult problems either not resolved or resolved at the cost of creating additional difficult problems. With a number of them we shall deal in this work.

It is assumed by the scholars who labor on the problem that the Peoples of the Sea came from the Aegean area, and since the scene is of the beginning of the twelfth century they must have been Mycenaean Greeks and their allies, dislocated from their native places. Ramses III enumerates the single tribes of which the Peoples of the Sea were composed, and efforts have been made to identify them with various Achaean tribes of early times.

Troy's fall was followed by migrations echoed in the wandering of Odysseus of the Achaean camp and of Aeneas from among the Trojan survivors. Although Odysseus visited an Egypt unruffled by war, it is conjectured that some great migratory wave of Achaeans carried them by land and sea to the kingdom on the Nile.

Besides the Peoples of the Sea, the other important people who took part in the war in Egypt were richly clad warriors named Pereset. They are referred to by this name and they are recognizable by their attire. Apparently they were the leaders of the expedition, the Peoples of the Sea being the mercenaries.

It is assumed that the Philistines, not mentioned as participants in the siege of Troy, took part in the subsequent migrations and wars, and grounds for such an assumption are found in the phonetic similarity of the names Philistines and Pereset; their wars with Egypt under Ramses III are placed in the time of their arrival on the Palestinian shore, and this arrival, only shortly before the Israelites' conquest of the hilly part of the country, is thought to refer to the very same events. This view required reducing the time of the Israelites' entrance into Canaan to sometime after −1200, a view not without supporters; in that scheme the time of the Judges is reduced to a little over one hundred years, instead of the traditional four hundred.

To discover the true relationship between the Mycenaean, the biblical, and the Egyptian sequences of events, the historical material left by Ramses III needs to be re-examined. We shall deal first with his palace at Tell el-Yahudiya, close to the apex of the Delta in the north, and then with his mortuary temple at Medinet Habu across the Nile from Luxor and Karnak.

Greek Letters on Tiles of Ramses III

Tell el-Yahudiya, or "The Mound of the Jew," is an Arab village east of the Delta, twenty miles northeast of Cairo on the road to

Ismailia. Over ninety years ago the Swiss Egyptologist Edouard Naville excavated there the ruins of a palace of Ramses III. Tiles, colored and glazed, once adorned its walls. They were found in great numbers on the site by traveling scholars and also by Emil Brugsch in the service of the Egyptian Department of Antiquities, before Naville, assisted by F. L. Griffith, came to dig there. The tiles have rich designs, mostly of flowers, and some bear the hieroglyphic name of Ramses III. On the reverse side of these tiles are found incised signs: these are apparently the initials of the craftsmen who produced them, inscribed before the tiles were fired.

There was no doubt that the signs on many tiles in the palace of Ramses III at Tell el-Yahudiya were Greek letters. "The most noticeable feature is that several of the rosettes have Greek letters at the back, evidently stamped on during the process of making," wrote T. H. Lewis, orientalist and art expert, to whose judgment the tiles were submitted.[1]

But how could Greek letters have been used in the days of Ramses III, early in the twelfth century before this era? The Greek alphabet was derived from the Phoenician or Hebrew much later; no traces of it have been found in Greece, on the islands, or in Asia Minor before −750. The problem of the Greek letters on the tiles of Ramses III cannot be solved even by assuming that the Greek alphabet derived from the Phoenician originated not in the seventh, eighth, or ninth century but a number of centuries earlier. What really matters is the fact that the Greek letters on the Egyptian tiles do not look like the early Greek letters of the seventh century but like the classical letters of the age of Plato.

Judging by these letters, the tiles must have been made in one of the later centuries before the present era. The peculiar form of the *alpha* was introduced only then;[2] and the forms of some other letters also indicate that they are of a late century. Thus *sigma* was designed C and not Σ. Following these obvious facts, scholars at first felt sure that the tiles had been made in the last century of the

---

[1] T. H. Lewis, "Tel-el-Yahoudeh," *Transactions of the Society of Biblical Archaeology*, VII, 1881 (1882), 182.

[2] Ibid., p. 189.

Late Kingdom (the fourth century before the Christian Era), possibly even during the period of Greek rule there after Alexander the Great, under the Ptolemies.

"The Greek letters, and especially *alpha,* found on the fragments and disks leave no room for doubt [*ne laissent aucun doute*] that the work was executed during the last centuries of the Egyptian Empire and probably in the time of the Ptolemies; but the matter becomes more difficult if we ask who the author of this work was."[3] So wrote Emil Brugsch.

Then who *was* the author of this work? Here was an intrinsic incongruity: judging by the titles and designs on their faces, the tiles were manufactured in the days of Ramses III; but judging by the Greek letters on their backs, in the fourth century at the earliest.

"There is a curious fact about the disks which have been found in such a large number; some of them are inscribed on the back with Greek letters, while others bear Egyptian signs. The Greek letters show that strangers were at some time employed in the work. . . . It is not likely that later kings, such as the Saites or the Ptolemies, would have taken the trouble to build for their predecessor, Ramses III, such a beautiful chamber, the walls of which were not only ornamented with representations of plants or animals, but also recorded the feats of war of Ramses III." So wrote Edouard Naville.[4]

The dilemma was very clear but it had no answer: the Greek letters could not have been written at the time of Ramses III early in the twelfth century; they could have originated only in the last decades of the Egyptian Kingdom or during the following age of the Ptolemies. But the tiles must have been manufactured by laborers of Ramses III, and the royal name of the pharaoh adorns the front of the tiles. Would it be possible to separate the tiles and to ascribe part of them to Ramses III and another part to a later epoch?

"The question involves a great difficulty. The potter's marks include, besides less definite cyphers, several hieroglyphics and the

---

[3] E. Brugsch, "On et Onion," *Recueil de travaux relatifs à la philologie et à l'archéologie égyptiennes et assyriennes,* VIII (1886), 5.

[4] E. Naville, *The Mound of the Jew and the City of Onias,* Egyptian Exploration Fund, 1887 (1890), pp. 6–7.

following, which may be interpreted as [capital] Greek letters, A E I Λ M O C T X. . . . I have found T endorsed on a captive's head, and on one of a similar series a label is attached to the girdle, bearing the name of Ramses III. . . . I do not see how the classes can be kept distinct as to date. *The hieroglyphic and figure tiles relate to Ramses III, but the figure tiles bear Greek letters.*"[5] Thus wrote F. L. Griffith, Naville's collaborator in the expedition.

Signs similar to those of Tell el-Yahudiya were found in molds at Qantir, one of the royal residences of the Ramessides in the Delta. These molds could have been, in the estimation of the archaeologists, fifty to one hundred years older than the tiles from the palace of Ramses III at Tell el-Yahudiya. The idea of a Ptolemaic restoration must be dropped. "The question of the origin of the faience disks of Tell-el-Yahudiyeh [Tell el-Yahudiya] is now solved. . . . They undoubtedly belong to the epoch of Ramses III without even any sign of Ptolemaic restorations." So wrote Mahmud Hamza, an Arab Egyptologist.[6] But the vigor of the statement did not change the form of the Greek letters, which are characteristic of the fourth century before the present era.

Two explanations of why late Greek letters should have been cut on the backs of twelfth-century tiles during the process of manufacturing have been proposed.

"A subject of much difficulty in the earlier accounts of the objects was the marking of 'Greek letters' on the backs of many of the tiles," Sir Flinders Petrie wrote.[7] According to an explanation offered by him, Greek letters had a pre-existence in Egypt.[8] This presupposes that the Egyptians, who used hieroglyphics, also had an alphabetic system which they used only on rare occasions to cut on jars or tiles and bricks. This script presumably was known in Egypt for a thou-

[5] F. L. Griffith, "The Antiquities of Tell-el-Yahudiyeh," in Naville, *The Mound of the Jew*, p. 41. Italics are mine.

[6] Mahmud Hamza, "Excavations of the Department of Antiquities at Qantir, 1928," *Annales du Service des Antiquités de l'Egypte*, XXX (Cairo, 1930), p. 58.

[7] W. M. Flinders Petrie, *A History of Egypt from the XIXth to the XXXth Dynasties* (1905), p. 160. Cf. G. A. Wainwright in F. Petrie, ed., *Ancient Egypt* (1917), p. iii.

[8] Petrie, *The Formation of the Alphabet* (London, 1912).

sand years or thousands of years; it was never used to write down an Egyptian text. Later on the Phoenicians and the Greeks received this script from the Egyptians.

This theory has long been forgotten. Nothing that is known from archaeological and epigraphic study supported it; everything was against it. The development of the Hebrew-Phoenician script, its transplantation to Greece, the further development of the script down to the formation of the Latin characters not much different from the types we use—all have been explored to such an extent that there can be no shadow of truth to Petrie's idea.

An escape from the difficult situation would be found, it seemed, if the genuineness of the letters as Greek letters could be challenged. After a succession of famous scholars had, for fifty years, read the letters on the tiles as Greek, an idea was born, and an attempt was made to interpret them as hieratic signs.[9] Hieratic writing was used by the priests as a simplified, flowing penmanship, the hieroglyphs being trimmed of their ornamental designs and adornments. Out of about ten thousand signs in hieratic paleography,[10] which comprises the most divergent and manifold forms used in a variety of handwritings of generations of scribes, a few might perchance resemble Greek letters. Despite the turning of ten thousand signs in different directions to facilitate a comparison, they still do not look like Greek letters.

$$\mathsf{A \; E \; I \; \Lambda \; M \; O \; C \; T \; X}$$

To illustrate this, I present here Mahmud Hamza's "equivalents." *Alpha*, turned with its base up, was interpreted as a new hieroglyphic sign in the form of a lotus, though it has never before been found on a papyrus or on stone and, of course, is not included in

---

[9] M. Hamza, *Annales du Service des Antiquités de l'Egypte*, XXX (Cairo, 1930), p. 58.

[10] G. Moller's *Hieratische Paläographie* (2nd ed.; 1927–36) contains 2145 hieroglyphic signs and about 10,000 corresponding hieratic forms.

the complete catalogue of hieratic signs. One has also to consider that on the backs of the tiles are only so many different letters and signs, and in this assemblage nearly all of them are well-shaped Greek letters. How does it happen that all the multitudinous hieratic signs were left out and only those seeming to resemble Greek letters were profusely used?

Greek letters, found on objects in Egypt ascribed to a time some four or five hundred years before Homer and belonging presumably to the age either preceding or contemporaneous with the half-legendary time of the siege of Troy, did not cease to evoke consternation. Did Achilles and Odysseus use the Greek alphabet as we know it, and the working-class people too? Why have no Greek inscriptions in the script derived from the Phoenician been found in Greece or Asia Minor of the thirteenth and twelfth centuries? And, most important of all, how could Greek laborers in Egypt in the twelfth century before the present era write letters of an eight- or nine-hundred-years-later design?

The problem of the classical Greek letters on the tiles of Ramses III of the twelfth century, and of older Greek letters dating from a century earlier, has never been solved, and is handled very much as though it were a parapsychological phenomenon. "Light will be thrown on the question someday," one of the quoted scholars wrote resignedly when he realized the scope of the problem and became aware of the impasse.[11] But for three generations now scholars have been turning away from the problem with no promise of a solution.

We have dealt mostly with the reverse side of the tiles. We turn them face up and contemplate their relief design on a blue field with a glaze that delicately and uniformly covers the relief and the field.

Naville says, "This work strikingly reminds us of Persian art, both modern and antique. In Persia it seems to have been made on a larger scale than in Egypt."[12] This observation adds a "Persian prob-

---

[11] Griffith in Naville, The Mound of the Jew, p. 41.
[12] Naville, The Mound of the Jew, p. 6. His authority is T. H. Lewis, Transactions of the Society of Biblical Archaeology, VII, 1881 (1882), 188. Lewis

lem" to the "Greek problem" if the tiles were manufactured more
than six hundred years before Cambyses subjugated Egypt. The
Greeks first came to Egypt and settled there in the days of Psammetich, in the seventh century, according to Herodotus, who himself visited Egypt in the fifth century. The Persians reached Egypt
in the later part of the sixth century and stayed there with short
interruptions until −332, when they were expelled by Alexander.

If, digging in the countryside, you find in the ground several
pieces of ancient armor with heraldic emblems of an early king
who died eight centuries earlier, but on the inside of the armor
you discover a clear trade mark of a Sheffield manufacturing firm of
Victorian days, and if you are certain of not being the victim of a
practical joker, and the best experts assure you that the armor was
wrought for Richard the Lionhearted, and other experts, equally
good in their field, assure you that the trade mark is genuine and
the Sheffield firm that used it was not in existence before the days
of the Hanoverian Dynasty in Great Britain, then you, too, would
say like Griffith, who subsequently became one of the great names in
Egyptology, the words quoted on an earlier page: "The question involves a great difficulty." However, the chances are that you
would be inclined to follow the opinion of the experts on the Sheffield steel trade mark.

Necropolis:
Twelfth or Fourth Century?

One mile away from Tell el-Yahudiya, Naville and Griffith found
the necropolis, the ancient cemetery of the site, with several artificial little mounds or tumuli built of basalt blocks and sand; almost
all of these tumuli tombs had been pilfered in the past by searchers
for utensils, scarabs, or signets, and jewelry. In each instance the
tomb consisted of an outer case of large crude bricks; a kind of
vaulted roof was made of bricks leaning against each other, inside

---

wrote of "the peculiar decoration in cement" found by Emil Brugsch, similar to
the "lily work, as at Persepolis."

was placed a terra-cotta coffin in the shape of a swathed mummy, made of one piece, with a large opening at the head through which the corpse was introduced, apparently not mummified. "This done, the head was covered with a facepiece on which were modelled the features, the hair, and sometimes the hands. The features were very coarsely executed, in the style of the numerous coffins found in the late cemeteries of Erment or Alexandria."[1] Some of the tombs had been "imperfectly rifled" because the excavators found in them bronze saucers and also small pots with a double handle at the top and "some good specimens of so-called Cypriote pilgrim-bottles." One tomb—it was a child's—was intact: in it was found a necklace of porcelain and glass beads and a ring set with a small scarab. On the breastbone of the child was a small Cypriote vase, placed at the time of interment over the child's heart.

Most of the coffins were painted. "The colours, which were sometimes very vivid," wrote Naville, "soon disappeared after having been exposed to the air. The painting was very coarse, such as we find on mummies of Greek and Roman time." It represented mummies enclosed in cartonnage (the dead were not mummified, but mummies were painted on the coffins); there were painted hieroglyphic bands and funerary genii with the heads of crocodiles. The hieroglyphs on the coffins were found to be "very faulty"—"they strike the eye at first sight as being of a very late epoch." In several instances the hieroglyphs looked "merely ornamental," not intended to be read or to make sense.

"These inscriptions show clearly the late epoch of the coffins, which is confirmed by the total absence of any sign of mummification." A hieroglyphic name on a coffin still partly readable had the Greek ending ος. "The hieroglyphs written on these coffins are so carelessly painted as to make it difficult to assign a definite date to the tombs, although the Greek or Roman period is indicated by the general style." Naville proceeded: "I could readily believe them to be contemporaneous with some of the Jewish burials which, from the style of the writing on the tablets, must be attributed either to the late Ptolemies or to the early Romans." This reference is to an-

[1] E. Naville, *The Mound of the Jew*, p. 16.

other cemetery, a little closer to Tell el-Yahudiya, where tombs were cut in rock with niches for interment; a few tablets inscribed in Greek were found in them, epitaphs with the names of the deceased, like Glaucias, Agathocles, Aristobulos, Onesimos, Tryphaena, Eiras, pure Greek names that "may be found in any country where Greek was spoken"; but besides, there were names "in Grecized Hebrew or pure Hebrew." Naville thought it very possible that both cemeteries were contemporary; at least, both originated not earlier than the Greek time in Egypt; the Jewish cemetery, not earlier than the late Ptolemies.

In the short preface to the volume with the record of the excavation which he published together with Griffith, Naville wrote:

"The reader will notice that our opinions disagree as to the age to which some of the objects discovered in the necropolis of Tell el Yahoodieh [el-Yahudiya] should be attributed. Each of us is alone responsible for the views he states on this point, which we submit to the judgment of the reader." Thus he concluded the preface.

And a great disagreement it was! Only some twenty pages after the passages quoted, Griffith thus described the same necropolis in the desert:

"Here the bodies, enclosed in coffins of painted earthenware, were laid on the surface of a natural or artificial heap of basalt blocks or on the sandy floor of the desert. Around each coffin, which was protected by a simple arch [of bricks], were placed a certain number of utensils in pottery, bronze, etc., and then the whole funeral apparatus was covered over with stones and sand to the depth of almost two feet." These piles of loose basalt blocks formed the little tumuli.

"The coffins were numerous, lying parallel to each other in rows. We found that the plunderers in ancient times had been busy amongst them, and all the coffins of adults had been opened and pillaged. On the other hand, the graves of children were intact—the thieves knew well that they contained no valuables. In one of these two pottery scarabs were found which *bear the name of Rameses III*, and thus give most satisfactory evidence for the precise date of the tumuli."

In one of the tombs two scarabs "set in silver and gold" were found. "The name of Setnekht [father of Ramses III] is crudely inscribed upon one of the scarabs." The other scarab was of Ramses VI, one of the closely following successors of Ramses III. Griffith described the contents of single tombs and the vases, jugs, and bottles of various shapes, as well as bronze bowls, found in them; the children's graves contained, besides the scarabs, necklaces of glass and glazed pottery. In two graves described last, a few "letter-like" marks M and C were found on the pottery; they were incised on a vase before firing; but no implication was derived from the finding of these letters on a vase, for Griffith wrote: "The remains in both of these graves are necessarily of the same date as the rest, viz., XXth Dynasty." He concluded his report:

"The general result of the excavations in the tumuli is to show that they belong to the XXth Dynasty," actually to the middle part of that dynasty. "Out of the first seven tumuli, there is nothing certainly later or earlier than this, while the finding of scarabs of Ramses III and VI, in agreement with the fact that the most striking type amongst the pottery, 'the false amphora,' is found in the paintings of the tomb of Ramses III, fixes the date."

In the tomb of Ramses III, more than three hundred miles away, in Thebes, in the Valley of the Kings, very similar amphorae (jars with two handles and a narrow neck) were painted on murals. But Naville claimed that the Cypriote flask pottery found in the tumuli tombs of the desert necropolis was precisely an indication of a late date for these tombs; and he could call to his support the fact that Flinders Petrie "had already found similar specimens at Nebesheh," the Greek military settlement in the Delta, one day's journey to the west of Deffeneh (Daphnae); the Greeks first settled in Egypt in the seventh century.

Griffith wrote also: "At the same period that the royal hall [of Ramses III] was built in the city [on the site of Tell el-Yahudiya] . . . there must have been many well-to-do people in the city who could afford themselves respectable burial in these tumuli." The hall of faïence disks described earlier was contemporaneous with the cemetery.

Now we have the same problem again—in the cemetery as in the royal hall. Do these tombs date from the time of Ramses III, which means of the twelfth century before the present era, as Griffith ably claimed? Or are these tombs of the Greek or even the Roman time, as Naville not less ably claimed?

Between the time of Ramses III and the time of the first Greek settlement in Egypt over five hundred years passed; but Naville, comparing the paintings on the coffins in the tumuli with those of Greek and Roman times, had in mind the age when Greek influence in Egypt was already growing strong, in the fourth century, or even under the Ptolemies, whose time started with Alexander's death in −323, and continued to the first pre-Christian century when in the days of Pompey and Cleopatra it was replaced by the Roman occupation and influence.

Certainly we are confronted with the same problem once more. The occupants of the tombs lived either under Ramses III in the first half of the twelfth century, as the scarabs of the pharaoh and that of his father testify, and likewise the amphorae, or they lived in the fourth century or even later: the span is at least eight centuries wide.

Strange, but now for the second time in the same surroundings the archaeologists faced the same dilemma. These were no amateurs, not untrained archaeologists, lighthearted or quarrelsome. In the annals of French-Swiss archaeology the name of Edouard Naville is one of renown. The name of Francis Llewellyn Griffith grew to become one of the brightest in the British constellation of Egyptologists. They have placed the problem of the age of the tumuli tombs before the readers, but on what basis can a reader decide when all the evidence was before the archaeologists who excavated and who studied it *in situ* and described their finds? Clearly there was evidence for the dating in the days of Ramses III, in the twelfth century. Clearly there was also evidence for the dating in Greek times.[2]

[2] W. F. Albright took a definite stand in favor of Griffith's view. "An Anthropoid Clay Coffin from Saḥâb in Transjordan," *American Journal of Archaeology* (1932), pp. 302–4.

The problem is not solved. Instead of having found in the necropolis a solution for the Greek letters on the tiles of Ramses III, we met there a very similar puzzle, with two archaeologists arguing in the same volume their opposite views before the readers.

Egypt Tributary to Arsa, a Foreigner

With two similar and perplexing divergences in scholarly estimates, first concerning the age of the porcelain tiles from the palace of Ramses III in Tell el-Yahudiya, second concerning the tumuli tombs in the nearby cemetery, the next proper step would be to reach for the texts that survived from the age of this pharaoh. He left extensive inscriptions carved in stone, accompanied by pictures in low relief, on the walls of his mortuary temple at Medinet Habu in western Thebes—they deal mainly with his military exploits. He left also texts on papyri. The largest of the latter is contained in the so-called Great Papyrus Harris, now in the British Museum—the longest papyrus in existence. It is a magnificent document, not a scribal copy, 133 feet long by 16½ inches high, comprising 117 columns of hieratic writing or fluent script used mostly for religious texts.[1] This document has the character of the king's last will and testament, and it has also been argued that it was composed in the name of Ramses III by his son and successor—though not first-born —known to modern historians as Ramses IV.[2] The king, though speaking in the first person, is also spoken of as "god," a designation usual for a dead king, though we know of instances when a reigning monarch was referred to as "god." The papyrus extolls the contributions Ramses III made to the temple of Amon-Re, Mut, and Khons, the triad of Thebes, also to the temples of Thoth in Hermopolis, of Osiris at Abydos, of Sutekh at Ombos, of Ptah in Memphis, of Horus at Athribis, of Re in Heliopolis, and to many other sanctuaries, some of which were also built by his order; his

[1] The facsimile of the text was edited by S. Birch in 1876. It was translated into English by J. Breasted, *Ancient Records of Egypt* (1906–7), IV, Secs. 182–412.

[2] W. Struve, in *Aegyptus*, VII (1926), 3ff.

munificence is narrated in great detail; the good will of the gods
and of the powerful priestly clan is thus assured. The text was
written by several hands and it concludes with a survey of past
times, preceding Ramses III and Setnakht, who chose him as his
successor: it stresses the great security the king achieved for his
land—the infantry, the chariotry, and the mercenaries are all idle
now that the king has been victorious over his enemies and pacified
the land, planted trees all over the Nile Valley, imported myrrh from
"the great sea of the inverted water" (separately we shall identify
it as the Dead Sea), brought copper from "Atika" on the ships of
that country (and the whereabouts of this unidentified place we
shall discuss, too), and made Egypt a land of delight: "I caused the
woman of Egypt to walk freely wheresoever she would unmolested
by others upon the road." The roll ends with an order and appeal
to all civil officials and military officers of the land to be loyal to his
son and heir, Ramses IV.

From the historical side the most important part of the papyrus is
in the survey of the times *preceding* the rule of Ramses and that of
Setnakht, his predecessor.

"The land of Egypt was overthrown from without and every man
was thrown out of his right; they had no chief mouth for many years
formerly until other times. The land of Egypt was in the hands of
chiefs and rulers of towns, one slew his neighbor, great and small."

The land was subdued by a foreign power ("overthrown from
without") and the population became depraved. The words "they
had no chief mouth for many years" mean that there was no king
and no central government; the local potentates, mayors, and others
acted lawlessly.

"Other times having come after it, with empty years, Arza, a certain Syrian (H-rw),[3] was with them as chief. He set the whole land
tributary before him together; he united his companions and plun-

---

[3] Because of the uncertainty of vowels in hieroglyphics the name can be
read Arsa, Irsu, or the like. J. Breasted suggests Yarzu, Arizu, or Arzu. W.
Hayes and J. Wilson, Irsu; A. Gardiner, Arsu. H-rw is a designation for a
Palestinian, Syrian (Aramean), or Hurrian. Cf. A. H. Gardiner, *Ancient Egyptian Onomastica*, Vol. I (1947).

dered their possessions. They made the gods like men, and no offerings were presented in the temples."

It was after these distressing times that Usikhaure-meramunsetpenre Setnakhte-merrere-meramun "set in order the entire land which had been rebellious; he slew the rebels who were in the land of Egypt; he cleansed the great throne of Egypt." The royal power was re-established and the state was orderly after the many years of subjugation and exploitation. Ramses III (Usimare-meramun Ramesse-hekaon, Life, Prosperity, Health!) was successful in further improving the order, welfare, and defense of the country.

The claims to glorious achievements for Ramses III and his predecessor, Setnakht, did not surprise the scholars who studied the document. The surprise was caused by the enigmatic reference to the overthrow of the country "from without," whereas, following the accepted version of history, nothing is known of Egypt having been subdued by a foreign power in the years preceding the Twentieth Dynasty, that of Ramses III. It is maintained that there exists no other written document, Egyptian or foreign, which would support this statement by Ramses III. "Not the slightest hint is to be found" that would corroborate Ramses' words pointing to foreign domination under Arsa.[4] Further, the accepted version of history leaves only a few years between the end of the Nineteenth Dynasty and the beginning of the Twentieth; yet the text of the papyrus speaks of a long period without a royal power, culminating in the domination of Arsa, who made the country tributary to himself and to his companions. Neither is the time thought to be available in the historical sequel for the events described, nor do the events suit the period. The person of Arsa is mystifying, yet "the rule of an otherwise unknown" foreign usurper "is certain"[5] and this because of the explicit statement in the papyrus.

Therefore it is referred to as a "strange passage"; it has much occupied the attention of historians. To establish the identity of

[4] H. Junker, "Die Aegypter," in Junker and Delaporte, *Die Völker des antiken Orients* (Freiburg, 1933), p. 153.

[5] J. Wilson in J. B. Pritchard, ed., *Ancient Near Eastern Texts* (Princeton, 1950), p. 260, n. 6.

Arsa, and to explain his provenance and his eminence, several strained ideas were suggested. "It is not unlikely," wrote one scholar, "that 'Irsu' was either an epithet ('the Self-made'?) for one of the last rulers of the Nineteenth Dynasty, who may have had a Syrian mother, or was one of several Syrian chancellors who in Ramesside times achieved power and importance."[6]

But times without a legitimate ruler in the country are spoken of; further, the name of Arsa is followed by a sign serving to designate a foreigner and would not follow the name of an Egyptian pharaoh even if his mother were a Syrian.

Was it a reminiscence of times much earlier, those of the occupation by the Hyksos, before the Eighteenth and Nineteenth Dynasties? asked A. H. Gardiner, making a desperate surmise:

"In this strange passage the glorious achievements of Dynasties XVIII and XIX are ignored and we are transported back to the conditions of pre-Hyksos times. The sole specific fact recorded is the emergence of a Syrian condottiere who gained mastery over the entire land; the identity of this foreigner has been much debated. . . ."[7]

It is baffling that Ramses III testifies to a conquest of Egypt "from without," or by a foreign power, in the time preceding that of his father, and nothing is known about such an important fact in the history of the imperial age of Egypt; it is amazing that Egypt should have been in vassalage to a foreign chief, and no source, no course of events as known from the accepted timetable, sides with or fits into a state of dependence under a foreign chief, least of all a Syrian. How should we understand this enigmatic and highly important information willed to posterity by Ramses III?

---

[6] W. C. Hayes, *The Scepter of Egypt* (1953–59), I, 363.

[7] A. H. Gardiner, *Egypt of the Pharaohs*, pp. 281–82. Another suggestion was made by J. Černý: Arsa might be identical with a man by the name of Bey, a "kingmaker" at the time of Sethos II. In the volume dealing with the Assyrian conquest of Egypt, it will be shown that Sethos II and Bey belong in the very beginning of the period that is known as the Nineteenth Dynasty, in this reconstruction, the first quarter of the seventh century.

Arsames

The Persian motifs on the tiles of Ramses III direct our inquiry to the Persian period of Egyptian history.

The Persian time in the Near East began with Cyrus' victory over Croesus the Lydian (−546), the capture of Babylon (−539), and his inheritance of the Babylonian Empire. Cyrus' son Cambyses (−530 to −521) subdued Egypt in −525. Darius (−521 to −486), successor to Cambyses, made Thrace and Macedonia into Persian provinces and twice invaded Greece. On the second expedition his army was defeated at Marathon (−490). He organized maritime trade and dug the canal from the Nile to the Gulf of Suez on the Red Sea.

His son Xerxes (−486 to −465) led another expedition against Greece (−480) and defeated the Greeks at Thermopylae, but the Greeks were victorious on the sea at Salamis. Beaten again at Plataea, Xerxes desisted from further attacks on Greece. He reigned "from India even unto Ethiopia, over a hundred and seven and twenty provinces," according to the book of Esther, who presumably was one of his queens. He never visited Egypt. When he was assassinated, his son Artaxerxes I (−465 to −425) followed on the throne. A few years later a revolt took place in Egypt, headed by Inaros, a local chief. The Athenian fleet of two hundred triremes sailed up the Nile to help Egypt in its struggle against the Great King. At first the Persian garrison was routed and took refuge in the citadel of Memphis, but after a few years a new Persian army freed the beleaguered garrison and defeated the Athenian fleet, leaving it high and dry by diverting the flow of a canal. The Athenians burned their fleet and retreated to Cyrene. Egypt remained in Persian vassalage.

The great and prosperous age of Pericles followed in Athens. In Palestine, Nehemiah, with the permission of Artaxerxes I, rebuilt the wall of Jerusalem, still in ruins since the capture and destruction of the city by the Babylonians, over two hundred years earlier.

Soon after the suppression of the revolt led by Inaros, Artaxerxes

I appointed Arsames, a member of the royal house, to take care of Egypt as its satrap. Of him and of his doings records and references survived in cuneiform on clay, in Aramaic on papyri and on scrolls of hide (there called Arsham), and in Greek authors, Ctesias and Polyaenus (there called Arsames). The earliest of the clay tablets referring to him is dated before the revolt of Inaros, actually in the first years of Artaxerxes I (-463 or -462).[1] Before his appointment as satrap of Egypt, and also, as it appears, of all the region between the Euphrates and Egypt, he had already occupied other positions of distinction in the far-flung Persian Empire.

Upon the death of Artaxerxes the Persian throne was seized by a son who assumed the name of Xerxes (II) and then by a half brother of his who murdered him and then was murdered in his turn. Arsames was instrumental in securing the throne for Ochus, who renamed himself Darius (II); chroniclers called him Nothus, a bastard, since he was an illegitimate son of the late king. He was cruel and vain. The support given by Arsames was decisive in Ochus' attaining the supreme power, and as Darius II he heaped on Arsames honors and riches, the latter in the form of large land possessions in Babylon and in Egypt.

The time from the earliest document referring to Arsames (under Artaxerxes I) to the latest (under Darius II) comprises fifty-three years; his influence during all this time was unchecked and impressed itself on the entire region "beyond the river" or west and south of the Euphrates. From farmers and herdsmen living and toiling on the immense tracts of land given to him, and also appropriated by him, he exacted heavy toll; the administrators (governors) and treasurers of the satrapies acted also as his private employees, collecting revenues chiefly for him but also for a few other privileged members of the royal family with residences in Babylon, Susa, or Persepolis.

On top of this exploitation by its satrap Egypt had to pay a yearly tribute to the Persian crown, collected by the administrator (gov-

[1] G. R. Driver, *Aramaic Documents of the Fifth Century B.C.* (Oxford, 1954).

ernor), who was also chief treasurer, and brought personally to Arsames in Babylon.

Since the time of Darius I each of the satrapies was bound by a regular tribute; Egypt, as Herodotus narrates and a modern scholar assesses, was "one of the heaviest income producers for the throne, bringing in 700 talents, twice as much as all Syria-Palestine combined."[2] Besides, Egypt had also to furnish the Persian garrison and the associated troops, mostly from the Anatolian region, with 120,000 rations.[3] In the days of Darius II the oppressive tributes, if anything, were made more so.

To modern historians Arsames was a well-known personality even before the inscribed hides, which we shall presently discuss, were made available to scholars. The scale of his business affairs in Babylon, where he had large cattle farms, can be judged from cuneiform tablets: in the eleventh year of Darius II (i.e., −413/2), on one day a transaction of his concerned 1809 head of cattle in Nippur in Babylonia and on two following days 582 more head. Cattle were usually leased and the lessee was responsible for tending and folding the herds and flocks.[4]

In 1932, L. Borchardt, whose main interest in Egyptology lay in the study of ancient calendars, was approached while in Cairo by a dealer in antiquities who offered to sell a leather pouch full of leather scrolls inscribed in Aramaic. The dealer would not or could not tell the locality in which the leather scrolls had been found but from their texts one could judge that they were dispatched from the chancery of Arsames, the satrap, in Babylon where he maintained his chief residence, appearing in Egypt only occasionally to look over his possessions and give instructions. His plenipotentiary in the administration of Egypt, or governor and chief treasurer, was, first, one Psamshek and then one Nekht-hor, both Egyptians. We

[2] E. G. Kraeling, *The Brooklyn Museum Aramaic Papyri* (New Haven, 1953), p. 32.
[3] Herodotus, III, 91. One hundred and twenty thousand rations "suggest an army of ten to twelve thousand men." (Kraeling, op. cit., p. 32.)
[4] Driver, *Aramaic Documents*, p. 44.

should notice these men and their names because we shall deal with them separately in appropriate places.

In all there were, besides a number of fragments, fourteen scrolls in the bag; one of them was practically lost in an effort to open it. The information found in Ctesias, a Greek physician at the Persian court of the early fourth century, and author of *Persica,* that official messages of importance were written in the Persian Empire on king's (royal) hides was confirmed by the find.

It was a surprise to learn that Aramaic was the official language of the correspondence between the Persian satrap and his subordinates in Egypt. E. Mittwoch, a Hebrew-Aramaic scholar, read the scrolls. *Aram* in Hebrew means Syria and Aramaic was a Syrian dialect. It came into use in the ninth century before the present era, as single relics seem to indicate; in the days of the Babylonian exile of the Jews it was one of the several languages in use at the court of Babylon (Daniel 2:4); in the fifth century, under the Persians, it was used in official correspondence, replacing also the Akkadian (Assyro-Babylonian) in Babylon, as the royal hides disclosed.[5] By the first Christian century Aramaic had become the spoken language of the population of Palestine, as certain expressions in the gospels, written in Greek, testify. Both the Jerusalem and the Babylonian Talmuds, creations of the first to the fifth century of the present era, are written in Aramaic.

The scrolls we discuss, written mostly from the chancery of Arsames in Babylon and preserved in the chancery of his plenipotentiary in Egypt, were addressed to various people: on the outside surface of a scroll the name of the addressee used to be written together with a note telling of the subject discussed in the letter. The letters of the collection are without dates but from their contents it can be deduced that they were written under Darius II Nothus, from about −424 to −410.

Ten of the missives are from Arsames (in most cases signed by his scribe in his name) and four of these are to Nekht-hor; the re-

<hr/>

[5] A. T. Olmstead, *History of the Persian Empire* (Chicago, 1948), pp. 116–17. Cf. also Ezra 4:7—letters to and from Artaxerxes were written in Aramaic (Syriac).

maining three letters are also to Nekht-hor but from different send-
ers, yet in all these Arsames is mentioned. Thus his name is present
in each of the preserved letters of the collection. The earlier letters
indicate that Psamshek preceded Nekht-hor in the post and one of
these missives contains also a strong reprimand to a commander of
a garrison because of insubordination to Psamshek. Arsames' letters
to Nekht-hor have no introductory salute, showing the satrap's
haughty attitude toward his plenipotentiaries of Egyptian extrac-
tion.

The letters deal mainly with exacting tribute from the land of
Egypt and even more with personal land and serf properties of
Arsames and of two or three of his entourage who, like himself,
were related to the Persian royal house.

A typical letter follows:

"From Arsham to Nekht-khor (Neḥtiḥur): And now previously,
when the Egyptians rebelled, then Psamshek the previous pekida
[governor] took strict care of our staff and property which were
[are] in Egypt, so that my estate suffered no sort of loss; he also
sought out enough staff of craftsmen of various races and other
property and made them over to my estate. . . ."

In the letter Arsames reprimanded Nekht-hor, the present governor, and his assistants for laxity and ordered: "Do you show your-
selves active and take strict care of our staff and property that my
estate may suffer no sort of loss; also seek out enough staff of craftsmen of various races from elsewhere and bring them into my court
and mark them with my brand and make them over to my estate,
just as the previous pekidia (governors) used to do.

"Thus let it be known to thee: if my staff [of serfs] or other property suffer any sort of loss and you [plural] do not seek out others
from elsewhere and add them to my estate, you will be called
strictly to account, and reprimanded." Arsames held an example
before Nekht-hor: certain agents of his in Lower Egypt are "showing themselves active and taking strict care of their lord's staff and
property and are also seeking out others from elsewhere and adding
them to their lord's estate, while you are not doing so"—and the
order to him to do likewise followed.

From such a letter of the satrap to the governor one learns that land property was unceremoniously confiscated and added, in Upper and Lower Egypt alike, to the satrap's private holdings; people from anywhere (from "elsewhere" in Arsames' language) were made bondsmen and marked with his brand, thus becoming his possessions.

Not even smaller holdings, or those in a state of disrepair, stood a chance of escaping the annexation policy of the satrap. Thus Arsames' chancery informed the governor that a man named Petosiri wrote to the satrap asking permission to take possession of his father's farm; his father, Pamun, perished with the women of his household when a "disturbance" occurred in Egypt. The abandoned farm "was not made over to my estate," wrote the scribe in Arsames' name. The governor was ordered to let the son occupy the farm but upon taking over the farm he should "pay the land tax to my estate. . . ." A scribe signed the letter.

In his greed Arsames did not think to alleviate the conditions that caused "the disturbance" but wished to enlarge his income by adding a ramshackle and possibly burned-down farm to his fief.

From these "royal hides" written in a Syrian idiom one learns of exploitation of Egypt by Arsames and his cohort.

Of Arsames we can justly say what Ramses III said of Arsa, the foreigner who, many years after the overthrow of Egypt "from without," following which event there was no native ruler in the country, "was with them as chief." Everything points to Arsames, the satrap and writer of the Aramaic letters, who exploited Egypt and abused his position, as being Arsa of the Harris Papyrus who "set the whole land tributary before him" and "plundered their possessions."

The name Arsames (Arsham in Aramaic or Syrian) could be easily rendered Arsa in Egyptian not only because the Egyptians habitually shortened private names (also of the kings[6]), but even more readily in this case where the ending -mes found in many Egyptian

[6] See *Ages in Chaos*, I, 141, n. 2.

names and meaning "son"—as in Thutmes (Thutmose)—could be considered dispensable.

Writing his letters in Aramaic, Arsames would be considered a Syrian. Besides, in those times, as we learn from Herodotus, the terms Syrian and Assyrian (Mesopotamian) were not distinct and the same term was applied to both.[7]

Artaxerxes II's private name, by which he was known before mounting the throne upon Darius II's death (−404), was Arsatis, in Persian-Aramaic texts spelled Arshu (Olmstead). He may well also contest for the role of Arsa (or Arsu) as an exploiter of Egypt. He actually lost Egypt in the fifth year of his reign (−399) when Nepherites' rebellion freed the country of Persian domination, and the Egyptians made war against him in −374.

In a Babylonian astronomical text dating from his eighteenth year (−387), he is still referred to as Arshu: "Arshu, who is called by the name Artakshatsu [Artaxerxes II] the king . . ." (Kugler). This was only a short time before the events that we are describing now. The career of Artaxerxes II was closely connected with Babylon: he, as crown prince, grew up in Babylon and had his second residence there, at that time the center of Aramaic culture. This may explain the reference to Arsu (Arsa) in the Great Harris Papyrus as a Syrian (Aramaean). He could have had a Syrian mother.

To whomever of the two, Arsham (Arsames) or Arshu (Arsaces), the papyrus referred, both deserved the description as violators of the population of Egypt of the period closely preceding the events we are now about to describe. However, Arsames, who died before Artaxerxes mounted the throne, was in charge of Egypt. Artaxerxes II never visited there, and therefore I saw a stronger argument for identifying Arsames (Arsham) with Arsa.[8]

[7] Herodotus, VII, 63. Also, Strabo, II, 1, 31 and XVII, 1, 1–3.

[8] Earlier in my work, before coming to this dilemma, I considered Ezra the Scribe for possible identification of Arsa or Erzu of the Great Harris Papyrus. He received from the Persian king a mandate to collect tribute from the treasurers of the satrapies "beyond [this side of] Euphrates" for the Temple in Jerusalem— Egypt was not excluded from the satrapies obliged to pay such tribute or tax. His jurisdiction included the prerogative of imposing the death penalty on offenders. He arrived in Jerusalem in the seventh year of Darius II (−417) or the seventh year of Artaxerxes II (−397). (See the discussion on a later page.)

With this identification we are almost closing the ring: it appears that all the problems we discussed find their solution if Ramses III —and the Twentieth Dynasty with him—are removed into the fourth century before the present era. But what about his wars and his annals of them?

Chapter II

PERSIANS AND GREEKS INVADE EGYPT

Pereset: Philistines or Persians?

IN WESTERN THEBES, more than three hundred miles up the Nile
from the Delta, Ramses III built a sumptuous mortuary temple
to himself. On its walls he had engraved for posterity the story
of his military victories and the record was profusely illustrated
with bas-reliefs.* The place, called Medinet Habu, is across the Nile
from Luxor, under the cliffs that hide the Valley of the Kings with
its royal sepulchers. Usimare-meramun Ramesse-hekaon (Ramses
III) defended and saved the country when it was in peril of being
conquered by large invading armies and navies.

Against Ramses III there gathered in Canaan-Palestine a huge
military force—an army composed of many peoples under the leadership of a nation whose name is read Pereset, and a fleet for the
invasion of Egypt. In accordance with the timetable of conventional
chronology the period was shortly after —1200, several years after
Ramses III mounted the throne, and in compliance with this timetable it is accepted that Pereset stands for Philistines. In the Egyptian script there is no letter L and the letter R may be pronounced
also as L. Yet in almost all cases where the letter appears it is usual
to pronounce it R, and thus we read Ramses, not Lamses.

Aside from the presumed mention of the Philistines in the war
annals of Ramses III, the Old Testament is the only literary source
of our knowledge of the Philistines. According to Deuteronomy
(2:23), Amos (9:7), and Jeremiah (47:4), the Philistines came from

* For simplification, the term "bas-relief" is used instead of the more tech-
nical "hollow relief."

the island of Caphtor to Canaan. Jeremiah speaks of the "Philistines, the remnants of the country of Caphtor." It is usually assumed that Caphtor means Crete; however, more probably it is Cyprus.[1] The Philistines reached the coast of Canaan in force only very shortly (a few decades or merely a few years) before the Israelite tribes coming from over the Jordan reached the hilly part of Canaan.[2]

Ramses III did not mention the Israelites or any of the Twelve Tribes in his detailed annals of the war and, reciprocally, no reference is preserved in the Books of Joshua and Judges to a war conducted by the Egyptians in Canaan. The Pereset being the invading hordes of the Philistines, it was argued that apparently the Israelites had not yet reached Canaan. This would explain the strange fact that Ramses III could have carried on a great and victorious war against the Philistines and their allies, partly on the terrain of Palestine, without the Israelite tribes having been involved on one side or another. It is usual to interpret the situation in this way: such a late arrival of the Israelites would explain their not being mentioned by the Egyptian annals of the war in Canaan and, equally, it would warrant the silence of the Scriptures about the events described in the annals.

The placing of the conquest of Canaan under Joshua after −1180 is not without a very serious complication: instead of the traditional four hundred years for the period embracing the wandering in the desert, the conquest of Canaan, and the time of the Judges, there remain only a little over one hundred years. By −1000 a part of David's reign of forty years had passed, and Saul, the first king of Israel, had reigned for several decades before David. One hundred years for the period of the Judges is decidedly far too little.

Ascribing the conquest under Joshua to a time after Ramses III's war in Palestine conflicts also with the preferred theories about the conquest during the Eighteenth Dynasty (in the Tell el-Amarna period) or during the Nineteenth Dynasty. But the reader of *Ages*

---

[1] Cf. *Ages in Chaos*, I, Section "Troglodytes or Carians," p. 201.

[2] "In no sense were they the descendants of those Philistines who had concluded a treaty with Isaac [cf. Genesis 21 and 26]; they had immigrated from Cyprus at a much later date." L. Ginzberg, *The Legends of the Jews*, IV (1913), 94.

in Chaos knows that the Exodus took place at the end of the Middle Kingdom, long before Ramses III of the Twentieth Dynasty, Merneptah of the Nineteenth, or Amenhotep III or IV (Akhnaton) of the Eighteenth. Then the riddle persists: how is it that Ramses III did not encounter the Israelite tribes during the war waged by him with the invading Peoples of the Sea in Egypt and in Palestine, and how is it that the Hebrew annals have not preserved any memory of that campaign either?

It was assumed that what had taken place was a vast wandering of peoples, the equal of which but few other epochs had known. "The year 1200 B.C. marked roughly the culminating of the disturbances in the political life of the Ancient East . . . a change unrivalled in its far-reaching effects, save by the conquest of Alexander," wrote a member of the many-season archaeological expedition to Medinet Habu.[3]

As no other people soon after −1200 seemed to fit better, the Pereset were identified with the Philistines; and in schoolbooks there are portraits of the Philistines, the people of Goliath, a nation prominent in the days of the Judges: these portraits are copied from the bas-reliefs of the mortuary temple of Ramses III.

On the murals of this temple at Medinet Habu the Pereset and their allies, the Peoples of the Sea, are easily recognizable by their apparel. The Pereset wear crownlike helmets on their heads and are dressed in rich garments. The soldiers of the Peoples of the Sea have horned helmets sometimes with a ball or disc between the horns.

The Pereset were a rich and cultured people, judging by their elaborate and colorful attire. Certainly the superbly clad and armored troops did not look like drifting hordes of migrants, as they are sometimes represented in the theories of migratory waves of displaced tribes that reached Egypt. A modern scholar expressed this very view and her conviction that these armies were forces of a well-organized state and not migrating hordes uprooted from their

[3] H. H. Nelson, *Medinet Habu, The Epigraphic Survey of the Oriental Institute* (University of Chicago, 1929), p. 1.

domicile.[4] Neither do the Peoples of the Sea look like wandering hordes: they are disciplined and organized troops.

We have no other ancient likeness of the Philistines to compare with; however, if we page through the records of excavations in various countries and photographs of ancient art, we find again the crownlike helmets that we know from the bas-reliefs of Ramses III as the headgear of the Pereset. We find them on the heads of Persian soldiers.

In Persepolis, the ancient capital city thirty miles northeast of Shiraz, there are ruins of the palaces of the ancient kings of Persia, with grandiose staircases still standing; many figures of Persian soldiers are preserved on the walls of the staircases in relief. They have crownlike helmets on their heads: this headgear consists of a number of facets or petals set on a strap wrought with ornaments around the head, and a small protective screen for the back of the head. The crownlike headgear of the Pereset on the Egyptian murals also consists of a number of facets or petals on a strap wrought with ornaments around the head, and a small protective screen for the back of the head.

Near Persepolis, in Nakhsh-i-Rustam, are the tombs of the great kings of Persia: these are sepulchral chambers cut into a mighty rock, high above the ground. The tomb of Darius has carved rock bas-reliefs showing the guard of the Persian monarch. Again it is easy to recognize the headgear of the Pereset.[5]

---

[4] L. A. Stella, *Rivista di Antropologia*, 39 (1951–52), 3–17.

[5] These types of headgear are unique; they were also characteristic of the Persian nation for centuries. In the palace of Kuyunjuk, built by the late Assyrian kings, were found bas-reliefs depicting some figures in headdresses not unlike those of the Pereset. See A. H. Layard, *Nineveh and Babylon* (London, 1882), pp. 76–77. De Clercq, *Catalogue des antiquités assyriennes* (Paris, 1883), p. 139 (*Palais de Koyaundjok*), speaks of "*une couronne de plumes.*" The petal-shaped sections are embossed with a feather design; the figures wear long tunics. The figures were either cut by the late Assyrian kings, who, as is known from their annals, carried wars into Elam, the Persian highland, and took prisoners, or fashioned by the Persian conquerors of Assyria, which fell to their domain together with Babylonia in the second half of the sixth century before the present era. A figure of a knight on a bas-relief in Nakhsh-i-Rustam, dating from the Sassanid Dynasty of the third to seventh Christian centuries,

Besides the royal guard with their many-petaled headgear, the bas-reliefs in Persepolis and in Nakhsh-i-Rustam show satraps and the king himself crowned with plain tiaras. On the Egyptian murals of Ramses III prisoners also wearing such plain tiaras are seen. They are not depicted in the course of the battle, but a few of the captives with plain tiaras are seen being led in a triumphal procession of the pharaoh. These captives were obviously of higher rank.

The typical and unique headgear seen on Persian guards and knights, seen also on the Pereset soldiers, and the tiaras of the Great King and his satraps, seen on the Pereset officers, make a strong argument for identifying the Pereset as Persians. But the Persian contact with Egypt and Persian wars with Egypt are limited to the years between −525, when Cambyses conquered Egypt, and −332, the year Alexander reached Egypt and terminated Persian domination there.

If we are to judge by the fact that the Pereset soldiers on the Egyptian bas-reliefs are beardless and only the officers have beards, whereas on the bas-reliefs of Darius of close to −500 the officers and soldiers of the royal guard have beards, then we are directed toward the fourth century: one hundred years separate Darius from the fourth century. In the meantime a reform had been introduced requiring the soldiers to shave their beards so as to deprive the foe of an easy hold.[6] But the officers of higher rank retained their beards. On the Egyptian bas-reliefs beards adorn the faces of the higher officers of the Pereset.

Are not the rich garments of the Pereset, which impressed modern scholars,[7] but the clothes of the Persians, which impressed contemporary Greeks?

In the days of Herodotus, in the mid-fifth century, the Persians "wore on their heads loose caps called tiaras, and on their bodies sleeved tunics of diverse colours, with scales of iron like in appear-

---

has headgear similar to the headgear on the head of Isis pictured as nursing Ramses III.

[6] Plutarch, *Lives*, Theseus, 5, says that Alexander introduced this custom of soldiers shaving their beards; in this he followed an oriental military custom.

[7] G. Maspero (*The Struggle of the Nations*, 1896, p. 463) speaks of "a taste for a certain luxury and refinement" of the Pereset.

ance to the scales of fish." The Syrians in the army of Xerxes wore "helmets upon their heads made of brass, and plaited in a strange fashion which is not easy to describe."[8] Ammianus Marcellinus, describing much later the armor of the Persians, tells us that they were clad from head to foot in pieces of iron fashioned *like feathers.*[9]

In some instances the petals on the crown-helmet of the Pereset are embossed with a feather design; this caused historians to speak of "feather crowns" of the Philistines in the manner of the American Indians. But from Ammianus we learn that the iron scales of the Persians were fashioned to imitate feathers.

The climate of Egypt forbids, for the larger part of the year, the use of mail. The soldiers of the Pereset were clad in light tunics, a few strips of mail, and helmets made of scales. At the excavations of Daphnae (Tahpenes of the Scriptures), the Greek military colony in Egypt, iron scales were unearthed. "The scale armour is the most unusual find of all."[10] But identical armor, actually "a corselet of scales, is shown in the tomb of Ramessu [Ramses] III," Flinders Petrie observed not without wondering.[11]

The fact that iron scales were unearthed by Petrie at Daphnae, founded in the seventh century for Greek mercenaries serving in Egypt, and a corselet of similar scales is shown in the tomb of Ramses III belongs to the growing collection of anachronisms with which the time of this pharaoh now seems to abound.

The Pereset were obviously not Philistines but Persians. This interpretation of the name is subject to control. For almost two hundred years Egypt was under Persian domination—or warred against it—and it should not be difficult to find by what name the Egyptian texts of the Persian and Ptolemaic periods refer to Persia and the Persians.

In the hieroglyphic texts of the Persian epoch between −525 and ca. −390 when Egypt won a temporary independence, there are a

[8] Herodotus, VII, 61, 63.
[9] Ammianus, XXIV, iv, 15.
[10] Petrie, *Tanis*, Pt. II, "Nebesheh and Defenneh (Tahpanhes)," p. 78.
[11] Ibid.

number of references to Persia—it is always called P-r-s (in Hebrew Persia is also called P-r-s, or Paras); the name, as usual in Egyptian writing, is supplied with the sign "foreign land."

Under the third Ptolemy, in −238, a priestly conclave made a decree and had it cut in stone—it is known as the Canopus Decree, for the place in Egypt where the conclave took place. It deals with a calendar reform: we shall occupy ourselves with its text on a later page of this book. A reference is found in the decree to the Persians as a nation and, significantly for our thesis, it is written P-r-s-tt.[12]

The Canopus Decree refers to the time when sacred images were carried away by the Pereset: "And the statues of the gods which the vile P-r-s-tt carried away from Egypt—his majesty [Ptolemy III] marched into the lands of Asia, he rescued them, and brought them back to Egypt."

The Canopus Decree is written in three scripts on a slab of stone, in Greek, in demotic Egyptian (cursive), and in hieroglyphics. The Greek text reads: "And the sacred images which had been carried off from the country by the Persians, the King, having made an expedition outside Egypt, brought them back safely unto Egypt, and restored them to the temples wherefrom they had been carried off. . . ."[13]

If there could be a doubt as to the meaning of Pereset, the Greek text of the Canopus Decree dissipates it. And with this there should no longer be any problem in identifying the Pereset of the inscriptions at Medinet Habu of Ramses III as Persians.

[12] Dr. N. B. Millet of the Royal Ontario Museum kindly compiled, at my request, some references in Egyptian texts to Persia and Persians. He suggests that the double *t* in Peresett was used for aesthetic purposes of the hieroglyphic design, as is not unusual in this script. Eddie Schorr points out that in the text of the Canopus Decree other geographical locations also have a second *t* added. Thus Keftíu (Cyprus) is Keftet, and in the case of Retenu (Palestine) the word is spelled Retenutet.

[13] E. A. Wallis Budge, *The Rosetta Stone in the British Museum* (London, 1929), Appendix: "The Decree of Canopus," pp. 256, 283. Cf. D. Lorton, "The supposed expedition of Ptolemy III to Persia," *Journal of Egyptian Archaeology*, 57 (1971), pp. 16off.

The Enormity of the Problem

Before we proceed any further, let us pause and visualize the enormity of the problem. Several times already we have been directed by the state of things toward the Persian period: first, when we discussed the tiles of Ramses III with Greek letters and Persian art motifs; then when we read that the graves built during the reign of Ramses III exhibit clear characteristics of the fourth or a later century; for the third time, when we observed that the subjugation of Egypt to a foreigner, Arsa, was unimaginable in the thirteenth or twelfth century, but that something very similar took place in the second half of the fifth century; and, last, when we approached the realization that Ramses III fought his war against the Persians; the Persians, however, first warred against Egypt in −525, and then again in the fourth century battled the Egyptians, who proclaimed their independence under native kings.

We can stop here, perplexed by the evidently inadmissible thought that there could be a mistake of eight hundred years, or frightened at the sight of the perturbation into which this inquiry may lead us. But should we not make up our minds to try to probe a little further and may we not perchance feel relieved if some new evidence should exonerate the centuries-old concept of ancient history? For this must be clearly understood: we cannot let Ramses III fight with the Persians and keep the hinges of world history in their former places. What a slide, what an avalanche, must accompany such a disclosure: kingdoms must topple, empires must glide over centuries, descendants and ancestors must change places. And in addition to all this, how many books must become obsolete, how many scholarly pursuits must be restarted, how much inertia must be overcome? It is not merely an avalanche but a complete overturning of supposedly everlasting massifs.

Now that the reader appreciates the consequences implied by the identification of the Pereset with the Persians, we invite him to follow closely the further evidence in order not to be persuaded of what is unproven, or guided to what is but an illusory picture of the past.

Do we describe the twelfth or the fourth century?

Since the beginning of the fourth century is no gray antiquity, and the wars in which the Greeks took part, even as mercenaries, are most certainly described by some of the Greek authors, we are putting our scheme of history to a most merciless test: all parts of the story must be told and explained in a Greek source. If this cannot be done, we have perchance made indefensible claims; but if the events pictured and annotated by the pharaoh are found in a Greek historian, event after event, with all the actors playing their proper roles in the very order established by the Egyptian murals and their accompanying texts, then the scheme we offer here is freed from an aspect of arbitrariness—

> Ah, love, could you and I with Him conspire
> To grasp this sorry scheme of things entire
> Would not we shatter it to bits and then
> Remold it nearer to the heart's desire?[1]

Should the revised scheme of history meet the challenge just offered, it ought to be recognized that a substantial gain has been made in the contest for the rightful title of true history.

In the revision of this portion of history we cannot turn for assistance to the Scriptures or to Assyro-Babylonian sources, and for very simple reasons: in the beginning of the fourth century before the present era the Old Testament was about to be or had already been concluded, and its latest historical portions—the books of Esther, Nehemiah, and Ezra—deal with the period prior to Ramses III; and Assyro-Babylonia no longer existed as a state. However, we may be able to find the necessary material for comparison in the writings of Greek authors.

It was the fourth century, and it was already a century less six years since the day Sophocles first competed with Aeschylus; Pericles, for whom the golden age of Athens was named, had been dead for about fifty years; Socrates, too, was dead. *The Frogs* of Aristophanes had been acted and read for a number of decades.

---

[1] From E. FitzGerald's translation of *Rubaiyat* by Omar Khayyám.

We shall not look in the books of the historian Thucydides for records on Ramses III; the historian died shortly after −400. Neither can we turn to the books of Herodotus: when he visited Egypt, Ramses III had not yet been born.

When the biblical sources cease to yield information, the Greek authors provide the contemporaneous annals. The Egyptian kings Nepherites, Acoris, Nectanebo I, Tachos, and Nectanebo II are familiar figures in these annals and chronicles, written by historians of a later generation than Herodotus and Thucydides. In Egyptological studies these late pharaohs are placed in the so-called Twenty-ninth and Thirtieth Dynasties of kings (the last before the short reconquest of Egypt by the Persians a decade in advance of the conquest of Egypt by Alexander). Nectanebo I, who reigned from −379 to −361, is the most imposing figure among these last native pharaohs. But if, as is maintained here, Ramses III lived not in the twelfth but in the early part of the fourth century, who, then, is Nectanebo who lived at the same time?

We are going to demonstrate that the pharaoh for whom, of his several names, modern historians have selected Ramses III was Nectanebo I of Greek authors. Since they lived at the same time and were not separated by eight hundred years, and since both were pharaohs in Egypt, there is no alternative but to identify them as one and the same person. And we shall see, as we compare the records of Ramses III and the writings of the Greeks about Nectanebo I, that the details of their personalities, their lives, their rules, and their wars are so much alike as to preclude arbitrariness in identification. Moreover, we will find that on certain inscriptions Ramses III used the name Nekht-a-neb as one of his royal, so-called Horus names.

Ramses III left annals of his war with the Pereset and the Peoples of the Sea. Diodorus of Sicily, a historian writing in Greek in the last century before the present era, narrated in detail the war of Nectanebo I against the Persians and the Greek mercenaries. Diodorus, who spent the years between −60 and −57 in Egypt, obviously had before him many documents and sources when he composed the history of the last native dynasties in Egypt. We shall subject the two records to a most rigorous test of comparison. These two annals must present a story of one and the same war unless we have drifted off the right course in our attempt to unravel the true history of the times.

"The Isles Were Restless"

Upon the death of Darius II (Nothus) his son Arsaces mounted the throne, adopting the name Artaxerxes II. Called Mnemon for his good memory, he occupied the throne from −404 to −358, a period of great events in history. Early in his reign his brother, the satrap of Anatolia, Cyrus, called the Younger, revolted and marched against the king. In this famous expedition a Greek mercenary army numbering ten to twelve thousand men participated; Xenophon the Athenian, one of their leaders, described the march and the retreat in the *Anabasis* (*Going Up*). Cyrus advanced as far as Babylon and died nearby in a battle (−401); the Greek army retreated and after many hardships reached the Black Sea.

During the next few years the Persian satrapies in Asia Minor were disturbed by rebellions of satraps and by the attempts of Sparta to liberate the Ionians on the Asian coast from Persian domination. This effort took a very aggressive course when in −396/5 the Spartan king Agesilaus was victorious in engagements in western and central Asia Minor.[1]

The exploits of Agesilaus anticipated those of Alexander. Cornelius Nepos wrote in his short biography of Agesilaus:

"Agesilaus . . . had taken many places, and secured abundance of spoil. . . . While he was thinking of marching into Persia, and attacking the king himself, a messenger came to him from home, by order of the Ephori, to acquaint him that the Athenians and Boeotians had declared war against the Lacedaemonians [Spartans]

---

[1] He came repeatedly into military but also diplomatic contact with the Persian hereditary satrap Pharnabazus, whose province was known in Persian as "Tyaiy Drayahya" or "Those [or the people] of the Sea." We note the man here because we shall meet him again a score of years later; we shall also recall then the name by which his satrapy in Asia Minor was known.

and that he should therefore not delay to return. Though he was at the head of a victorious army, and felt assured, to the utmost, of becoming master of the kingdom of Persia, he obeyed the orders. . . . . Agesilaus preferred an honourable name to the most powerful empire, and thought it much more glorious to obey the laws of his country than to subdue Asia in war."[2]

The eight-year-long Corinthian War began. The Persian king gave support to the Athenians; indeed he had been instrumental in instigating these hostilities; it was a stratagem to make Agesilaus return to Greece and to let the Greek states enmesh themselves in prolonged hostilities. In −394 the Spartans won battles at Nemea and Coronea, but their fleet was annihilated by the Persian fleet at Cnidus under the Athenian admiral Conon, and never regained domination at sea. The Ionians on the Anatolian coast revolted and declared their independence from Sparta. Athens recovered the islands of Delos, Scyrus, Imbros, and Lemnos and made alliance with Chios, Mitylene, Rhodes, Cos, and Cnidus.

Many famous incidents took place during the Corinthian War (−395 to −387), and many islands participated in it. Evagoras, king of Salamis in Cyprus, went to the aid of the Athenians, thus performing a service to the Persian king. But a few years later (−390) Evagoras rebelled against Artaxerxes, being provoked to this by the Great King, who resented Evagoras' courage and independence. Artaxerxes also needed a servile king on the island in preparation for a war against Egypt. But the war against Evagoras endured for ten years and was very costly to Persia; for a period of time Evagoras crossed over to Asia Minor, persuaded the Cilicians to revolt, and took several cities in Phoenicia.

At the other end of the eastern Mediterranean, in Sicily and southern Italy, a war was going on too. The Carthaginians invaded Italy. Dionysius, the tyrant of Syracuse in Sicily, made war against Croton, the Greek settlement in southern Italy; the Athenian fleet participated in this war, too, and the islands west of Greece entered the conflict.

---

[2] Cornelius Nepos, *Agesilaus* (3, 4), trans. J. S. Watson (London, 1910). The Ephori were the five magistrates exercising control over the kings of Sparta.

In the Corinthian War the Spartans were supreme on land; but one of the sensations of that war was the victory of the Athenian general Iphicrates, who in −391 destroyed a division of heavily armed and slowly moving Spartan troops with lightly clad and easily maneuverable Athenian regiments, whose defensive and offensive arms he had reformed so as to obtain greater mobility and thrust.

In Egypt, the Persian oppression before the death of Darius II caused Amyrteos to establish his authority over a part of Egypt. He is the sole representative of the very short Twenty-eighth Dynasty. After him, another secular leader, Nepherites, revolted. He obtained some measure of independence, which Egypt had not had for about a hundred and thirty years. When he died, after a few years of relative independence, Nepherites was not followed by a son of his; instead the throne was seized by one Acoris. Possibly a Persian intrigue was behind this seizure; at the beginning Acoris recognized Persian supremacy, but after a while he rebelled: when Evagoras, aided by the Athenians, revolted against the Persian king, Acoris chose to revolt too. In −381 Evagoras' fleet was defeated by the Persians. Acoris died in −379 or −378, and the throne was seized by Nectanebo I, who claimed Nepherites' parentage but who, it is asserted, was a son of a military man and an officer himself. It appears that he served on the Libyan front, scoring there some successes before he declared himself king.

The defeat of Evagoras, king of Cyprus, the improvement of relations between Athens and Persia, and the assistance given by Persia to Athens against Sparta influenced the state of affairs in Egypt. Nectanebo, too, at first recognized Persian overlordship but soon was building up his troops and fleet to meet the onslaught of the Persian army and navy. Only for a short time did he pretend to be loyal.

Diodorus wrote that (in −375/4) "Artaxerxes, King of the Persians, intending to make war on the Egyptians and being busily engaged in organizing a considerable mercenary army, decided to effect a settlement of the wars going on in Greece." By pacifying the western front (Greece), he hoped to be able to concentrate on the

southern front (Egypt); he hoped, also, "that the Greeks, once released from their domestic wars, would be more ready to accept
mercenary service." But the results of this so-called King's Peace,
which should have given autonomy to each Greek city, brought new
strifes, since the Thebans, led by Epaminondas, disagreed on proce-
dures; and besides, upon obtaining autonomy, "the cities fell into
great disturbances and internal strife, particularly in the Pelopon-
nese."[3]

The attempt to reach a general settlement resulted in new hostilities between Sparta and Athens; Sparta, blockading the Hellespont, coerced Athens to a peace with Persia; Sparta occupied the
citadel of Cadmeia in Thebes, capital of Boeotia; the Theban exiles
recovered Cadmeia by a coup. Athens allied itself with Thebes. In
−376 the Athenian admiral Chabrias destroyed the Spartan fleet
off Naxos in a decisive battle.

The next year "King Artaxerxes sent an expedition against the
Egyptians, who had revolted from Persia."[4] Giving a description of
this expedition and of its disastrous ending, which will be reproduced on the following pages, Diodorus reverted to the political
conditions among the Greek states and wrote: "Throughout Greece
now that its several states were in confusion because of unwonted
forms of government . . . many uprisings were occurring in the
midst of the general anarchy. . . ."[5]

This state of affairs shows Greece in turmoil. The Corinthian War
had scarcely ended before a new war between the Greek city-
states and islands was in progress.

On the second pylon of his mortuary temple at Medinet Habu
Ramses III wrote that "the islands" were restless, disturbed among
themselves.

> The countries . . . the Northerners in their isles were disturbed,
> taken away in the fray—at one time. Not one stood before their

[3] Diodorus, *The Historical Library*, trans. Charles L. Sherman (Loeb Classical
Library), XV, 40.
[4] Ibid., XV, 41.
[5] Ibid., XV, 45.

hands [arms], from Kheta (Ht), Kode [the "circling" of the Syrian coast at the Gulf of Iskanderun], Carchemish, Arvad [in northern Syria], Alasa [Cyprus], they were wasted. They set up a camp in one place in Amor [Syria].[6]

These words sound like a true description of the state of affairs preceding the invasion of Egypt by the Persians: from the days when the Spartans under Agesilaus subdued western Asia Minor, the Greek islands were in a state of confused war, and Sicily and Cyprus were involved in wars and insurrections.

Of the "camp set up in one place" in Syria we shall find a more detailed description in Diodorus. But before we proceed any further we shall pose a few questions and find answers.

Quid Pro Quo?

Study of the bas-reliefs of Ramses III discloses that complicated alliances and realliances were made among the factions that participated in the war. Relations between the Egyptians, the Pereset, and the Peoples of the Sea, during the years memorialized by Ramses III in his inscriptions and bas-reliefs, took various forms, with the Peoples of the Sea changing sides; however, the Pereset also changed sides, at one time being Ramses' supporters—at others, his enemies.

There was something odd in the relations between these peoples, the Egyptians, the Pereset, and the Peoples of the Sea. When the pharaoh at the beginning of his reign made war against intruders from Libya, the Peoples of the Sea with horned helmets and the Pereset with tiaras helped him and his army and one may see them killing the Libyans (Plate 4). Thus their first appearance is not that of enemies but of allies of Egypt.

Later on, in the second act, the Pereset are seen as the main foes of the Egyptians; in the war against the Pereset, the Peoples of the Sea aid the pharaoh, showing examples of heroism, a few going into battle against many (Plate 5). The bas-reliefs also picture them

[6] Cf. Breasted, *Ancient Records of Egypt*, IV, Sec. 64.

parading with the army of the pharaoh; their attire and their armor —helmets, shields, spears, and swords—are carefully reproduced in these scenes where they march to the sound of an Egyptian trumpeter, or where they advance swiftly in military array (Plate 6).

But in the great battle at the mouth of the Nile the Peoples of the Sea with horned helmets—now without discs between the horns—appear on hostile vessels and the Egyptian fleet puts to rout the vessels of the Pereset and the Peoples of the Sea alike. A number of warriors of the Peoples of the Sea and of the Pereset are on the Egyptian vessels but they are fettered captives (Plate 7).

After the battle we see processions of captives with arms and necks in stocks and bound by ropes; among them are the soldiers of the Pereset and the soldiers of the Peoples of the Sea (Plate 8).

What can this change in roles mean? At first the Pereset and the Peoples of the Sea are with the pharaoh. Then the army of the Peoples of the Sea is with the Egyptians, and the Pereset are the enemy. Finally, both the Peoples of the Sea and the Pereset are enemies who try an invasion.

The Pereset were lordly warriors. They helped the pharaoh but soon became his principal enemies. Why?

The Peoples of the Sea were mercenaries. They were valiant warriors. They changed camps. Why?

The texts that accompany the murals do not explain the reason for the strange reversal in the roles of the allies and the enemies in these battles and the repeated about-face.

In an attempt to identify the time of Ramses III as the fourth century and recognize him as an alter ego of one of the last native pharaohs on the throne of Egypt, we put our scheme to a very interesting test. In the beginning of the fourth century before the present era, shortly after the time when Arsames exercised the power to exact tribute from Egypt and administer law there, political and military developments took place in Egypt in which the Persians and the Greeks participated. If we are on the right track, the order of events requires that, at first, the Persians and the Greeks would be on the side of the pharaoh in his efforts to keep order on his western frontier; then the Greeks would remain his supporters but the Persians would be his enemies; in the third stage the Greeks and the Persians alike would be the pharaoh's enemies; and there would be a naval battle at one of the mouths of the Nile in which the Egyptians alone would fight against the Persians and the Greeks.

Greek Mercenaries Change Sides

At the time he mounted the throne Nectanebo I was on friendly terms with the Persians. It is even possible that he occupied the throne as a Persian puppet, since he was not the son of Acoris, who developed an unfriendly policy against the Great King. Early in his reign Nectanebo had to defend the western frontier of his realm; Cyrenaica and Libya seethed and Persia was also concerned, from the days of Darius on, that the western approaches to Egypt should stand protected and thus the growing might of Carthage be discouraged from moving in this direction. As it was the policy of the Persian kings to give support to the Athenians in their wars against the Spartans, though Athens maintained a relative freedom through having warred against Persia, so did the Persians help the Egyptian king, who had obtained a measure of independence, in his frontier conflicts with the Libyans.

But a few years later the pharaoh started a war with the Persians. Diodorus described the beginning of this conflict as having taken place under Acoris, but certain authorities disagree, placing the story in the days of Nectanebo, Acoris' successor.[1] In Diodorus' own words, these events in Egypt started at the very same time as the formation of the second Athenian maritime confederacy, which aimed at the overthrow of Spartan supremacy in Greece—and this was in −377/6. One or two years earlier Nectanebo had succeeded Acoris.

Diodorus related this:

> Whilst these things were acting in Greece, Acoris, king of Egypt, for some time before bearing a grudge to the Persian king, raised

[1] H. R. Hall, "Egypt to the coming of Alexander," *Cambridge Ancient History*, 1st ed. (1927), VI, 148.

a great army of foreigners from all parts: for, giving large pay, and being otherwise very bountiful, he got together a great number of Grecians in a short time, who listed themselves into his service. But, wanting a skilful general, he sent for Chabrias the Athenian, an excellent commander, and one highly honoured for his valour, who undertook the employment, but without the consent of the people [of Athens], and so prepared himself with all diligence for the war against the Persians.[2]

In the skirmishes that the army of Nectanebo had with the Persian detachments, Chabrias and his mercenaries played a leading role. The Persians were ejected from Egypt.

But Pharnabazus (declared commander-in-chief by the [Persian] king), having made great preparations of money for the war, sent messengers to Athens to complain against Chabrias, letting them know that, by his accepting of the chief command under the king of Egypt, he had greatly alienated the king of Persia from the people of Athens.[3] Then he demanded that they would send to him Iphicrates, to assist him in the command of the army. Upon this the Athenians (who made it their great concern to stand right in the king's good opinion, and to keep Pharnabazus firm to their interest) without delay recalled Chabrias out of Egypt, and commanded Iphicrates to assist the Persians.[4]

Here we see that the puzzling changes of sides that were depicted on the walls of the Medinet Habu temple by Ramses III have a perfect explanation. First the Persians and the Greeks supported the pharaoh. Under Chabrias the Greeks served the pharaoh in his war against the Persians. Then Chabrias was recalled to Athens, and Iphicrates with the Greek mercenaries arrived to help the Persians and together they battled the Egyptians.

Diodorus also related that when Socratides was archon at Athens, and Quintus Crassus (Servilius), Servius Cornelius, and Spurius Papirius were military tribunes in Rome, "at that time the king of

---

[2] *The Historical Library of Diodorus the Sicilian*, trans. G. Booth (London, 1814), XV, 3, p. 21.

[3] Hall (*Cambridge Ancient History*, VI, 148) places this adventure of Chabrias in —377; this is in conflict with his dating of the events (ibid., p. 146). See also the footnotes by Charles L. Sherman to his translation of Diodorus (Loeb Classical Library, 1952), Vol. VII, pp. 24–25.

[4] Diodorus, XV, 3.

Persia marched against the Egyptians who had revolted some time before." The year is clearly identified as −374–73.

> The army was commanded by Pharnabazus and Iphicrates the Athenian; the barbarians by Pharnabazus, and twenty thousand mercenaries by Iphicrates, who was in so much favour with the king for his excellent conduct [strategic skill] that he intrusted him with that command. Pharnabazus had spent many years in preparation for this war.[5]

Iphicrates, imaginative and impetuous, of a different disposition from that of Pharnabazus, urged immediate advance. Knowing "the readiness of his [Pharnabazus'] tongue," one day Iphicrates accosted him, saying that he wondered "that one who was so voluble in his speech should be so slow in his actions." Pharnabazus answered that "he was master of his words, but the king of his actions."

The Persian satrap and the Greek strategist mustered their armies in Acco in northern Palestine. Diodorus wrote:

> When the king's forces came to Aces [Acco], in Syria, and were there mustered, there were found two hundred thousand barbarians, to be under the conduct of Pharnabazus, and twenty thousand Grecians, under the command of Iphicrates.[6]

It appears that Ramses III referred to this camp when he wrote: "They set up a camp in one place in Amor [Syria]."

The Naval Invasion of the Delta

In this war, not the huge army outfitted and camped at Acco but a naval expeditionary force was destined to carry out a stratagem and to play the major role, though not a successful one.

> About the beginning of the spring the officers, with all the forces both at sea and land, made for Egypt. When they came near to the river Nile, they found the Egyptians ready and prepared for battle.[1]

[5] XV, 5.
[6] Ibid.
[1] Diodorus, XV, 5.

During the years when the Persian satrap was making his careful preparations for the assault on Egypt the pharaoh had time to prepare for its defense. The plan of the attackers was to force an entrance into one of the mouths of the Nile with the fleet.

It is possible to compare what Ramses III wrote about his preparations and the course of the war with what Diodorus related about the preparations and the course of the war of the pharaoh Nectanebo I. Diodorus wrote:

> In the mean time, Nectanebis, the king of Egypt, had perfect knowledge of the strength of the Persian forces; but he placed his greatest confidence in the strength of his country, the entrance into Egypt being very difficult on every side, and the passage blocked both by sea and land by the seven mouths of the Nile. For at every mouth where the Nile falls into the sea, was a city built, with large forts or castles on either side of the river. . . .
>
> . . . Of all these he had most strongly fortified Pelusium; for, being the next frontier town towards Syria, they conceived the enemy would first attempt to enter into the country that way; therefore they drew a trench round the city, and, where there was a place whereat any vessels might in any probability enter, there they raised walls to obstruct the passage; and, where there were any fords by which the way lay open into Egypt by land, he brought the water over them; and, where any ship might pass, he filled up those places with stones and rubbish: by which means it was very difficult, and scarce possible, either for ships to sail, or horse or foot to march.[2]

Ramses III wrote:

> They were coming, while the flame was prepared before them, forward toward Egypt.
>
> Their confederation was the Peleset, Theker, Shekelesh, Denyen and Weshesh, lands united. They laid their hands upon the lands to the very circuit of the earth, their hearts confident and trusting: "Our plans will succeed!"
>
> . . . I organized my frontier in Zahi. . . . I caused the Nile mouth to be prepared like [by?] a strong wall with warships, galleys and coasters, equipped.[3]

[2] Ibid.
[3] Edgerton and Wilson, eds., *Historical Records of Ramses III* (1936), p. 5.

The erection of fortifications at the entrance to the mouths of the Nile is described by both Ramses III and Diodorus; both tell how in order to obstruct a forced entrance of the mouths of the Nile, the pharaoh raised walls in them, a very singular engineering feat not known from the earlier or later history of Egypt.

Diodorus related that when the fleet of attackers realized the impregnability of the Pelusian mouth of the Nile it sailed for another, the Mendesian mouth. There the ships forced an entrance and after a sharp engagement with the Egyptian troops landed and occupied the fortress at the mouth of the river. Diodorus proceeded:

> They steered their course for Mendesium, another mouth of the Nile, where the shore runs a great way out from the main land. Here they landed three thousand men, and Pharnabazus and Iphicrates assaulted a fort built upon the very mouth of the river; but the Egyptians came down with three thousand horse and foot to the relief of the place; upon which there was a sharp engagement.[4]

A bas-relief of Ramses III shows a naval battle at the mouth of the Nile (Plate 7). Five vessels of the invading fleet are engaged by four Egyptian ships. This time the enemies of the Egyptians are the warriors in horned helmets and crownlike tiaras. The Egyptian text to this scene reads:

> Now the northern countries . . . penetrated the channels of the Nile mouths. . . . His majesty is gone forth like a whirlwind against them. . . .

Ramses III, like Diodorus, wrote that the enemy succeeded in entering the Nile mouths. This penetration of the Mendesian mouth of the Nile and the occupation of the fortress on the shore of the mouth was hardly a success. Ramses wrote:

> Those who came on land were overthrown and slaughtered. . . . They that entered into the Nile mouths were like birds ensnared in the net.[5]

Diodorus explained why the occupation of the now half-ruined

[4] XV, 5.
[5] Edgerton and Wilson, eds., *Historical Records of Ramses III*, p. 53.

fort became a trap for the invaders. Iphicrates and Pharnabazūs, the Greek and Persian generals, disagreed and quarreled over tactics. Iphicrates wished to try penetrating the Nile as far as Memphis and occupying that city before the Egyptians could gather an adequate garrison there. This Athenian general was one of the most ingenious strategists Greece ever had.

> He [Iphicrates] advised that they should sail with the fleet thither before the rest of the Egyptian army got together; but Pharnabazus and all his forces were for staying till all the Persian land and sea-forces came up, that so there might be less danger in the expedition. But Iphicrates then offered to undertake the reduction of the city with those mercenaries that were then with him if he might but have the liberty. Upon which, Pharnabazus grew envious at the valour and confidence of the man, and began to be fearful lest all Egypt should be conquered by his arms only, and therefore denied his request. Hereupon, Iphicrates made a solemn protestation against them, declaring that all this expedition would be fruitless and vain, through their neglect, if they let slip the present opportunity. But Pharnabazus envied him the more, and, very undeservedly, gave him opprobrious language.[6]

The old Persian satrap argued that they had to wait for the arrival of the main forces marching by land.

The rejection of the plan of the strategist who had been invited by the Persians to help in the conduct of the war against Egypt appears to have been referred to by Ramses III when he wrote:

> They asked a chief with their mouth, but it was not with their heart.

The Egyptians, said Diodorus, now had enough time to

> put a strong garrison into Memphis and marched with all their army to the little town before demolished.
>
> And, prevailing in sundry skirmishes against the Persians, they never let them rest, but, growing still stronger and stronger, made a great slaughter of them, and grew every day more obstinate.

Ramses III wrote:

> . . . As they were coming forward toward Egypt, their hearts

---

[6] Diodorus, XV, 5.

relying upon their hands, a net was prepared for them, to ensnare them.

They that entered into the Nile mouths were caught, fallen into the midst of it, pinioned in their places, butchered, and their bodies hacked up.[7]

Both Ramses III and Diodorus, in almost identical terms, described the slaughter of the invaders—the Pereset and the Peoples of the Isles, or the Persians and the Greeks.

In the bas-relief that carries this inscription Ramses III is shown standing on a rostrum before a fortress built at a mouth of the Nile. His officials present him with captives. Ramses is saying:

That which I commanded is come to pass, and my counsels and my plans are perfected.

Over the fortress is written: "Migdal." Migdal means in Hebrew a "tower" or "bastion." This must be the fort which, as Diodorus related, was built at the mouth of the river and was occupied by the invaders, where they underwent a siege; actually in the text of Diodorus the word *pyrgos* is "tower," the word Ramses III used. So also it is translated in a modern version of Diodorus.[8] It is also worth noting that Ramses III used a Hebrew term for a tower: of the impregnation of the Egyptian language by Hebrew terms in the days of this pharaoh, we shall have a little more to say later.

The expedition was a failure. The Persian army occupied the castle for a number of months, but when the Nile began to overflow "the commanders resolved forthwith to leave Egypt" (Diodorus).

Ramses wrote:

Their feet have ceased to tread the frontier of Egypt.

Diodorus wrote accordingly:

Thus all that large preparation for an expedition into Egypt came to nothing.

There was a dramatic sequel to the hurried retreat. Ramses wrote:

Their leaders —— fled wretched and trembling.

---

[7] Edgerton and Wilson, eds., *Historical Records of Ramses III*, p. 42.
[8] Diodorus, trans. Charles L. Sherman (Loeb Classical Library), XV, 42.

Diodorus confirmed that Iphicrates fled in secret from the Persian satrap, fearing that he might be blamed for the unfortunate turn of the campaign.

> As soon, therefore, as they returned into Asia, Pharnabazus renewed the quarrel with Iphicrates: upon which, Iphicrates . . . consulted how to withdraw himself privately from the camp. To this end (having prepared a vessel for his purpose) he went on board in the night, and so sailed to Athens: but Pharnabazus sent ambassadors after him, and accused him, as being the occasion of the miscarriage of the design relating to the reducing of Egypt; to whom the Athenians answered—That, if he were guilty, they would punish him according to his deserts: but, in a very short time after, they made him admiral of their whole fleet.[9]

Ramses III was very proud of his victory, not merely over a strong enemy but also over renowned generals, rich in successes and crowned with laurels. He knew the spirit of Greece, never wholeheartedly with the Persian king; she would hail this achievement.

> Their people are mine with praise.

Ramses III's sea and land war against the invaders from Syria, which ended in their expulsion, was described by himself. The Greek historians told the story of Ramses III as that of Nectanebo I.

"From the Egyptian inscriptions we learn nothing about the history of Egypt during the reign of Nectanebus I, and it is to classical authorities, especially Diodorus, to whom we must look for information concerning the progress of the war between the Greeks and Persians, and to the part which Egypt played in it."[10]

Of "Nectanebo's war" no Egyptian records will be found because the account is already in the records of the pharaoh for whom modern historians selected the name of Ramses III. Of Ramses III's war, neither Hebrew nor Greek historical data will be discovered because the record of it is in the history of Nectanebo I.

"Denien" or "Thenien" are named by Ramses III as first among his beaten enemies. These appear to be Athenians (and not Danaäns as sometimes surmised).

[9] XV, 5.
[10] E. A. Wallis Budge, A History of Egypt (New York, 1902), VII, 101.

Chapter III

THE ART OF WARFARE

Warriors of the Peoples of the Sea

THE SOLDIERS of the Peoples of the Sea, the Tjeker, the Shekelesh, the Teresh, the Weshesh, and the Sardan, were from the Asia Minor region. The Denien, however, are referred to by Ramses III as "Peoples of the Islands." The conclusion that these soldiers were archaic Greeks has already been arrived at by scholars who explain the events narrated and illustrated by Ramses III as a Greek invasion of Egypt that took place soon after the fall of Troy: more properly these particular warriors would be described as Mycenaean Greeks and their confederates or, if one prefers the classification, as Homeric Greeks, the Trojan War having been fought by the last generation of the Hellenes, whose leader, Agamemnon, son of Atreus, was king of Mycenae.

To support the identification of Denien with Mycenaean Greeks, it was argued that Denien (Dnn) stands for Danaäns (a Homeric term for archaic Greeks). Some texts, however, connect them with the Syrian coast, and others with Cyprus. I, however, lean toward identifying the "Peoples of the Isles," the Denien, with the Athenians, since *d* and *t* in Egyptian are one and the same letter.

The expression "Peoples of the Isles" also points to the Aegean area, and in a broader sense it would include Cyprus, Crete, Sicily, and also the Peloponnesus, for since antiquity the southern part of Greece, below the Corinthian Isthmus (Peloponnesus), was spoken of as an island; the plain of Argos (Argolis), Sparta, Arcadia, and Achaia were regarded as parts of an island; and actually the narrow isthmus of Corinth is but a bridge between continental Greece and the Peloponnesus (Pelops' Island).

The Hebrew prophets, Isaiah II, Jeremiah, and Ezekiel, used to refer to the Aegean archipelago and the Hellenic world in general as the "isles." "Listen, O isles, unto me; and hearken, ye people, from far" (Isaiah 49:1).[1] "And all the kings of Tyrus, and all the kings of Zidon, and the kings of the isles which are beyond the sea" (Jeremiah 25:22).[2]

The Peoples of the Sea is a general name for a conglomeration of tribes or a confederation of nations; Ramses III supplies the names of the various peoples covered by this generic name: Tjkr, Skls, Trs, Wss, and Srdn. Various efforts have been made to identify these tribes. The Tjeker may have been Teucrians, or Greeks who settled in the fifth century in Dor, a city of the Tjeker. The Shekelesh are possibly from Sagalassos in Asia Minor. The Teresh may be from Tarsus or Tyre. The Weshesh are perhaps from Assos or Iasos or Issos in Asia Minor. The Sardan are familiar as mercenaries of the pharaohs of the Nineteenth Dynasty, Seti and Ramses II. The phonetics of the name made one group of scholars look for Sardinia and another group for Sardis, the capital of Lydia in western Asia Minor. The Lydian kingdom, however, dates from the eighth and later centuries.[3]

In discussing the Sardan serving under the pharaohs of the Nineteenth Dynasty, I am able to show by independent sources that the people must be identified with the people of Sardis.

It is of importance to note that the province of Pharnabazus was called "Tyaiy Drayahya" or "Those [or the people] of the Sea." This satrapy was in Asia Minor and evidently designated the same area as the land of the "Peoples of the Sea" of Ramses III.

An inscription next to one of the bas-reliefs of Medinet Habu, with a group of prisoners clad in the attire of the Pereset, identifies them as Tjeker (Tjkr); another such group is identified by the

---

[1] See also Isaiah 59:18; 60:9; 66:19.

[2] See also Jeremiah 31:10, Ezekiel 27:35, Zephaniah 2:11.

[3] Hanfmann, excavating Sardis and finding a wall similar to the walls of Troy VI, argued that the antiquity of Sardis goes back to the thirteenth century. Should not his argument be reversed?

accompanying hieroglyphics as Denien. A third and largest group in identical dress and headgear is designated as Pereset.[4] From this we learn that soldiers and marines from the Persian satrapies in the imperial army of Artaxerxes II were dressed in the same fashion as the Persian warriors. These were conscripts; the soldiers with horned helmets, however, were mercenaries.

Since Herodotus visited Egypt in the middle of the fifth century, it looks as if the designation Teucrian was then current for the people of the western coast of Asia Minor in general, or, possibly, for one group among them. The Tjeker also appear as marines in the story of Wenamon, a subject discussed later in this book.

The facial type of the soldiers with horned helmets on the bas-reliefs of Ramses III closely resembles that of the Greeks in the age of Pericles, and this has also been noticed. "The European, in fact Greek, type is very noticeable: the face closely resembles that of a well-known head of a young man of the VIth–Vth century B.C. in the Acropolis Museum at Athens."[5] The art expert who thus described a warrior from a relief at Medinet Habu dated ca. −1190 did not intend to make any inferences about the time of Ramses III; he accepted the established chronology, according to which seven hundred years elapsed between the creation of two similar models.

However, there is a facial difference between the Greek models of the fifth or any other previous century and the Peoples of the Sea. The Peoples of the Sea, like the Pereset, are beardless. Surviving Greek art shows that, from the times of which any recollections or pictures are preserved, Greek men grew beards, and not until the late fifth or fourth century did they begin to shave their faces. The Mycenaean vases are often adorned with human figures in painted clay; the male figures are regularly bearded. The Homeric heroes, with the exception of Achilles, were depicted with beards by Greek artists of the seventh and later centuries: but it was Achilles who,

---

[4] Trude Dothan, *The Philistines and Their Material Culture* (in Hebrew) (Jerusalem, 1967).

[5] *Cambridge Ancient History*, volume of plates, C. T. Seltman, ed. (1927), p. 152.

to avoid taking part in the Trojan War, could pass for a girl and live among virgins at the court of Lycomedes, king of Scyros, where he was detected by Odysseus, who set arms before him, Achilles betraying himself by the fondness which he displayed for them. Under Pericles, the Greek men grew beards. This is true of full-grown men; the ephebes, youths at the time of their first down, like those on a Parthenon frieze, are, of course, pictured beardless. The warriors of the Peoples of the Sea were not ephebes who had just joined the army but full-grown men who made a habit of shaving.

As already mentioned, Alexander copied the oriental military custom of shaving when the Macedonians were marching through Asia Minor. Therefore it is to be expected that various ethnic groups in Asia Minor and the Greeks who were there were already accustomed to shaving. The appearance of beardless Greek soldiers on the bas-reliefs of Medinet Habu, ascribed to the early twelfth century, at the close of the Mycenaean age, presumably in the time of Odysseus' wanderings, is an anachronism. This feature alone suffices to cast grave doubt on the accepted view that the Peoples of the Sea were Mycenaean Greeks.

The armor of the Peoples of the Sea is also a good earmark. The helmets, the tunics, the corselets, the swords, the targets, the spears are those of Greek mercenaries in Persian service in the fourth century. A Greek warrior in a helmet with two horns is pictured on a vase found on the Acropolis of Athens.[6] But a helmet with horns and a crest was originally the headgear of the Lydian contingents in the army of Xerxes.[7] One hundred years after Xerxes came to the throne the helmets with horns but without ears apparently be-

[6] W. Reichel, *Homerische Waffen* (2nd ed.; 1901), Fig. 47. The portraiture of the warriors of the Peoples of the Sea on Medinet Habu bas-reliefs must have made Reichel ascribe the Greek portrait on the Acropolis vase to the Homeric age.

[7] After detailing the attire of the Asiatic Thracians or Bithynians, Herodotus wrote of the next Greek contingent, the name of which is lost in the extant copies of Herodotus (VII, 76): "They wore helmets of bronze, with the ears and horns of oxen wrought in bronze thereon and crests withal." This contingent was most probably from Sardis, a place that logically would follow Bithynia.

came part of the uniform of the Greeks in the Persian army and in overseas service in general.[8]

Horned helmets were worn by Athenian soldiers of the fourth century in mercenary service, first of the Egyptians and then of the Persians. There is a difference between the Athenian helmet worn by those who served under Chabrias (a disc between the horns) and the helmet worn by the troops under Iphicrates (no disc between the horns). This change in the form of the helmet indicates that the disappearance of the Peoples of the Sea from the ranks of the Egyptian allies and their appearance among the troops attacking in alliance with the Pereset was not a case of the same troops switching from one side to the other. The Athenian soldiers did not go over from the Egyptian to the Persian side; the soldiers of Chabrias were recalled from Egypt, and other troops, under Iphicrates, were commanded to sail to assist the Persians.

Forty years later a two-horn helmet was worn by Alexander in his campaign in Asia and Egypt. In Arabic, Alexander has the appellation "Dhul-Karnein" or "Two Horns." Alexander's horns, however, were more like ram horns.

An even more precise means for placing the Peoples of the Sea in their proper time is offered by their offensive and defensive armor—the swords and the shields.

We see swords of normal size, but then we see the Peoples of the Sea changing their short swords to very long ones.

The Peoples of the Sea were also in process of changing the length of their spears: we see short spears and long ones too; also shields of two different designs—an almost rectangular one that covers most of the body and a round target.

Next we shall read that such a change in the armor of Athenian soldiers took place early in the fourth century.

[8] A horns-and-disc helmet was occasionally used in Persia in later times: King Khusraw I of the Sassanid Dynasty of Persia (contemporary with the Roman Empire) was portrayed in such a helmet hunting ibexes. A. U. Pope, *Survey of Persian Art,* Vol. IV (1939), Plate 213.

The Reform of Iphicrates Pictured
by Ramses III

As already mentioned, Iphicrates, in the year −390 (or −391), acquired fame by gaining a victory with a regiment of Athenian soldiers over a Spartan *mora* of *hoplites* (heavy-armed warriors) near the wall of Corinth. It was his idea to give the soldiers more offensive power at the expense of their defensive armor. He clad them in tunics instead of heavy mail; he changed the shape of the shields; he had spears lengthened by half their former length; the swords also were made longer, to more than double, almost triple their length. At the first encounter the *mora* of *hoplites* was broken by the *peltasts* (light-armed troops), and the slow-moving Spartans were routed by the Athenians. Iphicrates devised a variety of other strategic innovations for the art of warfare.

In the pictures of Medinet Habu we have an opportunity to see the changes the Greek army underwent. The soldiers of the Peoples of the Sea are in tunics, some in light corselets, none in heavy armor. The development of sword, spear, javelin, and shield may be observed. We see rather short swords, as well as very long swords like those introduced by Iphicrates; short spears and long ones; also shields of two different designs—a square one that covers most of the body, and a smaller round target. The new Athenian arms were probably introduced into Egypt by Chabrias, who helped the pharaoh in his early campaigns.

In the period between −390, when the *peltasts* for the first time were put into action, and −375, when Egypt under Nectanebo clashed with Persia, the reforms of Iphicrates were adopted by other Greek generals, but old-fashioned arms survived in some detachments. Although heavy coats of mail were not used in the mercenary army, as shown on the bas-reliefs of Ramses III, next to battalions with the newly introduced arms—very long swords and round shields or bucklers—there are still soldiers with antiquated short swords and heavy shields, straight on the lower edge, curved at the top. The reform, as seen here, is in the making and is in the process of acquiring new adepts.

The Peoples of the Sea "engaged in the Land and Sea fight under Ramses III have immense swords," writes Lorimer,[1] and this is also what we had to expect from Greek mercenaries of the days when the reform of Iphicrates was introduced, and in the troops commanded by this strategist.

Ramses III himself described the unusual swords employed in the Libyan campaign as *five cubits long*.[2]

As Iphicrates joined Pharnabazus in −374 with twenty thousand Greek troops—now opposing Egypt—we can again compare and learn exactly what his latest military innovations were. Diodorus of Sicily inserted a few passages on the reforms of Iphicrates precisely in the record of the war between Nectanebo and the Persians, in which this Athenian general took part; he "especially employed himself in contriving the making of new sorts of arms" and made swords of almost triple length. "It was hitherto a custom among the Grecians to carry great and heavy shields; but, because these by their weight much hindered the soldiers in their march, he [Iphicrates] changed the form of them, and ordered targets of a moderate size in their room. . . .

"He changed likewise the fashion of their spears and swords. The spears he caused to be made half as long again as they were before, and the swords longer almost by two parts. This alteration was presently approved by use and experience, and the reputation of the general was highly advanced by the usefulness of his ingenious inventions. Lastly, he altered the very soldiers' shoes, that they might be sooner put on, easier to march with, and more readily cast off; and therefore they are called at this very day Iphicratics. He invented many other things belonging to martial affairs, which would be too tedious here to relate. But thus all that great preparation for an expedition into Egypt came to nothing."[3] The pictures

---

[1] H. L. Lorimer, *Homer and the Monuments* (1950), p. 267.
[2] F. W. von Bissing, *Studi Etruschi* (1932), IV, 75. Breasted reads "five feet."
[3] Diodorus, XV, 5.

in the temple of Ramses III at Medinet Habu illustrate Diodorus'
description.

Or were the reforms of Iphicrates already anticipated and carried
out eight centuries before he was born?

Carts with "Their Concubines"

On their military campaign toward Egypt the Pereset were accompanied by wagons with womenfolk. A bas-relief of Medinet
Habu, in the upper row of a battle scene, shows several wagons
with damsels, uncomfortably caught in the midst of the fracas.
Three women lift their arms in defense or in supplication and a
young girl is seen escaping or falling from the wagon. (See Plate 5.)

Herodotus, narrating the habits of the Persians in war, says that
when they went on military campaigns they were followed by carts
"wherein rode their concubines."[1]

The bodies of the carts occupied by the females are cubical in
form. These carts were drawn by oxen.

A royal chariot can be seen on coins minted in Sidon in the very
years of Pharnabazus' campaign against Egypt.[2] Sidon was under
Persian rule. The conveyance shown is driven by horses; but, inter-
estingly, its body is also of cubical form, very different from chariots of the Assyrians, "Hittites," Egyptians, Mycenaean or Ionian
Greeks, Etruscans, or Minoans.

In the naval battle as depicted on the walls of the temple at
Medinet Habu, the weapons used by the Pereset are chiefly swords,
not a convenient weapon for such an engagement; the Peoples of
the Sea, in boats of their own but in alliance with the Pereset, use
spears; but the Egyptians use bows and very long spears well
adapted for naval fighting at close range. One can see an Egyptian
reaching from his boat and piercing the enemy on another boat with
a long spear.

[1] Herodotus, VII, 83.
[2] Sir George F. Hill, *Catalogue of the Greek Coins of Phoenicia* (London,
1910), Plates XIX, 5, and others.

Herodotus (VII, 89) says that the Egyptians in the army of Xerxes "were armed with spears suited for a sea-fight and with huge pole-axes."

Fire Ships

A new interpretation may be given to a peculiar expression in a text of Ramses III. It is said of the approaching fleet of the enemy: "They came with fire prepared before them"[1]; and again in the description of the encounter at the mouth of the Nile: "As for those who came forward together on the sea, the full flame was in front of them at the Nile mouths."[2] In the twelfth century, flame throwers were unknown as weapons for storming or defending fortresses. The sentences were therefore explained as figures of speech, allegorizing rage. "When the text speaks of the 'full flame,' who could divine that it means the Egyptian fleet; or when it mentions the 'wall of metal,' who could infer that the Egyptian army is intended?"[3] It must be admitted that, in view of the flowery mode of expression peculiar to Ramses III, this explanation may seem plausible. Nevertheless, the narrative character of the passages about the "fire prepared" before the fleet and the "full flame" thrown into battle leads us to wonder whether these were indeed mere allegories.

Assyrians introduced "fire" warfare, using burning pitch and fire pots in sieges, as their bas-reliefs reveal. Herodotus[4] relates that the Persians used arrows tipped with burning tow when Xerxes captured Athens in −480. In the Peloponnesian War (−413), according to Thucydides,[5] fire ships participated and resinous torches were thrown.

"Aineias (c. 360 B.C.) describes the production of a violent fire by the use of pots filled with a mixture of pitch, sulphur, pine-

---

[1] Edgerton and Wilson, eds., *Historical Records of Ramses III*, p. 55.
[2] Ibid.
[3] Breasted, *Ancient Records*, Vol. IV, Sec. 21.
[4] Herodotus, VIII, 52.
[5] Thucydides, VII, 53. See also IV, 100.

shavings, and incense or resin; this incendiary mixture could also, he says, be attached to large wooden pestles fitted with iron hooks at both ends and thrown on to wooden decks of ships, to which they attached themselves, or on to the wooden protections of besieging troops."[6]

When in −332 Alexander the Great stormed Tyre on the cliff near the Phoenician shore, the Tyrians used a fire ship. They also erected towers on the wall and attacked ships with bursts of fire.[7]

The correct date when Ramses III met the enemy fleet in the Mendesian mouth of the Nile is the year −374; the employment of fire ships and flame throwers thirty-nine years after the siege of Syracuse, during the Peloponnesian War, and forty-two years prior to the siege of Tyre by Alexander need not necessarily be allegorical fiction.

Mariannu

There still remains a partner in the war of Ramses–Nectanebo against the Persians and the Greeks whose identity is intriguing. Ramses III wrote that, in strengthening the defenses of the land frontier, he fortified a place called Zahi on the Egypt–Sinai boundary, and this corresponds with the story told by Diodorus about the defense work done by Nectanebo I on the eastern land frontier. Ramses III mentioned the organization of the garrison:

> I organized my frontier in Zahi, prepared before them (to wit) the princes, the commanders of the garrison, and the Mariannu.[1]

Who were these Mariannu, the only trustworthy allies of Egypt? At first it was suggested that Mariannu is the Aramaic word *Mareinu*, meaning "noblemen." But who could they have been, the foreign warriors in the Egypt of the twelfth century, called by an

---

[6] J. R. Partington, *A History of Greek Fire and Gunpowder* (1960), p. 1.

[7] Arrian, *Anabasis of Alexander*, trans. E. I. Robson (Loeb Classical Library, 1929), II, 21. Cf. *Cambridge Ancient History*, VI (1927), 374–75.

[1] Edgerton and Wilson, eds., *Historical Records of Ramses III*. Wilson refers to Zahi as a point on the border. Some other authorities consider Zahi as designating a large part of Palestine.

Aramaic name? Aramaic is a Semitic language that supplanted Hebrew in Palestine after the Babylonian exile, in which parts of the Books of Ezra and Daniel, and later the Talmuds, were written; at the beginning of the present era it was the everyday language of the Jews in Palestine. The oldest Aramaic inscriptions date from the ninth and eighth centuries.

The presence in Egypt in the twelfth century of Semitic noblemen with an Aramaic title was conceded to be a phenomenon calling for an explanation. The idea was discarded as entirely inappropriate for the place and time, and theories were put forth that the word *Mariannu* originated in Mitanni or in Sanskrit.[2] Shifting the historical scene, we may ask again: Is not the Mariannu of Ramses III the Aramaic word for "noblemen"?

In 1906, among the debris of old buildings in the southern part of Elephantine, an island in the Nile opposite Aswan, papyri written in Aramaic were found. They were discovered only half a meter from the surface, unprotected in the sand and rubbish. These documents proved to have originated in the fifth century before this era, in the time of the Persian overlordship in Egypt; the oldest of them dates from the year −494 (or −483), the most recent ones from the year −407. Names of Persian kings are mentioned in many of them, together with the year of the reign of the king in which the documents were written, making possible the exact dating of the papyri.

These documents disclose the fact that in Heb–Elephantine there existed a Jewish military colony. The place was on the southern frontier of Egypt, and the permanent task of the settlement was to safeguard the land against invasion from Nubia. This colony had a temple where Yaho (Yahweh) was worshiped in a cult combined with that of Anath-Venus. The temple and the colony were already

---

[2] A. Gustavs, *Zeitschrift für Assyrologie*, XXXVI, Neue Folge, II (1925), 297 ff. Gustavs maintains that the language of the (Hurrian) *marjannu* was not Aryan (Sanskrit), as Winckler (*Orientalistische Literaturzeitung*, XIII [1910], 291) had surmised, but Subaraean (Mitanni). See literature in W. F. Albright, *From the Stone Age to Christianity* (Baltimore, 1940), p. 153; cf. Sidney Smith, *Early History of Assyria* (London, 1928), pp. 237–38. Cf. R. T. O'Callaghan, "New light on the Mariannu as 'Chariot Warrior,'" in *Jahrbuch für Kleinasiatische Forschung*, I (1950–51), 309–24.

in existence when Cambyses overran Egypt; when he destroyed the temples of Egypt he did no damage to the temple of Elephantine—this is stated in one of the papyri.

The social status of the members of the military colony was that of the privileged; they had slaves and generally they were treated with consideration as professional soldiers permanently garrisoned in the country.

But in the year −410 the priests of the Chnum temples in the vicinity, exploiting the absence of the Persian governor, prevailed upon the regional chief to permit the destruction of the temple of Heb-Elephantine. The notables of the military community had the satisfaction of witnessing the punishment of the offenders; but the temple was not rebuilt, and because of this they wrote to the Persian satrap Bagoas in Jerusalem, and to two sons of Sanballat, the satrap in Samaria. Bagoas was the man who succeeded Nehemiah,[3] and Sanballat is repeatedly mentioned in the Book of Nehemiah as his adversary in his pious endeavor to rebuild the wall of Jerusalem.

This particular letter was written in −407 and is the last in the unearthed collection. Very soon thereafter Egypt took up arms in revolt against Persian domination. It is not known what happened to the Jewish military colony. Did it survive the insurrection and continue to exist? Did it participate in the war for freedom and defend Egypt against the expeditionary forces of the Persians?

We have only to open the published text of the Elephantine papyri[4] to find an answer to the question: Who were the Mariannu of Ramses III? and by implication to find out what was the fate of the Jewish military colonists in Egypt after −407.

The very first words of the papyrus that was written in −407 are el-maran, which means "to the sir," and the word maran is repeated again and again in this and in others of the Elephantine papyri. The word maran or marenu ("our sir") was put before the name

---

[3] Josephus, Jewish Antiquities, XI, 297 ff.

[4] E. Sachau, Aramäische Papyri und Ostraka aus einer jüdischen Militär-Kolonie zu Elephantine (Leipzig, 1911). His preliminary publication is Drei Aramäische Papyrusurkunden aus Elephantine (Berlin, 1908). These papyri were found in Elephantine in the later decades of the last century.

of the satrap in Jerusalem when the chiefs of the colony wrote to him; they themselves were addressed as *mareinu* ("our sirs") by the ordinary members of the colony in their letters. The singular and plural possessive forms, *marenu* and *mareinu*, are used profusely in the papyri of Elephantine.

Here we have proof from the hand of Ramses III that the Jewish military colony still existed in Egypt in −374, that its members were loyal to Egyptian interests, and that in a time of emergency they were shifted from the quiet south to the threatened eastern frontier.

In 1953 and 1954 more Aramaic documents, found in Egypt, were published: they had been stored unpublished in European and American collections for decades and their existence was unknown to the scholarly world at large. Some, written on hides, date from −411 to −408 and were written by the Persian satrap Arsham;[5] a different group of private letters, written by the members of the Jewish colony at Elephantine, date from −499 to −399.[6] From this latter collection it can be seen that Artaxerxes II was still recognized as king in Elephantine in the year −401. Otherwise the same conclusions as to the identity of the *mareinu* can be made from these letters as from those published earlier in this century.

The Ore of the Land of "Atika"

In the days of Ramses III (Nectanebo I) traffic between Greece and Egypt was maintained at an unprecedented pace. In the days of earlier kings, since the first half of the seventh century, Greek mercenaries and merchants had settled in Egypt, and in the sixth century, under Amasis, intellectual exchange was fostered with Greek philosophers visiting the country that beckoned them in their desire to learn ancient lore and history. But in the days of Ramses III the contact became very close and Athens in Attica played an

---

[5] Purchased by L. Borchardt in the 1930s; published by G. R. Driver, *Aramaic Documents of the Fifth Century B.C.* (Oxford, 1954).

[6] Purchased in Aswan by C. E. Wilbour in 1893; published by E. G. Kraeling, *The Brooklyn Museum Aramaic Papyri* (New Haven, 1953).

important role in the military, political, and economical life of
Egypt. Mercenaries came and went and returned; vessels with the
produce of fields sailed to Greece and from there came vessels with
their merchandise.

These relations—quite subdued in the fifth century when Egypt
was ruled by Persia and then when Greece was torn in the Peloponnesian and Corinthian wars—bloomed as soon as Ramses III came
to power, even before he broke with the Persians.

In the Papyrus Harris, Ramses III says:

> I sent forth my messengers to the country of the Atika . . . , to the
> great copper mines which are in this place. Their galleys carried
> them; others on the land-journey were upon their asses. It has not
> been heard before, since kings reign. Their mines were found
> abounding in copper; it was loaded by ten-thousands into their
> galleys.[1]

Where was the land of "Atika" referred to in this text? Breasted
says that it designates an "uncertain region, accessible both by sea
and land from Egypt, hence probably in the Sinaitic Peninsula."

Sinai it could not be—Ramses III would not have said of it, "it
has not been heard before, since kings reign," or since monarchy
in Egypt, by then several thousand years old. Sinai mining for copper ore was done during the New Kingdom, Middle Kingdom, and
probably during the Old Kingdom too. Sinai chieftains under
Ramses III or at any earlier period were never capable of sending
ore in vessels of their own. Also no other reference to "Atika" in
hieroglyphic texts from these earlier times has ever been found—
and Sinai was at the doorstep of Egypt.

The mining products were carried in "their galleys," which means
that not Egyptian vessels but vessels from the land of the mining activities were employed. Phoenicians, Cyprians, Lydians, or
Greeks, all seafaring nations, come first to mind. Cyprus had and
still has great copper mines—the very name of the island gave the
name to the metal or, vice versa, received its name from the metal.
But the description of Atika as reachable by sea *and* by land routes
excludes Cyprus. The extended war carried on by King Euagoras

---

[1] Breasted, *Ancient Records,* IV, 408.

for decades against the Persians kept Cyprus from carrying on commerce, and new sources of ore were probably looked for in countries that normally would have imported it from Cyprus. The Phoenicians also depended on Cyprian ore for manufacturing.

If the problem of the location of Atika were dependent on the condition that the place could be reached by sea *and* by land, as Breasted understood it, then it could be shown that Attica in Greece, the state of which Athens was the capital, complies with such conditions. The crossing of the Hellespont (the Dardanelles) was a feat achieved regularly in peace and war, whether by galleys, rafts, or temporary floating bridges built of barges, a feat accomplished by Xerxes in −481 on his way to invade Greece, and repeated by Alexander going east one hundred and fifty years later.

But the text does not depend on such a condition. Actually, it speaks of the ore carried from the mines to the ships on "their" ("of the people of Atika") asses, and of transport by ships from there to Egypt, again on "their" ("of the people of Atika") ships.

The question of the identity of the land of Atika referred to in the papyrus and Attica of which Athens was the capital narrows down to the problem of whether unusually hard metal or alloys of it were found in Attica. In the Great Harris Papyrus, the metal from the mines of Atika is called *hmt*, translated by Breasted as "copper," although with reservations, since *hmt* is not the usual term for that metal. In another text this same word *hmt* is used for three different varieties of ore or alloy, all of which are unidentified, but the hardness of the ore or alloy is being stressed.[2] Thus this word was used for metal (or mineral ore) in general. Today Greece is not a copper-producing country, yet mineral ore is high on its export list and leading among the ores are pyrite and chromite.

Pyrite has the appearance of brass—it is a pale yellow mineral, the bisulphide of iron; other metals which sometimes replace a part of the iron are cobalt, nickel, and copper. Pyrite's nickname is "fool's gold," yet not infrequently it does contain gold.

Chromite is composed of iron and chromium. The latter element

[2] Alan Gardiner, "The Tomb of a Much Travelled Theban Official," *Journal of Egyptian Archaeology*, IV (1917), pp. 28ff.

is surpassed in hardness only by boron and by diamonds; with an admixture of lead, chromite is yellow. Metallic chromium is prepared by reduction of the oxide by carbon. It is used in plating other metals because of its hardness and non-tarnishing properties. In the steel industry chromium is widely used in hardening the alloy.

The hardening of iron found next to chromium in the chromite ore would make it very desirable in the manufacture of weapons and also of tools for working on stone. Actually the never solved question—With what tools did the Egyptians of the Bronze Age, from the Old Bronze on, cut hieroglyphics into hard granite, even harder basalt, and hardest of all, diorite (bronze, a copper and tin alloy, would be blunted after a few strokes), or chisel stone sculpture with exquisitely sharp lines of eyelids, lips, and ears?— may be answered if chromite ore was used in making tools, or even only as abrasive powder. During earlier times, since the time of pyramid building, chromite ore could have been brought from Rhodesia, which is rich in it.

It appears probable that Ramses III referred to chromite and also to pyrite, ores abundant in Greece, when he wrote of the metal ore brought on galleys from Atika to Egypt in preparation for the impending war with Persia. If such was the case, the ore of Greece was even preferable to the copper ore of Cyprus or Sinai.

Chapter IV

ON LANGUAGE, ART, AND RELIGION

Semitic Influence on the Language
and Religion of Egypt

FOR OVER two hundred years after the fall of Jerusalem there existed a Jewish colony in Egypt. The influence of the Hebrew-Syrian language, conspicuous in the sixth century, must have become prominent in the time of Ramses III. This is indeed the case. In many instances Semitic words displaced Egyptian words, and the scribes of Ramses III "often abandoned a perfectly good Egyptian word" in favor of a Hebrew equivalent. In the inscriptions of Medinet Habu—to take one example at random— the Semitic word *barekh*, "to bless," is used instead of the corresponding Egyptian word.[1]

"The Medinet Habu texts are extreme in their choice of words. They exhibit a straining after the unusual word or phrase. . . . They take an especial relish in employing foreign words, borrowed usually from the Semitic tongues. Here is exhibited a striving for an arresting effect, a rather childish display of erudition, and also an increased internationalism. That Semitic words should be so profusely present in Medinet Habu points to cultural interrelations on a very brisk scale throughout the ancient Near East."[2]

---

[1] In the Papyrus Harris the Hebrew *ashek* is used for "to oppress." Other examples are: *aliah* for "ramp," *keseth* for "cover," *marcheshet* for "pan," *tzaek* for "cry." See J. H. Bondi, *Dem hebräisch-phönizischen Sprachzweige angehörige Lehnwörter in hieroglyphischen und hieratischen Texten* (Leipzig, 1886).

[2] J. A. Wilson, "The Language of the Historical Texts Commemorating Ramses III," *Medinet Habu Studies, 1928–29* (Chicago, 1930), p. 32.

This characteristic is understandable when the influence of the Jewish colony in Egypt is taken into account; it becomes embarrassing, however, if Ramses III was a contemporary of the Judges Gideon, Jephthah, or Samson and especially since in the entire Book of Judges there is no mention of any contact with Egypt.

Ramses III wrote: "I am upon the ways . . . of the All-Lord, my august, divine father, the Lord of the gods."[3] The influence of the Jewish settlements in Egypt might also have left some imprint on Egyptian religious thought.

Ramses III often mentioned Baal, also, and it has already been stressed that the Baal cult, formerly but little known in Egypt, became quite prominent at that time. The flourishing of this cult in Egypt must be credited to the influence of the non-Jewish post-exilic population of Palestine and its intercourse with Egypt.

There was evidently nothing deep or permanent in the influence of the Hebrew religion on the Egyptian conception of the Supreme Being. The temple of Medinet Habu is full of pictures of gods with human bodies and the heads of birds and beasts to whom the king is paying homage; he also stands before the god Amon, who is pictured in a state of obscene excitement. But more than all these, Ramses III venerated his own person. The temple of Medinet Habu was built as the place of worship of his own august being. It is boring to read the endless self-glorifications. The simplest of all of them is his modest statement: "My character is excellent."

A question could be asked: Does the literary style of the period under discussion—that of the Twentieth Dynasty—exhibit close relationship with that of the two dynasties immediately preceding it on the conventional timetable? The answer to this question could be used as an argument for or against the reconstruction presented here and equally so for or against the conventional timetable according to which Ramses III lived in the first half of the twelfth century.

[3] "All-Lord" is, however, an expression already met in a coffin text of the early Middle Kingdom: Erman-Grapow, *Wörterbuch der ägyptischen Sprache,* II (1928), 230.

"A cultured Egyptian scribe of the twelfth century B.C., well versed in the classics of his literature, might have bewailed the degenerate style of the temple scribes of his day. Remembering the crisp campaign annals of Thutmose III, he would shudder at the florid bombast with which Ramses III choked his records. . . . He would be oppressed by the straining artificiality evidenced by a profusion of foreign words and far-fetched metaphor. Remembering, if he could, the more rigid rules of grammar which defended the purity of the classical literature, he would feel a lofty pity for these scribes who labored to employ the old grammar but whose efforts were defeated by ignorance, haste, and the sheer weight of the spoken language."[4]

But was there "a cultured Egyptian scribe" under Ramses III? If there was, he did not leave any vestiges of his ability or taste to posterity. "The temple compositions of his day"—as judged by the Medinet Habu texts—"are turgid, careless, and grammatically irregular." Besides, they are "stupidly pompous." The longer texts are full of "every complimentary comparison and every glorifying epithet that the hard-pushed scribes could devise" and the brief texts accompanying the reliefs "consist to a great extent of rather staccato eulogy of the king, complimentary dialogues between king and god, or laudatory chants of the Greek chorus of courtiers and captives."[5] (The word "Greek" was not intended by the author of this passage to indicate the age of the texts or the race of the courtiers and captives—it was used only to describe the impression made by such choral injections.)

The "insistent stressing of the magnificence and valor of the Pharaoh" could mean that a "mediocre ruler had to be raised to the standard of his predecessors or, more probably, that the jaded palate of his people demanded a more exotic and highly seasoned fare." The grandiloquent utterances are like "sounding brass and a tinkling cymbal."

As to the grammar, the scribe of Ramses III "was groping after a style which had passed out of general use." He employed false

---

[4] Wilson, *Medinet Habu Studies,* 1928–29, pp. 24 ff.
[5] Ibid., p. 26, n. 3. Other quotations that follow are from the same article.

archaisms, which indicated that not a few forms had already passed out of use. "A certain vagueness" in the use of proper etymology "tells us that current speech was equally vague or else already committed to a fairly general suppression of endings [suffixes]."

On the paleographic side, "the cutting of signs is coarse and careless. . . . Evidence of haste is universal." The scribes who prepared the outlines for the stone engravers were clearly more familiar with the hieratic signs, generally used on papyri but not in stone, than with the hieroglyphs and thus disfigured the latter. Their hieroglyphs "entirely lost sight of the genesis of individual signs."[6]

Finally, the Medinet Habu reliefs themselves suggest "a distinct break with the past." "A loss in dignity and orthodoxy is partially counterbalanced by a gain in force and variety."

Before we turn to architecture and its style, we take note: in the days of Ramses III the language—its grammar, its expressions, and the art of writing, especially on stone—was far removed from the classics of the generations supposedly just past.

Art: Hunting Scenes

Ramses III ordered his artists to decorate his edifices at Medinet Habu with hunting scenes as well as military ones. These hunting scenes show many features in common with Assyrian bas-reliefs depicting the royal game as executed by the artists of Assurbanipal and, before him, of Ashurnasirpal. "It is regularly assumed that the scenes of the Assyrian chase of the ninth-seventh centuries were inspired by the Egyptian scenes which served them as originals. Yet no proof for this was ever presented. The problem needs a thorough re-examination," and L. Speleers gave it one.[1] He scrutinized the Assyrian and Egyptian hunting scenes with regard to the realism of presentation, weapons employed in the sport, general scenery, and, of course, the animals hunted.

[6] Wilson offers several examples to illustrate this.
[1] Louis Speleers, *"Les Scènes de chasse assyriennes et égyptiennes,"* Recueil de travaux relatifs à la philologie et l'archéologie égyptiennes et assyriennes, Vol. 40 (1923), 158–76.

Speleers saw clearly that the Assyrian scenes were more realistic, with better portraiture of animals in their various poses, and that the motifs had been developed by the Assyrians in an original way. This cannot be said of the scenes of Medinet Habu. Although these have certain features that can be traced to older Egyptian models, of the Old and Middle Kingdoms, many new details reveal themselves as of Asian origin.

The difficulty of harmonizing the results of the analysis with the chronological sequence was, of course, seen from the start. "In order to grip the problem properly we must remind ourselves that the Assyrian hunting scenes are many centuries later than those of Egypt [of Ramses III]." The author had to repeat this warning to himself several times because everything pointed to a borrowing by Ramses III from Assurbanipal.

Assurbanipal invaded Egypt in −663 and Ramses III flourished, it is maintained, in the twelfth century. Yet Assurbanipal did not borrow from Ramses III—this became clear in the analysis: "It is difficult to find in the Assyrian scenes any motif whose borrowing from Egypt is incontestable." But more than this: "Far from claiming that the Assyrians have copied from the Egyptians, it ought to be asked whether the latter have not borrowed the motifs from the Asians because it is undeniable that certain Assyrian motifs that seemed to have pointed to an Egyptian origin actually came from Asia."[2]

The Egyptian scenes show borrowing from Asia and, on the other hand, the selection of the motifs, the conception and realization of the subject, assure that the Assyrian scenes were not borrowed from Egypt. The motifs were developed in an original way by the Assyrians, and if there was some adoption in them it was from the Elamite (early Persian), not Egyptian motifs.

The hunting scenes of Ramses III have disclosed upon detailed examination their dependence on Asiatic motifs; but as soon as we disclaim the twelfth century for Ramses III we are no longer beset by the difficulty of explaining how twelfth-century motifs could have been borrowed from scenes created in the seventh.

[2] Ibid., p. 173.

Speleers was also struck by the similarity in the portrayal of animals (lions) by the artists of Ramses III and by artists under the late Ptolemies—a characteristic case is seen in the figures created at Kom Ombo.[3]

This, too, is of no embarrassment for a chronological timetable in which Ramses III preceded by only a half century the beginning of the Ptolemaic Dynasty. It would be natural for art forms used in Egypt of the fourth century to be copied by the succeeding Ptolemaic kings.

Temple Architecture and Religious Art

Ramses III, after his victorious war against Pharnabazus and Iphicrates, conducted the remainder of his reign in peace and security. He built many magnificent buildings, enumerated in the long Papyrus Harris. Some of these buildings, like the temple at Medinet Habu, have been better preserved than other monuments of ancient Egypt.

How did it happen that the temple of Ramses III survived while temples of the "later" dynasties are in ruins? "This building [Medinet Habu] is the most completely preserved temple of Egypt, antedating the Ptolemaic period. . . . The Medinet Habu temple is therefore unique."[1]

An Elephantine papyrus relates that "when Cambyses came to Egypt, he found the [Jewish] temple [of Elephantine] already built. The temples of the gods of Egypt were demolished, all of them; only the said temple suffered no harm."[2] But the same papyrus informs us that the temple of Elephantine on the southern border of Egypt, left intact by Cambyses, was destroyed later by a mob.

The fact that the presumably twelfth-century buildings of Ramses III survived in a good state of preservation is in conflict with the information contained in the papyrus dating from the year −407 that

---

[3] Ibid., p. 170.
[1] Breasted, *Ancient Records*, Vol. IV, Sec. 1.
[2] Sachau, *Aramäische Papyri und Ostraka*, p. 21.

all the temples of Egypt that stood when Cambyses entered the country (−525) were ruined by this king. Medinet Habu, the mortuary temple of Ramses III, and the temple of Khonsu erected by him in Karnak are among the best-preserved structures of Egypt. Buildings of the twelfth century could hardly have escaped destruction in the seventh century by Assurbanipal; and if, by chance, one or a few of the temple and palace structures of imperial Egypt escaped destruction at the hand of the Assyrians, they were not likely to have survived the Persian conquest, too, one hundred and forty years later; at least their survival is denied by a document written in Egypt under the Persians.

It is a different matter if the dating of Ramses III is drastically revised. In order to judge the age of the surviving buildings of Ramses III on their own merits, they should be compared with those of the Hellenistic age in Egypt.

In this book are reproduced a pylon (portals) of Ramses' mortuary temple (Medinet Habu) on the plain across the Nile from Luxor and another pylon of the temple of Khonsu in Karnak; the latter pylon was erected by Herihor of the Twenty-first Dynasty, one hundred years (on the conventional timetable) after Ramses III built the temple before which the pylon stands.

The onlooker cannot but be impressed by the very close similarity of these pylons with those of the Ptolemaic temples in Edfu, in Kom Ombo, and other places. For the purpose of comparison the supposedly twelfth- and eleventh-century pylons and those of the third and second centuries are pictured in consecutive illustrations. A remarkable resemblance is revealed at first glance. On closer inspection the impression matures into conviction that we have before us monuments of one and the same era or of very close generations, certainly not generations separated by eight hundred to one thousand years. I leave it to the inquisitive reader to go over the many details—identical in the pylons of Ramses III and Herihor (who will be discussed on subsequent pages of this book) and in those of the Hellenistic age. Beginning with the general form and continuing through many characteristics, the comparison yields so striking a similarity that a claim on stylistic grounds that some of these buildings belong to the beginning of the twelfth century and the beginning of the eleventh and others to the third century and later cannot be maintained.

A modern author expressed his wonder at the close parallelism of the pylon of Philae (supposedly of the fourth, but actually of the fifth century) and the wall gate of Medinet Habu, and at the resemblance of certain carved scenes of harem life and of sacrificing prisoners.[3] And decades ago, Adolf Erman, the Egyptologist, stated: "And if we did not read the inscriptions, we could never guess that the temples of Esneh, of Edfu, of Denderah, and of Philae belong to the time of Lagides [from Lagus, father of Ptolemy I], the Caesars, and the Antonines."[4]

From our point of view it is only natural that the texts on the walls of the Ptolemaic temples should, too, bear close resemblance to the texts of the temples of Ramses III. Jean Yoyotte, who examined the Ptolemaic temple at Edfu, was surprised to find on the walls of this temple completed by Ptolemy VIII (Soter II) a text that speaks of the king destroying his enemies, "hacking to pieces the Meshwesh, slaughtering the Shasu, massacring the Tjeker." Yoyotte wondered at the use of names of peoples that Egypt knew almost a thousand years earlier and that supposedly were no more present on the historical scene long before Alexander.[5] An inscription in the Kom Ombo temple speaks of the Meshwesh, the Shasu, the Tjeker, the enemies known from the wars of Ramses III. "At the present state of historical documentaion, the only massive attack of the Tjeker, one of the Peoples of the Sea, against Egypt took place in the reign of Ramses III," writes Yoyotte. Then why should some of the Peoples of the Sea be called by name and referred to as enemies in the temple of one of the later Ptolemies?

The answer is: The war of the Peoples of the Sea took place only

[3] Philippe Derchain in *Bibliotheca Orientalis*, January–March 1961, p. 48; book review of H. Junker's *Der Grosse Pylon des Tempels der Isis in Philä*.

[4] Antonines is the collective name of seven Roman emperors of the second century (from Nerva to Commodus). The quotation is from A. Erman, in *The Historians' History of the World*, M. S. Williams, ed., I (1907), 195.

[5] J. Yoyotte, "Un souvenir des campagnes de Ramses III au Temple d'Edfou" in "Trois notes pour servir à l'histoire d'Edfou," in *Kêmi*, XII (1952).

half a century before Ptolemy I, son of Lagus, a general of Alexander, mounted the throne of Egypt and founded a new dynasty.

The question of how the temple of Medinet Habu survived the destructions of −663 and of −525 finds a ready answer: this temple was erected not about −1180 but about −370, and therefore, unlike the earlier temples and palaces, it did not suffer destruction at the hands of Assurbanipal or Cambyses. The other problem, of the close similarity of the structures of Ramses III to the Ptolemaic ones, finds its explanation in the same solution. The reference to the peoples enumerated in the register of the invading Peoples of the Sea, on the temples of the Ptolemies, is not baffling either.

Reciprocal Influence of
Persian and Egyptian Religion and Art

Of Persepolis the magnificent staircases remain, but of the palaces and temples on the great platform only a forest of single columns and many portals rise above the ground. The walls have been reduced to dust. The portals usually carry on the lintels the design of Mazda (Ormuzd) represented by a human head placed over a disc—the planet Jupiter; the disc has long wings—the god is flying on stretched wings.

The same design minus the head of Mazda, but with all the same characteristic details—a disc with stretched wings—can be seen on many portal lintels of Egypt under the Twentieth Dynasty (Ramses III and following Ramseses) and under the Twenty-first Dynasty (Herihor); the design can also be seen on Ptolemaic temple portals. And not only the lintel design but the entire form of portals shows striking similarities. Here, a reciprocal influence could well have taken place, because the original architectural design of a disc with spread wings goes back to the Eighteenth Dynasty and even to the Old Kingdom in Egypt. Persepolis was started by Darius and continued by Xerxes, but Egypt was invaded by the Persians several years before Darius mounted the throne, and Darius spent considerable time in Egypt.

Ramses III wanted the divine honors due to a pharaoh. Not being of royal birth, despite his repeated stressing of such descent, he needed to emphasize his divine bringing up. On a bas-relief he is shown as a lad of fourteen or fifteen standing next to Isis, who offers him milk from her breast, which he sucks.

Interesting and new is the attire of Isis. Her usual attire and horns with a planetary disc between them are familiar from innumerable pictures, bas-reliefs, and sculptures. The artist of Ramses III, however, placed a headgear on the goddess which is a complete departure from tradition. The headgear is similar to the multipetal helmets of the Pereset, but it is taller and of a more exquisite design, with a rim running over the petals.

The same design, though the headgear is not as tall, can be seen on a Persian bas-relief on the rock surface at Nakhsh-i-Rustam, in the area of the royal tombs, close to Persepolis. The relief dates from the time of the Sassanide Dynasty in Persia, thus from the second to the fifth century of the present era. The headgear adorns the head of a knight with flowing hair—it is unmistakably a Persian motif rooted in the national idea of the multipetal helmet.

A deep-rooted tradition about the way the goddess Isis should be represented was not followed by the artist of Ramses III and an entirely innovative approach was undertaken. It is comparable to the effect that would be achieved if an artist of our day should picture the Madonna in modern street dress.

In order to stray so far from tradition, the influence of Iranian art on the Egyptian artist must have been almost irresistible or, what is entirely possible, the picture was made by a Persian artist in the service of Ramses III. We know that in Persian times artists were exchanged between Persia and Egypt.[1] Is not a Persian headgear on Isis a sign of a most profound, not just accidental, influence of Persian art on Egyptian religious art concepts of the fourth century improperly removed by eight centuries into the past?

[1] Such references are found in the correspondence of the satrap Arsames.

Chapter V

FROM RAMSES III TO DARIUS III

The Later Ramessides

I**N THE PRECEDING** pages we confronted the historical material from Greek and Egyptian sources and arrived at the conclusion that Nectanebo I of the Greek authors is an alter ego of Ramses III of modern historians, or Usimare-meramun Ramesse-hekaon of the Egyptian royal monuments and official papyri. In his own time and especially among the Greeks he was known as Nectanebo, the name he might have occasionally used in less formal situations. Whether this was so or whether Ramses III had, as is known to have occurred with other pharaohs, more than one set of royal names, or different names as king of Upper and Lower Egypt, Nectanebo of the Greek authors was the name by which they knew this monarch. With this identification made we would expect that some of the admittedly difficult problems of the history of the later Ramessides could be disentangled. "If it is true that a people which has no history is happy, then Egypt ought to be reckoned as more fortunate under the feebler descendants of Ramses III than it had ever been under the most famous pharaohs."[1] The entire period of these descendants occupying the throne is supposed to have lasted only two generations (ca. −1170 to −1100), though there are after Ramses III eight more kings of the same name numbered IV to XI. Then the dynasty is thought to have expired in unknown circumstances.

Our identification of Ramses III as Nectanebo I of the Greek

[1] G. Maspero, *The Struggle of the Nations*, p. 483.

authors is to be regarded as conclusive, but our attempt to reconstruct the identities of the later Ramessides must remain hypothetical, owing to the sparseness of information concerning these individuals.

We shall make an attempt, even if only abortive, to bring some clarity to the history of the royal succession, helped in this by what we know about the successors to Nectanebo I and also about some of his predecessors; on the other hand, certain details unexplained in the Greek version of the history of Egypt are clarified when some of the material of the Ramessides is integrated.

It is, for instance, not known under what circumstances Tachos succeeded Nectanebo I and on what ground a nephew of Tachos based his right to succession, revolted against Tachos, and occupied the throne: he is known as Nectanebo II. Would the monuments tell us on what Nectanebo II based his claim to the throne?

Before Ramses III died, intrigues were already brewing among his wives, the functionaries of his harem, and the officers of the royal guard. After the pharaoh's death, a prince, probably the legitimate heir, his mother, and several other persons were accused of plotting against the deceased pharaoh: another prince, not in the line of succession, seated himself on the throne, arrested the commander of the army and certain palace officials, and instigated a trial of his half brother and his camarilla, in an effort to prove that the culprit had plotted against their father. An extensive document concerning this trial is in existence[2]; several supporters of the prince were condemned to die at the hand of the executioner, while others were mutilated. The accused prince, however, was made to die by his own hand by drinking poison, a verdict not unknown in fourth-century Greece: the death sentence in the process of the Athenians against Socrates (−399) stipulated drinking poison administered by his own hand.

The prince who mounted the throne is known to us as Ramses IV but we identify him as Tachos of Greek authors. Ramses IV "claimed that he was a legitimate king and not a usurper. Perhaps,

---

[2] "The Judicial Papyrus of Turin," Breasted, *Ancient Records of Egypt*, IV, Secs. 416–56.

indeed, he did 'protest too much,'" wrote a modern author. It is said that of Tachos no inscription is found, but if Ramses IV is the same as Tachos, there are plenty of inscriptions and the enigma disappears.

The kings who followed Ramses III regularly added the name Ramses to their other throne names and eponyms. There was a similar custom in Rome of the imperial age, when the name Caesar or Augustus, more in the nature of a title, was added as an agnomen to the names of Roman emperors. Actually it was Ramses II, before Ramses III, whose name was added to whatever name an occupant of the throne, or a pretender, had or assumed.

Ramses IV reigned for six years and was deposed under circumstances for which hieroglyphic texts supply no information. Of Ramses V almost nothing is known—he must have been a youthful co-ruler with his father, Ramses IV; he died of smallpox. Ramses VI, however, was a son of the condemned prince and a grandson of Ramses III. Upon seizing the throne he avenged his father by erasing the name of Ramses IV from all monuments and substituting his own; he also appropriated to himself the unfinished tomb of Ramses V and thus, having secured a throne for this life and a tomb for the life thereafter, attended to building activity in various parts of the country. We will recognize him in Nectanebo II of Greek authors. As we will read soon, he rebelled against his uncle and succeeded in mounting the throne.

Ramses VII and Ramses VIII were mere pretenders who left no marks in history except for their claims to the throne. There were also Ramses IX, X, and XI, but with them and their true positions in the succession of the Ramessides we shall occupy ourselves on a later page. It is, however, generally agreed that no link is known between Ramses III to VIII and those who go under the names Ramses IX to XI, and that therefore there is no evidence of their following the line from Ramses III to Ramses VIII.

With these meager facts known about the Ramessides we have undertaken to identify the successors of Ramses III-Nectanebo I.

The sixty years of Egyptian independence from the day Nepherites freed Egypt saw about nine or ten kings, some only for weeks, some only as pretenders to the throne.

"The Little One" in Support of the Pharaoh

When Artaxerxes II died (−359), his son Ochus was proclaimed king under the name of Artaxerxes III. To assure the throne against any attempted seizure by one of his brothers or half brothers, he let them all, eighty in number, be killed.

Artaxerxes regarded as his chief task the reconquest of Egypt, lost by his father, and early in his reign he was making preparations for a military expedition thereto. A year before Artaxerxes Ochus occupied the throne of Persia, Tachos (Ramses IV), having removed his elder brother from the succession, mounted the throne of Egypt. Alarmed by the prospect of a war with the Persian king, Tachos sent an invitation to the Spartan king Agesilaus to come to his assistance for pay. The old warrior was approaching his eightieth year.

Agesilaus accepted the role of a mercenary and sailed toward Egypt. Plutarch, writing four centuries later, relates that in his opinion and probably in that of the contemporaries of Agesilaus, this act was not befitting the waning years of the man who, for more than three decades, "was the greatest and most influential of Hellenes." But Xenophon, who knew Agesilaus personally, presented his motives in justification.

Agesilaus was a penetrating judge of character. Xenophon tells us that "It was his habit to associate with all sorts and conditions of men, but to be intimate with the good. . . . Whenever he heard men praise or blame others, he thought that he gained as much insight into the character of the critics as of the person they criticized. . . . . Slanderers he hated more than thieves."[1]

This glorified warrior and leader of men could not but adversely impress the Egyptians unfamiliar with the Spartan disregard for

[1] Xenophon, *Agesilaus*, trans. E. C. Marchant (Loeb Classical Library).

pomp and ceremony. Agesilaus was also of an ungainly appearance.

"As this great man had found nature favorable in giving him excellent qualities of mind, so he found her unpropitious with regard to the formation of his body; for he was of low stature, small in person, and lame of one foot. These circumstances rendered his appearance the reverse of attractive and strangers, when they looked at his person, felt only contempt for him, while those who knew his merits could not sufficiently admire him. Such fortune attended him, when, at the age of eighty, he went into Egypt to the aid of Tachos, and lay down with his men on the shore without any shelter, having merely such a couch that the ground was but covered with straw, and nothing more than a skin thrown upon it, while all his attendants lay in the same manner, in plain and well-worn attire. . . . The news of his arrival having reached the king's officers, presents of every kind were soon brought to him; but when the officers inquired for Agesilaus they could scarcely be made to believe that he was one of those who were sitting before them." When Agesilaus chose a few things from those offered to him and ordered other things to be carried back, "the barbarians looked upon him still more contemptuously, thinking that he had made choice of what he had taken from ignorance of what was valuable."[2]

Plutarch's account of Agesilaus' landing in Egypt also presents the unfavorable impression the Spartan made on the Egyptians, by his small stature, his apparel and demeanor:

"As soon as he landed in Egypt, the chief captains and governors of the king came down to meet him and pay him honour. There was great eagerness and expectation on the part of the other Egyptians also, owing to the name and fame of Agesilaus, and all ran together to behold him. But when they saw no brilliant array whatever, but an old man lying in some grass by the sea, his body small and contemptible, covered with a cloak that was coarse and mean, they were moved to laughter and jesting, saying that here was an illustration of the fable 'a mountain is in travail, and then a mouse is born.'"[3]

[2] Cornelius Nepos, *Agesilaus*, trans. Watson.

[3] Plutarch, *Lives*, Agesilaus, trans. B. Perrin (Loeb Classical Library).

No historical records by Pharaoh Tachos are extant and the story of his reign is known to us only from later Greek and Latin authors —this because the hieroglyphic record goes by the name of Ramses IV; as already said, the authorship of the Great Harris Papyrus is considered by many scholars to belong to Ramses IV, though the papyrus is written as if Ramses III was its author.

On a wall of the mortuary temple of Ramses III at Medinet Habu, the following entry is written in connection with the Libyan War:

"His majesty had brought a little one of the land of Temeh, a small one supported by his strong arms, appointed for them to be a chief, to regulate their land."

"A little one" was conjectured as a reference to a child; a child brought by the pharaoh to support him makes little sense and the passage is regarded as a "difficult text."[4]

The word "chief" in Egyptian stands for "king"; therefore it was assumed that the pharaoh, interested in the affairs of the neighboring Libya, made an alliance with its king, still a child. But the text speaks not of support given by the pharaoh but received by him. A "little one" for a child who comes to Egypt at the invitation of the pharaoh and enjoys the support of troops stands as a fanciful conjecture in some treatises on the subject.

The appearance of Agesilaus as depicted by his biographers and especially the impression his diminutive figure created upon his arrival in Egypt make the text in the temple of Medinet Habu not only understandable but also very appropriate.[5]

---

[4] J. A. Wilson, "The Libyans and the End of the Egyptian Empire," *American Journal of Semitic Languages,* January 1935.

[5] If the text relates to Ramses III (Nectanebo I) and his activities, and not to his son, Ramses IV (Tachos), our hypothesis that the "little one" meant Agesilaus can be maintained only if this warrior went to Egypt not only in the days of Tachos (Ramses IV) but also some fifteen years earlier, in the days of his father. Such an assumption could find support in the following circumstance: it is known that Eudoxus, the future famous astronomer, at the age of about twenty-three, carried a letter of introduction to Nectanebo written by Agesilaus. It appears that Agesilaus knew Nectanebo personally; it was calculated that Eudoxus went to Nectanebo in the year 367 or 366. (See Giorgio di Santillana, "Eudoxus and Plato: A Study in Chronology," in *Reflections on Men and Ideas* [Cambridge, Mass., 1968], p. 228.) This permits us to refer the inscription at Medinet Habu to the days of Ramses III (Nectanebo) and still identify the "little one" with Agesilaus. We know that the Athenian admiral

The name of the land or the nation, Temeh, from which "a little one" came, "supported by his strong arms," at the invitation of the pharaoh is, of course, a decisive factor in whether I am right or wrong in identifying Agesilaus as the person referred to.

The Egyptians called the population of neighboring Libya Tehenu. The Tehenu were pictured with dark complexion and curly hair. Since the First Dynasty of Egypt they had been known to the Egyptians by this name. But for some time another tribe, or race, named Temeh, was described and pictured as inhabiting Libya or its eastern part, Cyrenaica. "The Temehu were quite a different race whose skin was fair and who had blonde hair and blue eyes. The home of those people cannot be Africa and in all probability they came from Europe and settled in North Africa. . . ."[6] They were clearly not of Semitic or Hamitic but of Arian origin. Then who were they?

We shall have another occasion to discuss the early migrations of Greeks to Libya. Here, however, it is most appropriate to recall what was said by Plutarch in his biography of Lysander. This Spartan hero participated in the Peloponnesian War and captured the Athenian fleet at the battle of Aegospotami (-405); he aspired to become the king of the Spartans and had the support of the oracle of Dodona but failed to obtain the support of the oracle of Delphi; he sent presents to the oracle of Amon in the Libyan desert but failed again; however, the priests of Amon, on a mission to Sparta, announced that the Spartans would soon come to live in Libya— this according to an older oracle.[7]

We may conclude that the name Temehu was applied equally to the Spartans of Libya and those of Lacedaemonia in Greece. The "king [chief] of Temehu" whom the pharaoh brought to his support was a Spartan king; the description "a little one" points to Agesilaus.

Chabrias also twice went to Egypt to participate in military actions, first for Nectanebo and the second time for Tachos.

[6] Ahmed Fakhri, *Siwa Oasis* (Cairo, 1944), p. 23.

[7] Plutarch, *Lives*, Lysander, 20, 25.

The Last of the Native Pharaohs

Xenophon tells us that Tachos, bent on war with Persia, "was possessed of large forces of infantry and cavalry and plenty of money" and that Agesilaus "was delighted when a summons for help reached him from the Egyptian king who actually promised him the chief command." However, Agesilaus soon became outraged "when this suitor for his assistance failed to give him the command. Agesilaus felt that he had been grossly deceived." Tachos vested in him only partial command, giving the fleet into the hands of Chabrias, once more in Egypt, and retained for himself supreme command. Tachos was in Syria, part of which had been occupied by him following the death of Artaxerxes II. Meanwhile, in Egypt, a plot to place his nephew on the throne was being hatched. Chabrias wished to remain loyal to Tachos, his master, and conferred with Agesilaus. The old Spartan king, angered by the limitation of his command, asked his people at home what he should do but suggested that siding with the rebel, Nectanebo (II), would be better for Greek interests. Xenophon wrote: "At this juncture first a portion of the Egyptian troops, operating as a separate army, revolted from the king, and then the rest of his forces deserted him."

In terror, Tachos fled from the front in Palestine to Sidon in Phoenicia and from there proceeded to the Persian king to ask forgiveness. "The Egyptians split up into two parties, and each chose its own king. Agesilaus now realized that if he helped neither king, neither of them would pay the Greeks their wages." Therefore, "having decided which of them [the two pretenders] showed the stronger signs of being a friend to the Greeks, he took the field with him." By deserting Tachos and fighting against yet another rival, Agesilaus made Nectanebo II king of Egypt.

In Plutarch we read that when rival pretenders arose to dispute the throne vacated by Tachos and asked the help of Agesilaus, the Spartan thought it would be awkward to change sides again, and in an eventful campaign defended Nectanebo II, the last native king of Egypt.

From this order of events, known to us from Greek historians, we recognized Ramses IV, the usurper of his father's throne, in Tachos and Ramses VI in Nectanebo II of the Greeks, as we earlier recognized Ramses III in Nectanebo I. Nectanebo II was the son of the legitimate heir to Nectanebo I, as Ramses VI was the son of the legitimate heir to Ramses III. The father of Nectanebo II failed to mount the throne because of the usurper, Tachos-Ramses IV, a half brother.

The pretenders who tried to induce Agesilaus to go over to their side were probably the persons known as Ramses VII and VIII. Neither of those two actually reigned, unless the short-lived seizure of power in some part of the country can be counted as a reign. Of them almost no inscription is left.

Upon the failure of the expedition headed by Pharnabazus, and the withdrawal from Palestine of the forces under his command, Nectanebo I (Ramses III) was able to occupy this practically defenseless country. And this also happened: in Megiddo, in a heap of refuse left by earlier excavators, a pen case belonging to a messenger of Ramses III was found; also a scarab of his was discovered.

In Lachish too a scarab of Ramses III was "picked up," and in Beth Shan a statue of him. These finds confirm that he actually took possession of Palestine upon his victory over the "Pereset."

The next king Tachos (Ramses IV) was in Palestine when the revolt of Nectanebo II supported by Agesilaus caused him to flee to Sidon and from there to proceed to the Persian king. Between the first unsuccessful campaign of Artaxerxes (III) Ochus against Egypt in −350 and the second, successful campaign in −343, Palestine was in the domain of Nectanebo II (Ramses VI). Therefore we could expect that some sign of his occupation of this country would be found too. And actually in Megiddo during the 1934 campaign a base of Ramses VI's bronze statue was discovered. Certain conclusions were made, once more, as to the stratigraphical chronology of Megiddo. A revealing footnote by the excavator, G. Loud, supplied to a short paper by James Breasted on the statue, says that it was found "under a wall in Stratum VIIB room (number) 1832 as if deliberately buried there and therefore intrusive."[1] From this kind of estimate it is difficult or even impossible to derive proper chronological conclusions. The diggers' Stratum VIIB represents "Nineteenth and early Twentieth Dynasties."

The unfortunate results of excavations in Beth Shan, Megiddo, Lachish, and other biblical sites will be the subject of a more comprehensive discussion in a volume re-examining biblical archaeology. It is enough to say here that the Beth Shan, Megiddo, and Lachish excavations have been the subject of much discussion among archaeologists, with great recrimination and even vituperative exchanges—all, in our opinion, because of the wrong synchronical timetable between the Palestinian and Egyptian chronologies. The findings of objects datable to Ramses III (Nectanebo I) and Ramses VI (Nectanebo II) could not but contribute to the chaos in Megiddo's stratigraphical archaeology. In the Memphis excavation by the University of Pennsylvania Museum expedition, the surprising fact was that the Twenty-first Dynasty layers were found immediately under the Ptolemaic layers.

A Comedy of Errors

On the strength of the evidence presented in the preceding pages, the pharaoh known in books on Egyptology as Ramses III vacated the royal throne erroneously assigned to him in the twelfth century and moved to his rightful place in the fourth: he became one with King Nectanebo I of the Greek historians. His immediate successors on the throne of Egypt followed suit to find their true alter egos in the same century, only a short time before the advent of Alexander.

Looking through the nomens and cognomens of Ramses III, we find that one of his so-called Horus names was Nectanebo (Ka-

[1] J. H. Breasted, in G. Loud, *Megiddo II* (1948), p. 135.

nekht-mau-pehti-nekht-a-neb-khepesh-Sati).[1] Budge, who compiled
the list of names used by this and other kings, did not raise any issue
on reading Nekht-a-neb since he had no inkling that a clue for a
portentous identification was before him. It seems that Ramses III
is the only pharaoh of whom we know positively that he had among
his royal nomens this name familiar from Greek authors writing on
Egypt of the fourth century. The part Neb is found also in the name
of Ramses VI (Nebmare-meramun Ramesse-itamun-nutehekaon);
"Nekht" (or "Nect" in the Greek version of the names) being a usual
part in princely names meaning "mighty," it is the part Nebo that
is striking.

The identity of Ramses (III)-Nekht-a-neb as Nectanebo of the
Greek historians was established on preceding pages on grounds
much more compelling than an identity of names: but coming on
top of all other evidence, the identity of names is most welcome, too.

It is, however, not enough to reunite Ramses III and Nectanebo
I: it is necessary to perform another act of detective work, namely,
to divest Nectanebo I of any association with a person whom modern historians assumed to be the Egyptian version of Nectanebo.
By searching among the personalities on the Egyptian scene of the
Persian period who left monuments in Egypt with claims to princely
positions, two potentates with names containing some part of the
name Nectanebo were found, and actually much more than just a
couple of monuments associated with their names survived—these
are Nekht-hor-heb and Nekht-nebef.[2] In the last century the first
of them was selected to be Nectanebo I of the Greek historians and
to the second the role of Nectanebo II was assigned.

What was disturbing about these identifications was the fact that
neither of them mentioned in their many inscriptions anything about
the wars that both of them carried on, Nectanebo I against Artaxerxes II and his mercenaries, on land and on sea, and Nectanebo II
against Artaxerxes III before he was defeated in the final campaign.

[1] E. A. Wallis Budge, The Book of the Kings of Egypt (London, 1908),
Vol. II, p. 1.
[2] F. K. Kienitz, Die politische Geschichte Ägyptens vom 7 bis zum 4
Jahrhundert vor der Zeitwende (Berlin, 1953).

Their inscriptions are vainglorious, and therefore an absence of any reference to war exploits crowned by victories seemed enigmatic. In view of the great number of inscriptions left by them, it could not be claimed that only by chance did their many building and donation inscriptions survive while the monuments dedicated to the conduct of wars and the memorials to their triumphs all perished. Yet, for lack of better choices, the identifications were made. Then early in this century W. Spiegelberg, a German Egyptologist, found reason to rearrange the identifications and Nekht-nebef was pronounced to have been Nectanebo I, while Nekht-hor-heb, who before that had occupied this role, was relegated to the role of Nectanebo II, a less lucky ruler.[3] Since the publication of Spiegelberg's work, most Egyptologists have agreed with his construction though dissenting voices are still occasionally heard in defense of the previous matching.

Since Nectanebo I has his real match in Ramses III and Nectanebo II, with almost equal certainty, his match in Ramses VI, we need to find for Nekht-hor-heb and Nekht-nebef their real historical identities. We will now embark on this detective task: before definitely installing Ramses III and Ramses VI in their homesteads we have to evict the squatters.

A careful reader of this volume will be quick to announce the solution for Nekht-hor-heb. We have already met him on a previous page—a governor and treasurer of the state but also the administrator of the estates of Arsames, who was the all-powerful satrap residing in Babylon, Egypt being only a part of his immense satrapy. In his letters Arsames repeatedly admonished Nekht-hor to take better care of his private fief by increasing the number of bondsmen on his estates and by enlarging the estates as well, by whatever means, lawful or not. The letters addressed to Nekht-hor displayed little personal respect for the *pekida* (functionary), a native subordinate. Nevertheless, this functionary was rather powerful against his own countrymen and, besides, had access to large sums—all the money flowing through his hands before it reached the satrap in

---

[3] W. Spiegelberg, *Die Sogenannte Demotische Chronik des Papyrus 215 der Bibliothek Nationale zu Paris* (Leipzig, 1914).

Babylon. I have quoted in the section "Arsames," in Chapter I, a typical letter from the satrap to his administrator.

An exacting critic may ask: does Nekht-hor stand for Nekht-hor-heb? The letters of the satrap were addressed "From Arsham to Nekht-hor." Conceding the unceremonial way the satrap wrote to his functionary in Egypt, it is well conceivable that Arsames dropped the last part of the name of the addressee (he dropped also all salutation in a letter from him to a Persian nobleman visiting Egypt that will be cited soon). Yet for a definite identification it would be better if proof could be supplied that Nekht-hor stands for Nekht-hor-heb. This, fortunately, can be done too.

In an article published in 1933, Abbé P. Tresson applied his expertise to two figures from a private collection.[4] One statuette represents a kneeling man (the head is missing), holding in his arms a small naos (icon) with the figure of Osiris in it. The base of the figure is inscribed in hieroglyphics.

"—[making offering] to Neith, the great, divine Mother . . . for the soul [ka] of the noble Lord, hereditary prince—of the King of the North—[makes offering to Neith], the great Mother Divine, that she grant funerary meals, every perfect thing . . . for the ka of the noble lord, hereditary prince, the carrier of the seal of the King of the North, a unique patron, chief commissioner of estates—governor of the entrances [to Egypt] by land and by sea, Nekht-hor-heb, born of Nes-en-per-Mut."

Nekht-hor-heb proclaims further: "I was truly distinguished in manners, excellent of character, a functionary free of reproach, my heart was (always) harmonious, my thoughts without disguise and there was nothing in my breast to conceal. . . ."

Nekht-hor-heb claimed in the inscription to have been a loyal functionary of the holder of the royal seal—in the latter we recognize Arsames. The prayer for the soul of this "noble lord and hereditary prince" suggests that the figure was commissioned at the occasion of Arsames' death. The icon of Osiris, the god of the dead, and the prayer for the meals for the dead points to the same. Having

---

[4] Paul Tresson, "Sur deux monuments égyptiens inédits," *Kêmi*, IV (1931, published 1933).

functioned for over half a century, Arsames, last mentioned in an
Elephantine letter written in −407, must have died soon thereafter
or even before, probably in Babylon, or possibly in Persepolis since
the Elephantine letter refers to his visit in −410 to the king. Darius II
(Notus) died in −404.

The reference to the King of the North in the inscription on
the statue unquestionably means the Persian monarch. In the
Manethonian list of dynasties, the Persian kings constitute the
Twenty-seventh Dynasty; however, Manetho does not give their
names. From monuments the pharaonic names of only Cambyses
and Darius the Great are known; as for the following Persian kings,
the Egyptian scribes preferred to refer to them in such terms as King
of the North, without naming them. Of the Persian kings only
Cambyses and Darius visited Egypt, and, from the priestly view,
in order to be a sanctified king and bearer of the Double Crown,
one had to go through a ceremonial in the southern and northern
sanctuaries of the land. Not having even visited Egypt, the Persian
kings after Darius could not properly acquire an Egyptian throne
name.

It was assumed that the governor-agent circumvented the un-
easy situation, and in the inscription he asks the Divine Mother that
the "son of Re," Aahmes, may achieve "a thirty year festival on the
Horus throne."

"Son of Re" Aahmes mentioned in this passage made Abbé Tresson assume that King Amasis, the next to the last of the Twenty-
sixth Dynasty (who died a few months in advance of Cambyses'
conquest of Egypt), is meant. Placing the statue in the time of
Amasis, Abbé Tresson had to assume that, besides King Nekht-hor-
heb, putative Nectanebo II of the fourth century, there was a namesake of his, two hundred years earlier, in the days of Amasis. Such
interpretation of the reference to Aahmes must stumble over the
reference to the King of the North in the same inscription: the sup-
plicant could not in the days of Amasis have paid homage to the
"King of the North."

The name Aahmes (Amasis) encircled by an oval (cartouche)
may refer to somebody else, not the King of the North, and we can

trace the person: in the Persian times, in the fifth century, "a general whose business it was to summon all the mayors of the country to bring gifts for the embalmment of the Apis bull bore the same name as King Amasis and wrote it in a cartouche, although his stela alludes to the Persian invasion [occupation]."[5] This man, the military commander over Egypt, is probably referred to by Nekht-hor-heb in the text incised on the kneeling figure with the icon, unless the name refers to the King of the North himself.

From this votive statue we learned that Nekht-hor-heb, besides his duties as an agent of the deceased and other positions, was also in charge of collecting import duties ("governor of the entrances [to Egypt] by land and sea"). Actually, Nekht-nebef, with whom we will deal next, erected a stele in the seaport city of Naucratis in which he decreed duties on import.

We learned, in addition, the name of Nekht-hor-heb's mother, Nes-en-per-Mut. The very extensive text on the sarcophagus of "King" Nekht-hor-heb, never translated or published, should be read, for it is reasonable to assume that it may also contain the name of his mother. But the evidence as to the identity of Nekht-hor-heb, a satrap's agent and governor, is already at hand in the collation of the letters by Arsames and the text on the icon-bearing figure.

The time of Nekht-hor-heb is thus established—he functioned in the later part of Arsames' life and was at his post when the latter died, in −407 or shortly before.

In order to show that Nekht-nebef lived and acted a little earlier but also in the days of the satrap Arsames, we will need to occupy ourselves with the person of Psamshek.

In one of the letters written by Arsames to Nekht-hor and quoted in this book, he referred to Psamshek as the man who occupied the positions of the addressee immediately before him. In another, earlier letter, addressed to a Persian prince, Artawant, who happened to be in Egypt, Arsames wrote:

I send thee much greetings of peace and prosperity.

[5] A. Gardiner, *Egypt of the Pharaohs*, p. 366. G. Posener, *La première domination perse en Egypte* (Cairo, 1936), pp. 41ff.

And now in regard to the grant which has been given by the king and by me to Ah-hapi my servant, who was an officer in my domains which are in Upper and Lower Egypt—Psamshek the son of Ah-hapi, who now has been made an officer [*pakida*] in his stead in my domains which are in Upper and Lower Egypt, has asked me for it.

Now in regard to that provision which has been given by the king and by me to Ah-hapi: —Psamshek his son shall be allowed to take up that grant there in Egypt.

We are before the disentanglement of one of the most bizarre confusions in Egyptian history, or, if a scholarly work permits the language, the apprehension of the person who played, undeservedly, not just the role of one of the later kings, as in the case just discussed, but who has personified probably one of the greatest of Egyptian kings. The momentous significance of what we have to discuss may easily overshadow the problem for which we seek a solution here—namely, the historical place of Nekht-nebef (no more Nectanebo I), with whom we will deal first, though we will establish his time only by his association with Psamshek.

Basalt slabs of a balustrade with likenesses of Psamshek and Nekht-nebef were found and described; from them we learn that Psamshek and Nekht-nebef were contemporaries, and since Psamshek immediately preceded Nekht-hor-heb in his post, Nekht-nebef must have been another high functionary under Arsames. I have already mentioned his stele with a decree concerning import duties, found in Naucratis, the commercial colony of Greeks established in the seventh or sixth century.

Nekht-nebef and Nekht-hor-heb enriched the Persian crown, Arsames the satrap, and, before anybody else, themselves. From their own description we learn that each of them showed munificence toward the priestly class and endowed temples and cloisters with land grants and with serfs.[6] Both of them and so also Psamshek wrote their names in cartouches, thus pretending to have royal titles —the Persian Great King did not care; he was King of Kings.

A finely wrought sarcophagus of Nekht-nebef was found in an

[6] Kienitz, op. cit.

Alexandrian private palace where it had been used for generations as a bathtub; now it is on display in the Cairo Museum.

The sarcophagus of Nekht-hor-heb also saw many adventures before it found its permanent place in the British Museum. It once served as a font in a church of St. Anastasius, which was later turned into a mosque, where it was shown in a kiosk as the coffin of Alexander.

It is worth noticing that the sarcophagus of Ramses III, now in the Louvre, was built on the model of Nekht-hor-heb's sarcophagus; the similarity extends from the semi-oval shape at one end to many other features, and no wonder—the possessors, as we have learned by now, were separated in life by only one generation, not by many centuries.

The great confusion in the conventional history of Egypt can be illustrated through many cases, in all periods from the end of the Middle Kingdom on. Yet one of the most confused spots is in the history of the Twenty-first Dynasty, not only because it was placed six to eight hundred years before its true time but also because some of its figures were wrongly identified with personalities of earlier or later epochs.

King Psammetich of Egypt is a most prominent figure in Egyptian history as narrated by Herodotus and other Greek historians. Modern historians placed him in the seventh century and assigned him room in the beginning of the Twenty-sixth Manethonian Dynasty. In the present, reconstructed version of history he is Seti-Ptah-Maat of the Nineteenth Dynasty and this is a matter of extended discussion assigned to the volume of *Ages in Chaos* dealing with the period of Assyrian conquest and domination; the continued discussion of the identity of the Nineteenth and Twenty-sixth Dynasties is the subject of the volume dealing with the time of Chaldean domination. Therefore this theme will not occupy us here. It is enough to say that the story of the Nineteenth Dynasty is written on the basis of Egyptian monuments and the (same) story of the Twenty-sixth Dynasty is written following the evidence of Greek authors.

Seti-Ptah-Maat of the monuments is Psammetich of Herodotus' story but modern historians looked for Psammetich's monuments

apart from Seti's monuments. Relics with the name read as Psamshek were discovered. Yet most puzzling was the fact that among
those rather numerous relics there was nothing that would call to
mind the story found in Herodotus and other classical historians.
Why did Psammetich omit to narrate his great deeds in peace and
war: how he succeeded in overcoming the other eleven regional
rulers of Egypt, how he returned from Palestine where he escaped
from the Ethiopians, how he received help from Carians and Ionians who arrived by sea, how he built military camps for them and
was first among the pharaohs to allow Greeks to settle in Egypt;
how he freed Egypt from Assyrian hegemony; how, now as an ally
of his former overlord Assurbanipal, he made war in Syria? Nothing
even remotely like such events was found in the relics carrying the
name Psamshek in hieroglyphics.

The other puzzle was in the very name—Psamshek as it is written
in hieroglyphics looks rather strange for a royal name. Gardiner
mused: "The name, for all its outlandish appearance, is an Egyptian
one meaning 'the negus-vendor.'"[7]

But a pharaoh would not adopt the name "vendor of negus
[lemonade]." Ptah and Maat in the royal name and cognomen of
Seti are Egyptian deities and this is what one would expect a royal
name and cognomen to be. But "vendor of negus"—if this is the
best that can be formulated to make sense in the Egyptian language, it only suggests that the name is not Egyptian at all. Since,
besides the famous Psammetich, the Greek authors referred to several more rulers of the same name but of lesser stature, in subsequent times, one would be led to assume that "vendor of negus"
became quite a preferred royal name, almost like Caesar in Roman
times.

The true situation is different. The relics with the name Psamshek in hieroglyphics can be safely ascribed to Psamshek, the administrator of Egypt under the satrap Arsames—and it is because
of this that we deal here with the man and his position. From the
letters on leather from Arsames' chancery in Babylon, addressed
to his subordinates in Egypt, we learned that, before Nekht-hor,

---

[7] *Egypt of the Pharaohs*, p. 352.

Psamshek was the administrator of Upper and Lower Egypt.

Psamshek needs to be returned back to his true time, the middle of the fifth century. His name, ending with *ek*, has a Persian ring—as I was told by Professor Martin Dickson of Princeton University. His time can also be figured out by a reference we have in Greek sources. In the year −445, "King Psammetich" sent grain by boats to the people of Athens. It is assumed that this reference is to a fifth-century namesake of the famous Psammetich of the seventh century and that otherwise nothing is known of him. This is not true—this "King Psammetich" is nobody but Psamshek, governor under Arsames. It is quite certain that Psamshek did not send grain to Athens without the knowledge and even directives of Arsames. It must have been a time when the Persian interests dictated support to Athens.

The rebellion of Inaros against the Persian domination of Egypt, which began in −463 and continued till −454, was supported by the Athenians and their fleet (see p. 122). The Athenians succeeded in occupying the citadel of Memphis, then proceeded to Prosopitus and there were starved by a prolonged siege, during which the Persians diverted the water from the canal. The war was terminated by a peace treaty in −448 between the Persians under Artaxerxes I and Athens. Athens left Cyprus and Egypt to the Persians and Persia promised not to attack the Greeks on the coast of Asia Minor. As the result of this non-intervention policy and improved relations, a peace followed in −446 among the Greek states—Attica (Athens), Boeotia (Thebes), Lacedemonia (Sparta), and others—that later received the name of the Thirty-Year Peace. Artaxerxes I regained full control of Egypt and gave it as a satrapy to Arsames, who continued his residence in Babylon (the third capital of the Empire, after Persepolis and Susa), and Ah-hapi, mentioned in a letter I quoted before, was, from some date on, his plenipotentiary there; after Ah-hapi's death, his son Psamshek was appointed in his father's stead. Having reconstructed this, we have two fixed dates—Psamshek sending grain to Athens in −445 and Nekht-hor-heb, his successor in Arsames' service, deploring his master's death in −407 or thereabout.

With these two fixed dates we will be able to disentangle quite a
few more problems: quite a few other historical personalities, having lost their historical anchors, have been unceremoniously moved
across the borders of centuries. How confusing the situation is for
the accepted chronological scheme the reader may judge by reading the deliberation of an expert in Egyptian art and history, W. S.
Smith, concerning the slabs of the balustrade with portraits of
Nekht-nebef and Psamshek.

> Strange portraits of two kings, Psamtik I and Nectanebo I [Nekht-
> nebef], are to be found in royal reliefs, and these seem to indicate
> that the taste for representing individual characteristics had not
> disappeared in the time between early Dynasty XXVI and the
> Ptolemaic Period. They appear on basalt slabs, 4 feet in height,
> which seemed to have formed a balustrade for a single monument.
> It is not easy to visualize the original appearance of this monument
> or to explain how a large part of it came to be left uninscribed for
> over 200 years until Nectanebo took up the work again. The same
> scheme of decoration is carried out on the two sets of slabs which
> are carved on both sides. On one side, closely spaced kneeling fig-
> ures of the king make offering to various deities, with a hawk frieze
> above. On the other side of the slab a single figure of the king is set
> against a black background, and there is a uraeus cornice.

As the reader may realize, the two personalities, Psamshek and
Nekht-nebef, both wrongly identified—one with a pharaoh of the
seventh century, the other with a pharaoh of the fourth century—
were not separated by "over 200 years" (nearer three hundred
years, actually): both belong to the fifth century.

Nekht-nebef, portrayed in a set of bas-reliefs parallel with those
of Psamshek, must have been his contemporary and therefore also
a functionary under Arsames; it is possible that they served, one as
governor, the other as chief treasurer, or one in the north, the other
in the south; or their functions under Arsames could have been divided in some other way.

1. Persian guard from bas-reliefs at the palace of Darius at Persepolis.

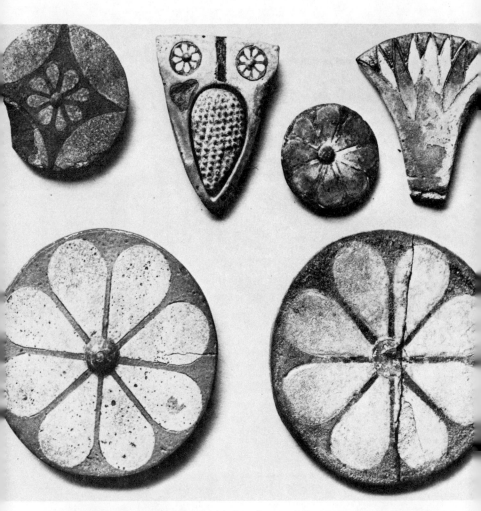

2. Tiles of Ramses III. The front sides of some of the tiles with Persian motifs found in the ruins of a palace of Ramses III at Tell el-Yahudiya in the Delta. *Courtesy of the British Museum.*

3. Reverse of some of the tiles of Ramses III with Greek letters, carved before firing. The top row of letters, from left, are *alpha*, *chi*, *lambda*, and *lambda*. The mark on the large tile, lower left, may be *iota*; the other is clearly *epsilon*. *Courtesy of the British Museum.*

4. The Egyptians, supported by the Pereset and the Peoples of the Sea, assault the Libyans. Observe the head-gear, the small shields of the Peoples of the Sea. *From Medinet-Habu*, Vol. II, *Courtesy of the University of Chicago Press.*

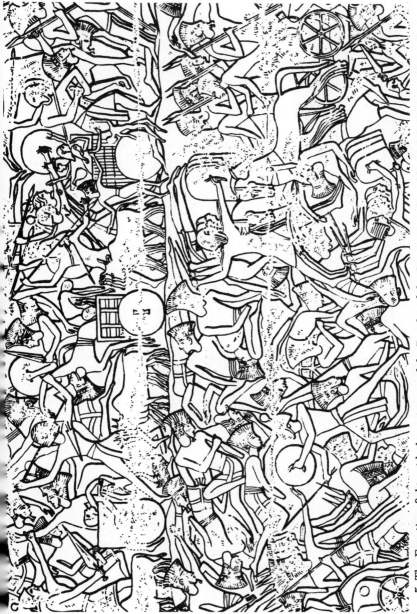

5. The Egyptians fight, with the assistance of the Peoples of the Sea, against the soldiers of the Pereset. This reflects the situation when Chabrias was in the Egyptian service and the Persians were ejected from the country. *From Medinet-Habu, Vol. I, Courtesy of the University of Chicago Press.*

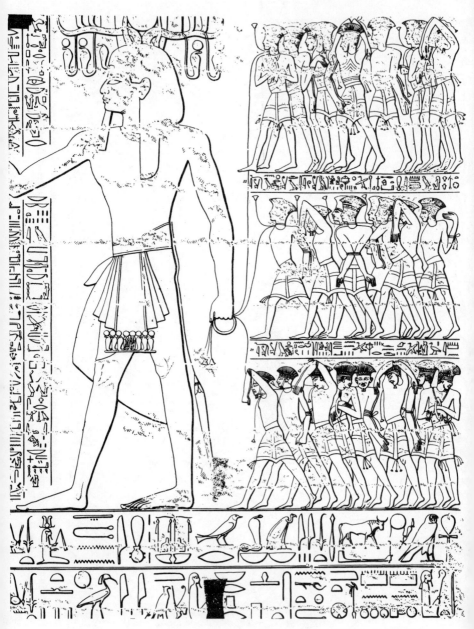

6. The Pereset as prisoners of the Egyptian King. *From* Medinet-Habu, Vol. I, *Courtesy of the University of Chicago Press.*

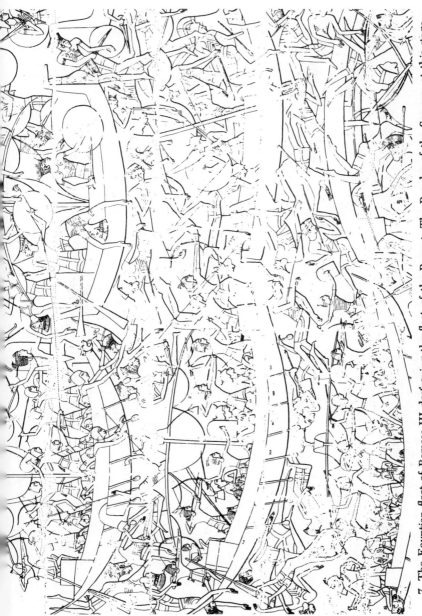

7. The Egyptian fleet of Ramses III destroying the fleet of the Pereset. The Peoples of the Sea are, at this stage, allies of the Pereset. The helmets of the Peoples of the Sea have horns but not the disks between the horns. *From Medinet-Habu, Vol. I, Courtesy of the University of Chicago Press.*

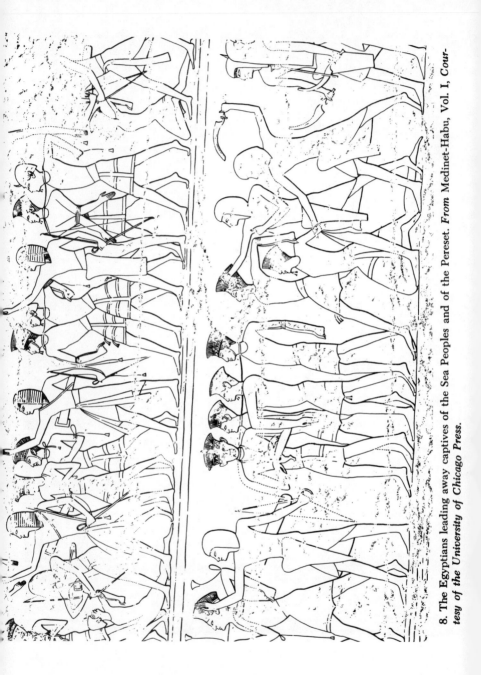

8. The Egyptians leading away captives of the Sea Peoples and of the Pereset. *From Medinet-Habu*, Vol. I, *Courtesy of the University of Chicago Press.*

Relocated by Eight Hundred Years

In the section titled "The Enormity of the Problem," we stood perplexed by the thought that there could be a mistake of eight hundred years in the accepted history of the Twentieth Dynasty and frightened at the sight of ever greater perturbations into which this inquiry leads us. We were struck by a series of discordant facts, each of which pointed to the necessity of a drastic reduction of the age of Ramses III and of the entire dynasty by this enormous stretch of time. Among these facts were Persian motifs and enamels and Greek letters of the classical period, of the age of Plato, on the tiles of Ramses III's palace in Tell el-Yahudiya; nearby tombs that, to one member of an archaeological team, revealed relations to the Twentieth Dynasty and therefore to the twelfth century and, to another member, ties with the fourth century at the earliest; the reference in an official document, composed by Ramses III or in his name by his son Ramses IV, to the domination by Arsa, an Aramean, to whom the kingless Egypt, one or two generations earlier, had paid tribute and who showed disregard for the gods of the land—a situation unthinkable in the accepted version of history, which does not know of any such event or even the possibility of such event between the Nineteenth and Twentieth Dynasties when Egypt is supposed to have been at the very apogee of its imperial power.

In order to find out whether these indices were illusory and spurious or meaningful and true, we undertook to compare the annals of Ramses III in which he described his war against the nation called Pereset, richly clad warriors, and their allies, Peoples of the Sea, with the description found in Diodorus of Sicily of the war of Nectanebo I, a pharaoh of the first half of the fourth century. We have shown that the identity of the Pereset can be determined by comparing their characteristic headgear with that of the guard of Darius on the sculptures at Persepolis, and we documented this identification by the fact that the very same name Pereset was applied in Egypt to the Persians as late as the composition of the Canopus Decree under the Ptolemies. The "Peoples of the Isles" did not resemble the Mycenaean Greeks, in either their weapons, their armor, or their shaved faces; the Greeks were known also to the Hebrew late prophets as "Peoples of the Isles."

The occupation of a bastion in the Mendesian mouth of the Nile by invading troops; counterattacks by the pharaoh and the slaughter of many of the besieged invaders and the siege of attrition; the discord into which the leaders of the invading forces fell, their retreat without an attempt at further penetration of the land, the flight of the chief strategist, and many other details—all were described by both Ramses III and Diodorus.

The events that preceded the war, the state of internal strife among the Peoples of the Sea, the military support delivered by the Pereset to the pharaoh in the early part of his reign; the mustering of the soldiers of the Peoples of the Sea and their parading in the service of the pharaoh; their participation alongside Egyptian troops in the ensuing war with the Pereset; finally, the fighting of Egyptian soldiers and marines against the combined forces of the Pereset and the Peoples of the Sea—all this is pictured in bas-relief by Ramses III and is also described by Diodorus, who tells in detail how in the year −377 the pharaoh revolted against the Persian overlordship and invited the Athenian admiral Chabrias and his mercenaries to his service, in which they helped to eject the Persians from the land; but the Athenians recalled Chabrias and his troops and sent Iphicrates to help the Persians in their war against the Egyptians. We found the very same happenings—with many details given by Ramses III and by Diodorus: a large camp assembled by the Pereset in Palestine for the assault on Egypt by land forces and by a fleet of many galleys, with the Peoples of the Sea acting as mercenaries; the fortification of the land frontier (at Zahi) by the pharaoh; his correct guess that the enemy would try to force one of the mouths of the Nile and his strengthening them by armed vessels and walls (dikes) and forts; a naval battle in a mouth of the Nile in which coastal fortifications and fire-shooting vessels were employed.

The stories told by Ramses III and by Diodorus are not of two wars separated by eight hundred years but of one and the same war.

Iphicrates' reforms of arms and armor known from Greek historians are illustrated on Ramses' bas-reliefs; the swords were made twice as long, and Ramses also refers in his inscriptions to swords five cubits long—twice the usual length—introduced in the army; the rectangular shields of the soldiers of Chabrias are replaced by round targets and both kinds of shields are seen on Ramses' bas-reliefs.

The use of fire ships also places the events in the fourth century as does the reference to the Mariannu garrison on the Egyptian frontier.

If all this is not enough—and it is, by every standard of scholarly pursuit—to establish the identity of events and persons separated in accepted history by eight hundred years, then we may also recall the observations of the authorities on art who recognized that Assyrian and Persian hunting scenes appear to have served as likely originals for Ramses' artists when depicting such scenes. The temples erected by Ramses III bear a singular resemblance to the temples of the Ptolemaic period; the Egyptian language and religion in the days of Ramses III underwent Semitization; the religious art exhibits a distinct Iranization.

Parallels were drawn in the next generations, those of Tachos (Ramses IV) and of Nectanebo II (Ramses VI). The arrival of Agesilaus with his troops and the diminutive stature of the old Spartan warrior are described on a papyrus by Ramses IV and by Greek authors. Nekht-nebef and Nekht-hor-heb, usually identified as the indigenous kings Nectanebo I and II of the Greek historians, were shown to have been administrators under a Persian satrap and not these kings.

The reader may wonder: How could such errors in writing history come to be? Who was the first to commit the blunder and place Ramses III and with him the entire dynasty that goes under the name of the Twentieth in the twelfth century? Ramses III and his dynasty were placed where they are found in books on chronology long before—actually centuries before—the first hieroglyphics were deciphered in the first quarter of the nineteenth century. We shall concern ourselves with this when we examine the foundations on which Egyptian chronology was erected.

Part II

Chapter I

THE DYNASTY OF PRIESTS

IN PART II we shall endeavor to reconstruct the history of the dynasty that goes under the misnomer of Twenty-first. It is a period rich in documents, mostly legal or sacerdotal, rarely of any historical content, and consequently it is admitted that historically it is one of the most obscure periods in Egyptian history; many efforts have been made to establish order in this succession of princely priests and to find meaning in their political activities. "The Twenty-first Dynasty is, still, a particularly obscure period of Egyptian history," writes J. Černý in the new edition of the *Cambridge Ancient History*.[1] And no wonder: the period, being displaced by many centuries from its proper place in history, is recalcitrant about disclosing its historical connections with the world outside Egypt or its political links inside the country. It is conceded here that it was not without sustained effort that understanding of these connections and sequences was achieved, an effort that was responsible for my repeatedly postponing the publication of this volume.

As the reader will find, the dynasty that comes now under discussion existed before the Twentieth (the same as Twenty-ninth and Thirtieth); it also ran parallel with the Twentieth and survived it by several generations, actually past the time of Alexander.

This being so, it appeared preferable not to deal with the two dynasties, partly contemporaneous, simultaneously, but to consider first the Twentieth, then the Twenty-first. This means, at least to

[1] "Egypt from the Death of Ramesses III to the End of the Twenty-first Dynasty," *Cambridge Ancient History* (Cambridge, 1975), Vol. II, Part 2, Chap. XXXV, p. 643.

some extent, going over the same ground twice, especially when dealing with the Persian succession.

A Chimerical Millennium

The Twenty-first Dynasty of Egypt is, on the accepted timetable, assigned to the eleventh century and to the first half of the tenth, or from ca. −1100 to −945. In Israel this was the time of the later Judges and of Kings Saul, David, and Solomon. This period in Israelite history is the most glorious of all. Great is the number of pages in the Old Testament dealing with the events of the time: the wars of Saul and the liberation of the country and of the entire ancient East "from Havilah until thou comest to Shur that is over against Egypt" (I Samuel 15:7), or from Mesopotamia to Egypt, from the domination of the Amalekites; the subsequent defeat of Saul at the hands of the Philistines; the occupation of Jerusalem by David, and the wars against Amon, Moab, and Edom; the splendid era of Solomon, who built in Palmyra and in Jerusalem and who participated with King Hiram of the Phoenicians in building harbors, in great maritime expeditions, and in overland trade in chariots and horses; cedars of Lebanon were shipped by sea to build Temple and palaces. Queen Sheba (Shwa) came to verify the astounding reports; and "all the earth sought to Solomon" (I Kings 10:24). But in Solomon's time, also, plots were hatched with the intent to dismember his empire, and the center of the plotting was in Egypt. Hadad of Edom, who escaped to Egypt when his country was devastated by Joab, general of David, returned to Edom, leaving his son Genubath in the pharaoh's palace in Egypt; Jeroboam, a subject of Solomon, who had run away to Egypt and married the queen's sister, returned to rend Israel from Judah. Five years after Solomon's death Pharaoh Shishak invaded Judah and took Jerusalem and carried away everything of value from the palace and the Temple. It was a stormy time of ascent and descent, with neighboring nations, first among them Egypt, involved in the policies of Israel and Judah, with their great peace and war enterprises, building activities and commerce, plotting and warring, an empire expanding and falling apart. The histories of Israel and of Egypt are interwoven through all this period.

In Volume I of *Ages in Chaos,* I identified with detailed documentation the contemporaneous period in Egyptian history: the end of the time of the Judges and their efforts to liberate their land from the Amalekite-Philistine domination corresponds to the final phase of the Hyksos (Amu) domination in Egypt and Palestine-Syria. Saul was a contemporary of Kamose and Amose, founders of the Eighteenth Dynasty, and together they besieged and took Avaris, the fortress-capital of the Hyksos-Amalekites; I also identified Avaris in el-Arish. There Saul took the last Hyksos king, Agag, prisoner. David was a contemporary of Amenhotep I and both lived in the memory of their nations as saints, whether deservedly or not; Solomon was a contemporary of Thutmose I, whose daughter he married and whose other daughter and heir—Hatshepsut—became the sovereign of Egypt. The illustrated description of her travels to the Holy Land (Divine Land) and Phoenicia (Punt) corresponds in every detail to the description of the visit of Queen Shwa (Sheba) whom the historian Josephus described as Queen of Egypt and Ethiopia. The reader need only reread those pages in Volume I of *Ages in Chaos* to become aware of the multitudinous and interlaced evidence. The terraces she saw, the trees that never were seen before, apes and peacocks, and even people of Ophir, all is narrated, and also shown in pictures, presents she received in God's Land—all this is narrated in the books of Kings and Chronicles. Paruah (P'-r'-hw) received Queen Hatshepsut at her arrival in the Holy Land, and it was Paruah, father of Jehoshaphat, who governed Ezion-Geber under Solomon (I Kings 4:17). Thutmose III (Shishak of the Scriptures) invaded Palestine, besieged its fortified cities, and accepted surrender of the king of Kadesh-Jerusalem; the vessels and furnishings that he removed from the Temple and the palace and had depicted on a wall of the Karnak temple were compared piece by piece, number by number, with the description of such vessels in the Temple of Solomon. Hadad's son Genubath (of

I Kings 11:20) is mentioned in inscriptions of Thutmose III;
Ano, the wife of Jeroboam (her name is given in the Septuagint),
was a princess of the household of Thutmose III, and a canopic jar
of hers is preserved in the Metropolitan Museum of Art. In small
details and in great designs the two histories harmonize one with
the other, and pages of description of times preceding this special
period (the time of the Exodus and of the collapse of the Middle
Kingdom of Egypt) and following it (the time of the el-Amarna correspondence) are nothing but a tight procession of synchronisms,
correspondences, and identifications, thus extending the frame to
centuries before and after.

In conventionally written history the Twenty-first Dynasty occupies the place opposite the end period of the time of Judges and
the reigns of Saul and David and the major part of Solomon's regnal
years. What can this scheme offer by way of contact between two
neighboring countries? Is there a single point of contact? The
Twenty-first Dynasty is exceptionally rich in papyrus documents.
What is the evidence for keeping the Twenty-first Dynasty opposite
Kings Saul, David, and Solomon?

To present the accepted view I shall follow Černý's "Egypt from
the Death of Ramesses III to the End of the Twenty-first Dynasty,"
Chapter XXXV of the third (1975) edition of Volume II of the
Cambridge Ancient History.

"Little is known of the relations between Egypt and the outside
world during the Twenty-first Dynasty," is the preamble. "Syria and
Palestine were politically independent, a fact which is confirmed
by the biblical tradition of the rise of the kingdom of Israel. An
unnamed pharaoh of the Twenty-first Dynasty, however, gave asy-
lum to Hadad, the young prince of Edom, when King David seized
his country, and later gave him in marriage to the sister of his queen.
Hadad's son Genubath was brought up at the court with the pharaoh's sons. After David's death and in spite of the pharaoh's objec-
tions Hadad returned to his own country as Solomon's bitter enemy.
The identity of the pharaoh is uncertain.

"It is equally uncertain which king of the Twenty-first Dynasty was on such friendly terms with Solomon that he sent his daughter to Jerusalem to become one of Solomon's wives."[1]

Is this not a *testimonium paupertatis?* No relations with Israel were recorded in Egypt: is the silence justified and explained because Syria and Israel were independent states? According to that scheme, the great sweep of David's and Solomon's activities left Egypt unaccountably unaffected. Whereas in Palestine, Phoenicia, and Syria great buildings were erected, fleets were sent to faraway countries, wars fought, and victories won, in Egypt at the same time political intrigues were woven, and the disintegration of the empire on its northern border was being prepared, and we are invited to believe that no Egyptian record of any contact or any such activities is preserved under the entire, rich-in-papyri Twenty-first Dynasty.

Under this dynasty Egypt was a picture of decay and wretchedness. The main occupation of the population, priesthood, and administration was looking for ancient tombs and their contents. The population, plagued by "foreigners," called also "barbarians," waited for nightfall to embark on illicit digging; the priests, under the pretext of rewrapping the mummies of the ancient kings, cleared them of any jewels that could still be found between the swathings, and the courts, as many papyri records testify, occupied themselves with tomb-robbery processes. The land had no industry, no foreign commerce. The miserable errand of Wenamon in an effort to purchase cedarwood in Byblos for a single barque of Amon, a vessel used by priests in their processions, is all that the Twenty-first Dynasty's papyri can report of relations of Egypt with Syria or Palestine. We shall soon examine Wenamon's travelogue and realize how wretched Egypt's position was in international relations and trade. It can hardly qualify as a documentation of "friendly trade relations with Palestine and Syrian coastal towns" (Černý), with no other evidence in view.

On what a different scale was the trade of Solomon, when forests of cedar trees of Lebanon were moved by sea to Jaffa—an operation not only different in scope but also in period.

One hundred and fifty-five years (−1100 to −945) of no contact,

[1] Ibid., p. 656.

not even a semblance of a contact, not even the remotest evidence!
Two histories stand here before the bar of justice. Is "No argument,
no evidence" the entire plea of one of the contenders for the title
of true history?

On the pages to follow, the so-called Twenty-first Dynasty—a
misnomer that we unwillingly retain for the priestly succession it
denotes, is placed in its proper historical position; when integrated,
it finds many contacts with foreign countries of the same period,
namely the period of Persian domination of Egypt extending into
the Ptolemaic period, past the advent of Alexander.

What goes by the name of Twenty-first Dynasty was a succession
of hereditary priest-princes who resided in Thebes, in Tanis, but
mainly in the oases of the Libyan desert—el-Khargeh, the southern
oasis, and Siwa, the northern. Their dynasty preceded, was contemporaneous with, and followed in time the Twentieth Dynasty,
that of Ramses III-Nectanebo I.

Cambyses' Conquest of Egypt

The Persian period of ancient history begins with Cyrus the Great.
From rather humble beginnings as a princeling in Anshan, a de-
pendency in the Median kingdom of Astyages, he rose to be the
supreme ruler of an empire unequaled in its confines by any earlier
known realm of antiquity. His conquest of the Lydian kingdom
of Croesus took place in −546 and his conquest of Babylon, ruled
jointly by Nabonidus and his son Belshazzar, in −539, an event that,
according to the Book of Daniel, occurred on the night of the writing on the wall.[1] But Egypt remained outside Cyrus' domain.

Cyrus fell in a war with tribesmen on the northern frontier of his
empire, east of the Caspian sea. His son Cambyses, mounting the
throne and defending it against other pretenders, early devised the
conquest of Egypt, ruled by Pharaoh Amasis II.[2] But before Cam-

[1] The Book of Daniel ascribes the conquest of Babylon to Darius. The possibility is not excluded that Darius, who at that time served under Cyrus, actually stormed and took Babylon.

[2] Amasis I (Ahmose) reigned upon the expulsion of the Hyksos from Egypt

byses reached Egypt in −525, Amasis died and was followed on
the throne by his son, Psammetich II, called Psammenitus by
Herodotus. The battle at Pelusium was fought and lost by the Egyptians. Memphis surrendered and the king was taken prisoner. Cyrenaica in the west sent ambassadors to Cambyses with a declara-
tion of submission. Not satisfied and planning the conquest of all
Libya, he dispatched an army into the Libyan desert but himself
went up the Nile and occupied Egypt to its southern border and
engulfed it from all sides.

Herodotus gives a vivid description of the conquest of Egypt by
Cambyses: it is a story of cruelty and desecration bordering on mad-
ness on the part of the conqueror; it is also a scene of deprivation
among the conquered population exemplified by the destitute state
of a dispossessed elderly nobleman openly begging soldiers of the
occupation for bread. Many a scholar has expressed skepticism concerning the truth of Herodotus' narrative; especially his story of
Cambyses stabbing the sacred bull, Apis, met severe criticism since
conflicting evidence was discovered by A. E. Mariette when in 1851
he opened large sepulchral chambers with no less than sixty-four
sacred bulls mummified and laid in magnificent sarcophagi, with
the dates of their births and deaths written on their swathings.

The name of Cambyses written in Egyptian script was found on
papyri and in stone but only one hieroglyphic record mentioning
the conquest and occupation of Egypt is known to exist—it is from
the hand of one Udjeharresne—an autobiographical sketch inscribed
on a statue and preserved in the Vatican. He was in command of
the Egyptian fleet in the Mediterranean; upon the fall of Memphis
and the surrender of the pharaoh, he alone of the native population
gained Cambyses' confidence: he became his adviser on Egyptian
affairs and was also appointed to be a royal physician, a startling
career change from the office of admiral.

Udjeharresne caused to be written on the statue:

There came to Egypt the great chief of every foreign land

as the first king of the Eighteenth Dynasty. Amasis II deposed Pharaoh Hophra
(Apries) of the Twenty-sixth Dynasty and is counted as its next to last king,
though he was not related to Apries.

Cambyses, the foreigners of every country being with him. When he had taken possession of this entire land they settled down there in order that he might be the great ruler of Egypt and the great chief of every foreign land. His Majesty commanded me to be the chief physician and caused me to be at his side as companion and director of the palace, and I made his titulary in his name of King of Upper and Lower Egypt Mesutire.[3]

All that Udjeharresne dared to say of the great misery of the populace was limited to a single sentence: "Great trouble had come about the entire land of Egypt." Something can be learned from the fact that he succeeded in obtaining a royal order to evict "all those foreigners who had settled down in the temple of Neith," of which he was a custodian: "His Majesty commanded that the temple of Neith should be cleansed." The temple was located in Sais.

Such an attitude on the part of Cambyses, as revealed by his Egyptian physician and adviser, together with the find by Mariette, undermined trust in Herodotus' version of what took place in Egypt upon its conquest.[4]

In whose record should we put our trust, in the story of Udjeharresne, the contemporary but an apostate who lets it appear that the burden of occupation was alleviated by law and royal decree, or in Herodotus, who came to Egypt to collect material for his history three quarters of a century after Cambyses and who was apt to overstate so as to make his narrative more interesting to his readers? How can we know?

But is it, first of all, true that we do not possess any other Egyptian contemporary record of the conquest of Egypt by Cambyses the Persian?

Ourmai's Letter of Laments

In 1891 the Russian Egyptologist, V. S. Golenishchev, bought from an antique dealer in Cairo several papyri, one of which, a

[3] Trans. by A. H. Gardiner, *Egypt of the Pharaohs* (Galaxy ed., 1966), p. 366.
[4] Posener, *La première domination perse en Egypte*.

letter written by Ourmai, son of Khevi, was published in 1961, seventy years after its acquisition. It is preserved in the state museum named for A. S. Pushkin, the Russian poet, in Moscow; its existence was known to specialists, but the publication of the text and a translation into Russian waited until M. A. Korostovtzev undertook the far from easy task[1]; the translator admits his uncertainty as to a number of words or sentences.

The papyrus of Ourmai dates from the early Twenty-first Dynasty. Ourmai, "god's father" of the temple in Heliopolis, wrote his letter to Re Nekht, a royal scribe in Heracleopolis. The title "god's father," it is assumed on good grounds, means an intermarriage relationship with the royal house—more definitely, king's father-in-law[2] (a king could have many fathers-in-law, according to the number of his wives). Obviously, both the recipient and the sender of the letter belonged to the aristocracy of the land.

The beginning of the letter is preserved completely; but from the middle of the third page on there are many lacunae: altogether there are five pages and a short postscript on the back of the papyrus. The entire first page and the beginning of the second, practically half of the surviving text, are taken up with polite expressions offering all kinds of blessings to the addressee, including a life span of a hundred and ten years, with no attending infirmities, and, thereafter, preservation of his mummified remains among the great dead ones of Heliopolis. The greetings and benedictions concluded, the writer immediately starts the story of his woes:

> I was carried away unjustly, I am bereft of all, I am speechless [to protest], I am robbed, though I did no wrong; I am thrown out of my city, the property is seized, nothing is left [to me]. I am [defenseless] before the mighty wrongdoers. . . .

Ourmai is only one of many victimized people. In the next sentence he apparently speaks of his colleagues or faithful employees:

> They are torn away from me; their wives are killed [before them];

---

[1] M. A. Korostovtzev, *Hieratic Papyrus 127 from the Collection of the State Museum of Arts* named for A. S. Pushkin (Moscow, 1961).

[2] C. Aldred in *Journal of Egyptian Archaeology*, XLIII (1957), 30–41. See also my *Oedipus and Akhnaton*, pp. 84–85.

their children are dispersed, some thrown into prison, others seized as prey.

I am thrown out of my yesterday's domicile, compelled to roam in harsh wanderings. The land is engulfed by enemy's fire. South, north, west, and east belong to him.

The "marines withdrew" from the country conquered by the enemy, and the latter "traverses the land along the flow of the river."

Ourmai enumerates the places he passed—all on foot because "seized are the horses, taken away the chariot and the harness"; "I am compelled to march an entire day from my city, but it is no more my city."

By his city is meant Heliopolis, where he was an important priest, related to the royal house. But apparently there is no royal house any longer in Egypt—the enemy has seized power in the land together with the private property of its prominent citizens. Possibly, at Heracleopolis, the site of the addressee, eighty miles to the south, things were not yet as bad as in northern Heliopolis, at the apex of the Delta, a little distance north from Cairo of today.

Not only were people dispossessed, their children abducted, and their wives murdered, but sacrilege was performed by the enemy against the gods and the dead.

Bodies [of the dead] and bones [are] thrown out upon the ground, and who will cover them? . . .

Here many lines are undecipherable in the papyrus, but then it continues:

Their altars disappeared, and [so also] offerings, salt, natron, vegetables.

The dispossessed priest complains, "I suffered hunger." He also mentions "my grain that was given to me by soldiers," and it sounds as if Ourmai had to beg for grain from the soldiers of the occupation.

The land is subjected to heavy taxation by the enemy ("his taxes are heavy") and a "great crime against god" was committed. He prays:

Thy power, O lord creator, should manifest itself. Come, save me from them.

Who could these invaders in the beginning of the Twenty-first Dynasty have been? In conventionally written history, no invaders are known to have had hold of Egypt when the Twenty-first Dynasty came to the throne, at the beginning of the eleventh century. It is assumed that, with the extinction of the Twentieth Dynasty, the Twenty-first peacefully took over the reins of state. Therefore the text of the Ourmai Papyrus, as soon as it was published, caused wonder; an explanation of the strange tale of woe told by Ourmai was sought, but in vain.[3]

However, in the present work of reconstruction we locate the time of the Twenty-first Dynasty not in the eleventh–tenth centuries but in the Persian period of Egyptian history; we are therefore bound to expect that some complaints of this kind would have been preserved from the beginning of the Twenty-first Dynasty. Ourmai described Upper Egypt as just conquered; the writer of the letter bears titles that attest to the recent existence of monarchy in Egypt, terminated by the conquering enemy.

As already said, one of the main historical sources on the conquest of Egypt by Cambyses, son of Cyrus, is Herodotus. He visited Egypt only a few generations later, when Egypt was under Persian rule and the time of conquest by Cambyses and the sufferings that went with it were still very vivid in the memory of the people.

In Herodotus' language, Cambyses committed "many wild outrages while he still stayed at Memphis; among the rest he opened the ancient sepulchers and examined the bodies that were buried in them. He likewise went into the temple of Hephaestus, and made great sport of the image. . . . Cambyses was raving mad; he would not else have set himself to make a mock of holy rites and long-established usages" (Herodotus, III, 37–38).

He killed children; "you even put children to death" are the words Herodotus puts in the mouth of Croesus, the Lydian, who accompanied Cambyses as a prisoner (Herodotus, III, 36).

After a stay in Memphis, Cambyses undertook a campaign toward the south, moving along the Nile. Returning to Memphis, he "dis-

---

[3] G. Fecht, "Der Moskauer 'literarische Brief' als historisches Dokument," *Zeitschrift für Aegyptische Sprache*, 87 (1962).

missed the Greeks, allowing them to sail home" (Herodotus, III, 25).

In the story of Herodotus and in the laments of Ourmai we find similar complaints of sacrileges against gods and the dead, of sepulchers opened, and bodies of the dead thrown out, of cruelties committed against the population, even the children; both the papyrus and Herodotus refer to the campaign along the river; both sources tell of the departure of the marines. A story told by Herodotus about the first days of conquest by Cambyses makes us think of Ourmai and his complaints:

> Ten days after the fort [of Memphis] had fallen, Cambyses resolved to try the spirit of Psammenitus, the Egyptian king, whose whole reign had been but six months. He therefore had him set in one of the suburbs, and many other Egyptians with him, and there subjected him to insult. First of all he sent his daughter out from the city, clothed in the garb of a slave, with a pitcher to draw water. Many virgins, the daughters of the chief nobles, accompanied her, wearing the same dress. When the damsels came opposite the place where their fathers sat, shedding tears and uttering cries of woe, the fathers, all but Psammenitus, wept and wailed in return, grieving to see their children in so sad a plight; but he, when he had looked and seen, bent his head toward the ground. In this way passed by the water-carriers. Next to them came Psammenitus' son, and 2000 Egyptians of the same age with him—all of them having ropes round their necks and bridles in their mouths—and they too passed by on their way to suffer death. . . . King Psammenitus saw the train pass on, and knew his son was being led to death, but, while the other Egyptians who sat around him wept and were sorely troubled, he showed no further sign than when he saw his daughter. And now, when they, too, were gone, it chanced that one of his former boon companions, a man advanced in years, who had been stripped of all that he had and was a beggar, came where Psammenitus, son of Amasis, and the rest of the Egyptians were, asking alms from the soldiers. At this sight the king burst into tears . . . "my own misfortunes were too great for tears; but the woe of my friend deserved them. When a man falls from splendour and plenty into beggary at the threshold of old age, one may well weep for him."[4]

[4] Herodotus, III, 14. Trans. G. Rawlinson.

The letter of Ourmai gives supporting evidence to Herodotus' account. It is testimony against the consensus among modern historians that Herodotus painted too dark a picture and that the story of sacrileges by Cambyses in Egypt has been invented. It may even appear that the plight of Ourmai, a relative of the king, served as a basis of the here cited scene as found in Herodotus; Ourmai, too, begged bread from the soldiers of the occupation.

From Darius I to Artaxerxes I

With the fall of Memphis, Egypt offered no further resistance to Cambyses. The Persian intended to attack Carthage but the Tyrians refused to lend their ships to the conquest of the state established by colonists from Phoenicia. Cambyses then sent from Thebes a force of fifty thousand men on a westward march to the oases of the Libyan desert as a first step in the strategy to add the northern seaboard of Africa to the empire bequeathed to him by Cyrus. The army passed the oasis of el-Khargeh (Kharga) but never reached the oasis of Siwa. It perished in a desert sandstorm and, according to Herodotus, not a single man survived to report the disaster.[1]

Not yet abandoning the plan to conquer Carthage, Cambyses devised a plan to conquer Nubia and Ethiopia and marched southward. The words of Ourmai, "the land is engulfed by enemy's fire; south, north, west and east belong to him," truly depict the situation. Cambyses led an army too large for a march through a country naked and poor in provisions: he apparently selected a course that cut across a desert to Napata, the capital of Nubia. When the beasts of burden were consumed and cases of cannibalism occurred, he gave orders to return north. In Egypt he went raving mad and, if Herodotus can be trusted, it was then that he opened ancient sepulchers, burned sacred statues, and slew the Apis. He also caused the death of his pregnant wife Roxana and ordered Croesus, the prisoner-king of his entourage, to be slain but changed his mind

[1] Herodotus, III, 17, 25–26; also Diodorus, X, 14.

and rescinded the order when he found that it had not been carried
out, yet he slew those who dared not carry it out. Before that he
had sent his brother Bardiya (Smerdis) home from Egypt but also
dispatched with him a murderer to dispose of him. When in Palestine, himself on his way home, he heard that Smerdis had occupied
the throne of the empire and believed that his assassination plan
had not been executed; he died near Mount Carmel possibly by
his own hand. However, the newly proclaimed king was not
Smerdis, who had been killed by Cambyses' secret order, but a
magus, Gaumata, who looked much like Smerdis.[2]

Darius, son of Hystaspes, served under Cyrus and accompanied
Cambyses on the Egyptian expedition; he went up against Gaumata, killed him, and became king in −521. Like Cambyses, he was
a fifth-generation descendant of Achemenes, through whom he
claimed his right to the crown. Next he fought against a usurper
who pretended to be an incarnation of Nebuchadnezzar, already
dead for several decades. He also suppressed insurrections in various parts of the empire and, crossing the length of Asia Minor,
traversed the Bosphorus, passed Thrace, and invaded the land of
the Scythians; but having experienced the vastness of the country,
he turned back, marched across his empire, and soon conquered
the land on the Indus. From there he sent an expedition to circum-
navigate Arabia and find passage to Egypt; there he ordered the
digging of a canal connecting the Mediterranean with the Red Sea
by linking the Nile to the Suez Gulf.

Darius did not build in Egypt proper and left the destitute population as squatters in towns and villages, many of them devastated
by the army of his predecessor, but he did not oppress the population. Early in his reign he ordered the codification of the Egyptian
civil law. He also took certain steps to appease the Egyptian priesthood: he erected a fortress-sanctuary in el-Khargeh, or the Great
Oasis, known as Hib or Heb oasis in the papyrus texts: it is the
southernmost in the string of oases facing Libya.

Buildings erected by Darius' order in el-Khargeh still stand,
though the ravages of time have left their marks. Long hieroglyphic

[2] Herodotus, III, 30 ff.

inscriptions, hymns to the celestial bodies and to the king, proclaimed divine, were chiseled into the walls. Their decipherer, Heinrich Brugsch, admitted that, if it were not for direct statement in the texts, there would be no way of guessing that Settu-Re means Darius: but he was invoked also by his Persian name, Endarius. "Amon of the Strong Arm" was worshiped in the temple of el-Khargeh and it appears that a syncretism with the Mazdaic pantheon was well under way.

Brugsch, who visited el-Khargeh in 1877, observed that, according to a text on a stele found at Luxor, the oasis was used in antiquity as a place to exile political prisoners. There they were far from the populated Nile Valley and under the supervision of military priests. On a subsequent page we shall discuss this stele found at Luxor.

Taking care of the military outposts entrusted to the command of priests who had the status of princes, Darius obviously was concerned with the protection of the western frontier of Egypt against the incursion of Libyan bands; or it is entirely possible that he was mindful of the growing might of Carthage, farther west.

It is not known when a similar outpost—a fortress and a temple —rose in the northern oasis of Siwa, but most probably it was built at the same time as the southern outpost and also by order of Darius I. It soon became famous because of its oracle, and "Ammon of the Oracle" (the Greeks wrote the name with a double *m*) was highly regarded among the Libyans and the Egyptians and its fame spread abroad. Aristophanes in *The Birds* (−414), in passages telling of oracles, mentioned Amon's oracle, next to those of Delphi and Dodona. The answers of Amon's oracle were usually cunning: occasionally, subsequent events could be interpreted as fulfillment of the oracle's words. So it was when during the war of the Athenians and the people of Syracuse, Amon prophesied that the Athenians would take all Syracusans captive but all they captured was an enemy ship with the census lists of the inhabitants of Syracuse. Pindar, at an earlier date, wrote a hymn or ode to Amon and a three-sided stele with the hymn was seen in the oasis by Pausanias six hundred years later. The Egyptian priests seized on the pop-

ularity of their oracle among the Greeks and spread the tale that
Heracles himself asked its advice. Philip of Macedonia, father of
Alexander, saw a dream that troubled him and asked the oracle
of Delphi its interpretation and was told to honor Amon—so Plutarch says; how true the story is we have no way of judging.

Egypt, which had lost its independence under the Persians and
been made into a satrapy, had, nevertheless, a measure of self-rule
as a theocratic state. Priests were made into military commanders,
the temples enjoyed certain protection, and the land, without an
autonomous civil government of its own, fell into a fief-like dependence on the temples and their priesthood.

A similar policy of creating a theocratic vassalage was pursued
by the Persians in Judah. Cyrus issued a decree licensing the re-
building of the Jerusalem Temple destroyed by Nebuchadnezzar,
and permitting the return of the exiles; these were led from Babylon
by Zerubbabel, appointed to be governor, and by Jeshua, son of
Jozadak, appointed to be high priest. They built an altar for burnt
offerings "but the foundation of the temple of the Lord was not
yet laid" (Ezra 3:6). They gave money "unto them of Zidon, and
to them of Tyre, to bring cedar trees from Lebanon to the sea of
Joppa [Jaffa], according to the grant that they had of Cyrus king
of Persia" (3:7). But the people of the land, mostly descendants
of the colonists brought into the country by Sargon, Sennacherib,
and Esarhaddon, the Assyrian kings, "hired counselors against them
[the repatriates], to frustrate their purpose, all the days of Cyrus
king of Persia, even until the reign of Darius" (4:5). When Darius
came to power, the prophets in Judah, Haggai and Zechariah, urged
the renewal of the work of building the Temple. Soon the satrap
Tatnai, with misgiving, reported to Darius the resumption of the
work; a search was made in the state archives, and in the palace
of Achmetha in the province of the Medes a roll with Cyrus' original
decree was found and Darius confirmed it. The prophets saw the
Messianic time coming: "Jerusalem shall be called 'a city of truth.'"
Zechariah proclaimed: "Yea, many people and strong nations shall
come to seek the Lord of hosts in Jerusalem, and to pray before
the Lord" (8:3, 22).

In the sixth year of Darius the Temple was completed. "They set the priests in their divisions and the Levites in their courses" (Ezra 6:18). The early Messianic expectations first focused on Zerubbabel, a civil leader, were soon stifled, and the priesthood took over the leadership of the "prisoners of hope" (Zechariah 9:12). Thus Judah of the "children returning from captivity" was molded into a theocratic state with a hereditary caste of priests.

The last prophet was Zechariah; Malachi, the last in the canon, was but an oracle whose prime concern was in sacrifices and sacerdotal purity; not unlike the Egyptian temple oracles, he was a mouthpiece of the priestly caste. "Will a man rob God? Yet ye have robbed me. But ye say, Wherein have we robbed thee? In tithes and offerings."[3]

The tribes of Israel—the Northern Kingdom—led into exile by the Assyrian kings, never returned and were lost to history; most of the population of the Southern Kingdom—Judah, Benjamin, Simon, and Levi—led into the Babylonian exile, stayed there. From the returnees under the Persian kings a nation was re-created on the ruins of its former glory, harassed by settlers who had supplanted the exiled ancestors, a budding commonwealth with a modest house of worship as a focal point. They inaugurated a period that was to endure about six hundred years and is known as Bait Sheni—the Second House, or second commonwealth.

Before Darius died he made the first inroads into Greece and suffered his first reversals in military fortune. His son Xerxes summoned the resources of the empire and concentrated the efforts of his reign on what is known as the Persian War—a military confrontation of Greece torn between its city-states, Athens, Thebes, Sparta, and others, with the Persian colossus, a war narrated in detail by Greek authors. Xerxes (in Persian Khshayarsha) was the biblical Ahasuerus who "reigned from India even unto Ethiopia, over an hundred and seven and twenty provinces" (Esther 1:1). According to Herodotus, "not one was for beauty and stature more worthy to possess this power." The story of the harem romance concerning

[3] Malachi 3:8.

Queen Vashti, Queen Esther who replaced her, Mordecai, her uncle, and Haman, the Agagite (of the seed of Agag, the Amalekite), is narrated in the Book of Esther. The names of the Jewish participants in this intrigue and counterintrigue, being derived from those of Babylonian deities (Marduk, Ishtar), point toward the process of assimilation that was eroding the national identity of those who chose to remain in the Diaspora.

Xerxes continued the building of Persepolis begun by his father. In a great plain, about forty miles northeast of Shiraz, in front of a steep mountain, Darius erected a platform of stones, some of which measure fifty feet in length, approached by a staircase wide enough for a troop of ten horsemen to ride up. On the platform he built a royal palace and a hall of a hundred columns for royal audiences. The walls of the staircases are adorned by bas-reliefs showing the royal guard composed of equal numbers of Persian and Median nobles or "immortals"; other bas-reliefs show the nobles of the conquered nations paying homage to the king of Persia, or King of Kings, on New Year's Day, when with great festivity the kingdom was "renewed."

At Susa Xerxes built another palace and harem, and at Nakhsh-i-Rustam, close to Persepolis, next to the tomb of Darius hewn in rock, Xerxes prepared for himself a similar tomb, which can be seen from afar. There he was laid when assassinated.

When Artaxerxes I mounted the throne, the population of the Delta under one Inaros rebelled. Achaemenes, related to the Persian king, was entrusted with crushing the insurrection; in the first encounter, Achaemenes was victorious, but the Athenians ordered a fleet of two hundred vessels then at anchor at Cyprus to sail to Egypt to side with Inaros. They sailed up the Delta to Memphis, attacked the Persian garrison, and occupied most of the city. In −460 a large army under Megabyzos, supported by three hundred Phoenician ships, fought the Egyptians and their Greek allies, forcing the latter to retreat to Prosopitis, where they withstood a siege of eighteen months. Then the Persians diverted the water of the branch of the Nile in which lay the Athenian fleet, and the Greeks burned their stranded fleet. The besieged surrendered.

Some time later Herodotus visited Egypt, going as far south as Elephantine; he described a land that appears to have been well governed.

In the reigns of Cyrus, Darius, Xerxes, and Artaxerxes, accusations against the Jews, who were "building the rebellious and the bad city" of Jerusalem, were repeatedly made "in the Syrian tongue" by the representatives of the descendants of the colonists settled in the land of Samaria by Assurbanipal (Asnapper of Ezra 4:10) and other Assyrian kings. "This city of old time hath made insurrection against kings."[4]

In the twentieth year of Artaxerxes, Nehemiah, his cupbearer, asked the king to send him to Jerusalem, "the city of my fathers' sepulchers" that is waste "that I may build it." The king, moved by the "sorrow of heart" of his cupbearer, consented and gave Nehemiah horsemen to accompany him on the perilous journey and handed him a letter to the keeper of the king's forest in Lebanon, saying that timber should be given for beams to restore the gates of the wall encompassing Jerusalem, broken down and burned by Nebuchadnezzar a hundred and forty years earlier.

On arrival in Jerusalem, Nehemiah made a solitary survey of the city and its walls, slowly riding on a charger through the night, and in the morning he spoke to the elders. They said, "Let us rise up and build." With Eliashib, the high priest, building at the Sheep Gate, numerous groups of builders divided the entire circumference of the walls with the many ruined gates and worked while others, with arms, watched over them. For weeks "none of us put off our clothes, save for washing," for Sanballat, the governor of Samaria, and his associates threatened them: "What is the thing that ye do? Will ye rebel against the king?"

Nehemiah's governorship lasted twelve years, from the twentieth to the thirty-second year of Artaxerxes I, and all this time he was harassed by the ill-wishers from among the Samaritans and the Arabs. After forty-one years on the throne, Artaxerxes died (−429)

[4] Ezra 4:19.

and soon was succeeded by his son Xerxes II, who, in a matter of weeks, was supplanted by Darius II.

"Barbarians Came and Seized the Temple"

The Amon cult continued as the dominant cult of Egypt through the entire Persian period. Amon (Jupiter) being the equivalent of the Iranian Mazda (Ahuramazd), the Persians showed equanimity toward the continuation of the Theban cult. Amon priests of the oases were also in charge of the sacred center in Karnak (Thebes). Since there was no native dynasty in Egypt and the Persian kings who followed Darius the Great—namely, Xerxes, Artaxerxes I, and Darius II—never visited Egypt but kept satraps there, the authority of the Amon priests, entrusted also with the command of garrison troops, was very pronounced.

In a document of the Twenty-first Dynasty it is said that in the year 1 of some king—it is just described as "Year One" (the month and day are named)—there was an investigation concerning the plunder of the royal tombs of the great kings of the Eighteenth and Nineteenth Dynasties. At the hearing before a commission appointed to investigate the tomb robbery, among several other witnesses and accused, a certain porter, Ahautinofer, was interrogated. The so-called Mayer A Papyrus, now in the Liverpool Museum, records:

"He said, 'The Barbarians came and seized the Temple while I was in charge of some asses belonging to my father. Peheti, a barbarian, seized hold of me and took me to I-pip, it being for as long as six months (already) since Amenhotep, who used to be High Priest of Amon, had been suppressed." The witness testified that he was permitted to return to his domicile after "nine whole months of the suppression of Amenhotep who used to be High Priest of Amon."[1]

---

[1] Papyrus Mayer A, 6, published in T. E. Peet, *The Mayer Papyri A and B* (London, 1920); Peet, *The Great Tomb Robberies of the Twentieth Egyptian*

This is the only known reference to the removal of the high priest Amenhotep; from the time when he held office, first as the Third Prophet, then as the Second, finally as the First Prophet, there are several inscriptions extant. One bas-relief shows him as offering a homage of flowers to a king, Neferkere-setpenre, designated by modern historians as Ramses IX. Since on this bas-relief the priest's figure is as large as that of the king, a situation otherwise unknown in surviving Egyptian art, it was conjectured that Amenhotep was competing with the royal house for authority, which was the cause of his downfall.[2] A rather extensive literature on the subject of Amenhotep's downfall has developed no other surmise as to the causes that led to it.

However, the obvious connection between the seizure of the temple (of Amon in Karnak) by the "barbarians" and the suppression or the removal of the high priest is contained in the testimony of Ahautinofer.

The seizure of the temple was carried out by barbarians "who appear to have been organized at least to the point that they had *hryw-pdt*, 'troop captains.'"[3] These barbarians were neither Arabs nor Libyans: those neighbors of the Egyptians were usually designated as "tent dwellers"; neither were the Ethiopians, the southern neighbors, ever called "barbarians."

The accepted chronological scheme, with the Twenty-first Dynasty reigning in Egypt while Saul, David, and Solomon reigned over Israel, needs to find out who these "barbarians" were; and since they were not referred to by the terms applicable to Libyans, Ethiopians, or Arabs, should the conclusion be made that they were Israelites? A conclusion of this kind was not made and rightly so. Should David or Solomon have held sway over Egypt, such an achievement would not have been left unmentioned in the Scriptures.

But, again, the accepted version of Egyptian history knows noth-

---

Dynasty, Vol. 2 (1930), p. xxiv. E. F. Wente, "The Suppression of the High Priest Amenhotep" in *Journal of Near Eastern Studies*, XXV, 2 (April 1966).
   [2] A. H. Gardiner, *Egypt of the Pharaohs*, pp. 299, 301.
   [3] Wente, *Journal of Near Eastern Studies*, XXV, 2 (April 1966), p. 84.

ing of an invasion and occupation of Egypt in the eleventh century, at the end of the Twentieth Dynasty or at the beginning of or during the Twenty-first; yet a contemporary document refers to barbarians behaving like conquerors.

Since these "barbarians" were organized in troops led by captains it would not do to see in their activities the "discontent" of some foreign minorities settled in Egypt, as some historians for lack of a better idea have suggested.

About the time that the "temple was seized" and the high priest Amenhotep was "suppressed," the leader of the captains was a man named Pinehas, who is regarded as responsible for the removal of the high priest. He appeared in Upper Egypt at the head of a strong contingent of troops, ousted Amenhotep, and restored order.

In Papyrus Mayer A, it is also said that some of the tomb robbers were "killed by Pinehas." They were killed upon being convicted. One would assume that a man who restored order would be highly regarded by the population, but it was not the case. "The name Pinhasi [Pinehas] is written in such a way as to make it certain that he was an enemy of the loyalists at Thebes, and the absence of any title shows that he was a very well-known personage."[4]

If, upon their trial, Pinehas severely punished the thieves and also established order in Egypt, why should he be regarded as "an enemy of the loyalists" or nationalists? But he is known also to have imposed or collected taxes in towns south of Thebes and occasionally made the population scatter in fear of some people who are described in hieroglyphic texts by a foreign word, *mdwt-'n*. "The exact nature of these *mdwt-'n* is obscure."[5] The first time the word is written with the determinative for men, which leads to the conclusion the Medes may be meant.

Pinehas is also credited with appointing Herihor, a man of military profession, with no known pedigree, to the post of the high

[4] Gardiner, *Egypt of the Pharaohs,* p. 302.

[5] J. Černý, "From the Death of Ramesses III to the End of the Twenty-first Dynasty," *Cambridge Ancient History,* Chap. XXXV, p. 631. Cf. also T. E. Peet, "The Chronological Problems of the Twentieth Dynasty," *Journal of Egyptian Archaeology,* 18 (1928), 68. Peet reads *mdw-'n.*

priest, in Amenhotep's place. To Pinehas was sent a royal order (the name of the king is unknown to us) to co-operate with the royal butler Yenes in supplying a quantity of semiprecious stones for the workshop of the Residence City.

Who were these "barbarians" who collected taxes, removed the high priest from his office and appointed another, a man of military upbringing; who punished offenders and were responsible for maintaining order and were organized in troops under captains; who kept the population in fear of search or seizure; and who occasionally collected semiprecious stones for an unmentioned king in the unidentified Residence City?

"Barbarians" was the designation of the Persians among the Greeks: it is invariably applied in the writings of the Greek authors of the fifth and fourth centuries to the Persians under Darius, Xerxes, Artaxerxes, and other kings of the Achaemenid Dynasty; they were referred to as "barbarians" instead of "Persians" and this despite the exquisite luxury of their court at Persepolis and the richness of the attire of their soldiers. In all their satrapies the troops of occupation were under captains and the captains under satraps.

The "barbarians" in Egyptian documents of the Twenty-first Dynasty were Persians; they collected taxes, executed court trials "unto death, or to banishment, or to confiscation of goods, or to imprisonment" in the words of a Persian decree quoted in the Book of Ezra (7:26). The Residence City was the Persian capital; Pinehas, whatever his nationality—Egyptian or foreigner—was a Persian governor. He, at the head of the "barbarians," seized Thebes and its temples.

If we were to try to establish more closely the time and the circumstances of Amenhotep's removal, we would first of all inquire which time point in the scheme of reconstruction best fits this description of the seizure of the temple by the "barbarians." It is the moment when Artaxerxes I occupied the throne and dealt harshly with the efforts of the Egyptians to regain their independence. If the surmise is true, it was about −458. It would follow that Herihor was appointed not immediately after the removal of Amenhotep from the high priesthood of Amon, but a number of years later.

Chapter II

"THE BASEST OF THE KINGDOMS"

"A Miserable Journey"

SINCE THE DAYS of the Persian conquest under Cambyses, Egypt had been "the basest of the kingdoms" (Ezekiel 29:15). The prophecies of Jeremiah and Ezekiel concerning the debasement of Egypt were fulfilled, not in their time, but at the close of Amasis' reign, when Cambyses subjugated Egypt, humiliated its people, and ruined its temples, and for generations thereafter, through most of the Persian period.

When Golenishchev purchased the papyrus with Ourmai's letter of laments, he obtained in the same transaction a papyrus containing another tale of woe—the story of Wenamon's errand to Byblos on the Syrian coast. Like the letter of Ourmai, the travelogue of Wenamon dates from the Twenty-first Dynasty; both were copied by the same hand; but it is understood that Wenamon's story relates events several generations more recent. Whereas Ourmai's letter was translated and published only recently (in 1961), Wenamon's story was published long ago, actually by Golenishchev himself in 1899.

No document better pictures Egypt's lowly international position during the later part of the Persian domination than Wenamon's description of his experiences.

The priest Wenamon was sent by his superior, the high priest Herihor, to purchase cedarwood in Lebanon for building a sacred barge of Amon. When he reached Tanis in the Delta he gave letters of mandate or introduction to Nesubanebded, the governor of Lower Egypt, and to Ta-net-Amon, his wife, and the letters were read in their presence. They sent him off with the ship captain Mengebet.

Before Wenamon reached Byblos, the goal of his travel, he lost gold and silver that he was carrying for the purpose of paying for the wood for the holy barge: when the ship entered Dor, "a town of the Tjeker" on the Palestinian coast, a sailor disembarked and carried away a golden vase, four jars of silver, and a "sack of silver" —apparently a purse with silver coins. Wenamon stayed in Dor for nine days complaining to the local prince, Bedel, and holding him responsible for finding the thief. Yet Bedel rejected the plea that he should make restitution for the loss and pointed to the fact that the thief was not a resident of his city but a sailor from the ship. Wenamon continued his travel toward Byblos.

The misfortunes that befell him on the way, the intolerance and disdain he encountered in the Syrian cities because of his Egyptian origin and citizenship, the lack of protection when on the high seas, are vividly described in the diary of his journey.[1]

At that time, traveling in Syria was perilous. Nehemiah (2:7) and Ezra (8:22) both mention the insecurity of the highways, even for one on the king's errand. Ezra admits his uneasiness about asking the Persian king for a "band of soldiers and horsemen" to protect him on the road through Syria because previously he had assured the king that the Lord Himself protects those who seek Him; but he felt frightened. Nehemiah, however, took with him a letter from the king to governors "beyond the River" (Euphrates) and a horse-mounted detachment to protect him on the insecure roads.

When Wenamon arrived by a different boat at Byblos the city's prince Zakar-Baal gave him orders to leave the place. "So I spent twenty-nine days in his harbor, while he spent the time sending to me every day to say: 'Get out of my harbor!'"

The Egyptian emissary waited for a ship to take him home. At last, on the evening when he was about to depart, a young man of the prince's entourage fell into a trance and delivered an oracular

---

[1] J. Breasted, *Ancient Records*, Vol. IV, Secs. 563 ff; J. A. Wilson in J. B. Pritchard, ed. *Ancient Near Eastern Texts* (1950), pp. 25ff. M. A. Korostovtzev, *Pooteshestviye Un-Amuna v' Bibl* (Akademiya Naook S.S.S.R., Moscow, 1960).

prophecy on Wenamon's mission. Then came an invitation to stay on. The ecstatic frenzy of the youth is called "the earliest instance of prophetic ecstasy known to us."[2] But the last prophets of Israel were already dead.

The prince of Byblos agreed to grant an audience to Wenamon. "I found him sitting in his upper chamber leaning his back against a window, while the waves of the great Syrian sea beat against [the shore] behind him."[3] Wenamon describes the scene so vividly that we see it as though we had been present.

"How long, up to today, since you came from the place where Amon is?" asked the prince. Wenamon answered: "Five months and one day up to now."

Zakar-Baal asked Wenamon where his credentials were; the answer was, with Nesubanebded in Tanis. The prince became angry and interrogated further—Where was the ship which Nesubanebded put at Wenamon's disposal? Where was its Syrian crew?

The prince, most probably, knew that Wenamon had left the ship captained by Mengebet when his gold and silver were stolen in the Palestinian harbor of Dor.[4] The emissary who came to obtain cedarwood for the holy barque of Amon had neither credentials, nor ship, nor gold or silver to pay for the wood.

Diplomatically, Wenamon switched the subject to the problem of the nationality of the crew of the ship on which he had left Tanis —"Wasn't it an Egyptian ship?"—and he went on to say that ships sailing from and to Egypt had no Syrian crews. To this the prince retorted that in his own harbor there were twenty ships that regularly sailed to Egypt and he continued:

"As to this Sidon, the other place which you have passed, aren't there fifty more ships which are in commercial relations with Werket-El, and which are drawn up to his house?"

Werket-El or Birkath-El "was apparently a Phoenician merchant resident in Egypt, trading particularly with Sidon," writes the trans-

[2] Breasted, *Ancient Records*, Vol. IV, Sec. 562.
[3] This passage follows Breasted's translation; in other quoted passages, Wilson's translation is followed.
[4] On Dor in Persian times see T. C. Mitchell, "Philistia" in *Archaeology and Old Testament Study*, D. W. Thomas, ed. (Oxford, 1967), p. 417.

lator of the text.[5] The name is an important clue and we shall return to it after relating the rest of that conversation between Zakar-Baal and Wenamon and the events that followed.

The prince said indignantly that "If the ruler of Egypt were the lord of mine" he could ask for a gift. But "I am not your servant. I am not the servant of him who sent you either!" And he snorted: "What are these 'miserable journeys' that they have sent you to make?"[6]

Wenamon answered that there was not a ship that did not belong to Amon: "The sea is his and the Lebanon is his!" He asked the prince to allow a dispatch to be sent to Tanis with a request from Wenamon to Nesubanebded for a loan that would be repaid (by Herihor) upon Wenamon's return. The prince consented and after a few weeks Nesubanebded sent some gold, some silver, five hundred rolls of papyrus, five hundred cowhides, five hundred ropes. The prince sent three hundred men to cut trees in the mountains and to drag the logs to the sea. The prince told Wenamon to get the logs and to depart. Wenamon vacillated. The sea was stormy and he was afraid of Tjeker ships. Zakar-Baal lost patience: "Don't come to look at the terror of the sea! If you look at the terror of the sea, you will see my own, too!"

The wrathful prince told Wenamon that he should be thankful to his fate: the emissaries that came from Egypt in a former generation, in the days of Kha-em-waset, to buy cedarwood were detained by an ancestor of the prince and upon having spent seventeen years in Byblos they died there. "And he said to his butler: 'Take him and show him their tomb in which they are lying.'" To which Wenamon said: "Don't show it to me."

Ordered again to leave, Wenamon was seized with fear that the "ships of Tjeker" would capture him on the open sea. "I spied eleven ships belonging to Tjeker coming from the sea, and saying: 'Arrest him, don't let a ship of his go to the land of Egypt.' Then I sat

[5] J. A. Wilson. He also comments: "The 'drawn to his house' would mean either drawn up on the shore at his Sidonian office or towed along the waterways of Egypt."

[6] Breasted's translation; "silly trips" in Wilson's translation.

down and wept." The prince of Byblos had compassion for the frightened man. He replied to the captains of the Tjeker ships who demanded his extradition: "I cannot arrest the messenger of Amon in my land. Let me send him away and you go after him to arrest him."

In Persian times piracy on the Mediterranean was quite legal.[7] Athenians, Spartans, Sicilians sailed their ships in all directions across the sea. Sidon was the great shipbuilding harbor and the sale of vessels there was not confined to honest merchants alone.

A plan to go by a roundabout route and a stormy sea threw Wenamon and his ship on the shores of Cyprus at a town ruled by a Princess Heteb. How he reached Egypt is not known, as the end of the papyrus is missing.

It is of interest that quite a number of Hebrew words are used by Wenamon in the story of his travels: for "assembly" he used the Hebrew "*moed*" and for "league" or "alliance" the Hebrew term "*hever*"; other such instances of preference given to Hebrew words over Egyptian vocabulary are exhibited by Wenamon.

Two names in the text of the papyrus caused deliberation among scholars. One was Khaemwise (Kha-em-waset), in whose days messengers sent from Egypt were detained in Byblos against their will. The other was the name of the shipowner Werket-El or Birkath-El, who maintained commercial traffic between Sidon and Tanis.

No answer was found to the question of the identity of Khaemwise. Ramses IX or Neferkare-setpenre Ramesse-khaemwise-mereramun and Ramses XI or Menmare-setpenptah Ramesse-khaemwise-merer-amun-nutehekaon were considered but rejected. Khaemwise was "certainly a king"[8] but, Ramses IX and Ramses XI having reigned only very recently, Wenamon, a priest and official, would not omit in referring to either of them the title "king"—such titling being a matter of civility a priest and scribe would not violate.[9] Declining the insulting invitation to visit the graves of the messen-

---

[7] See Max Cary, "Piracy," Oxford Classical Dictionary (Oxford, 1949), p. 694. In the Peloponnesian War privateering became "a serious scourge."

[8] Gardiner, "The Twentieth Dynasty," *Egypt of the Pharaohs*, p. 311.

[9] Korostovtzev, *Pooteshestviye*, p. 34.

gers who arrived in the days of Khaemwise, Wenamon says: "Don't show it to me! As for Khaem-Waset[10]—they were men whom he sent to you as messengers, and he was a man himself." Wilson comments: "This should rule out the possibility that Khaem-Waset was Ramses IX as Wen-Amon would probably not refer to a pharaoh as a 'man.'"[11]

The pharaoh who goes under the name of Ramses IX was a contemporary of Herihor, but the Ramses known as Ramses XI must have preceded him since he was shown in a relief being offered flowers by the high priest Amenhotep. Both these kings belong to the fifth century; both use the nomen Khaem-Waset. In the papyrus of Wenamon the reference must be to the earlier of these two, who was deposed together with the high priest Amenhotep in the earlier part of the reign of Artaxerxes I. He was most probably Inaros of the Greek sources who rebelled against Artaxerxes I. A hypothesis that Khaem-Waset stands for Cambyses would meet with philological difficulties.

The other name found in the Wenamon Papyrus that caused deliberation is that of the shipping magnate with headquarters in Tanis in the Delta. Of him the prince of Byblos said that in Sidon alone fifty ships "are in league with Birkath-El" and sail "to his house."

In his book on Wenamon's travel, A. Erman, the eminent German Egyptologist, arrived at the conclusion that the proper reading of the hieroglyphics w-r-k-t-r is Birkath-El, the hieroglyphics having but one sign for both r and l, and w and b being interchangeable.[12] The name Birkath-El, Erman concluded, points to the Semitic origin of the shipping magnate, most probably a Phoenician; it means "God's blessing," and is construed not unlike many other Semitic names ending with el.

M. Burchhardt added arguments in favor of Erman's reading of the name but also questioned it on the ground that, though the

---

[10] In his translation of the papyrus, Gardiner uses the spelling Khaemwīse.
[11] Wilson in *Ancient Near Eastern Texts* (1st ed.), p. 28, fn. 35.
[12] A. Erman, *Aegyptische Literatur* (1923), p. 230.

Egyptians of later times interchanged the consonants *b* and *w*, the eleventh or tenth century before the present era was much too early for such lexicographic laxity.[13]

In 1924, R. Eisler published a paper, "Barakhel Sohn und Cie, Rhedereigesellschaft in Tanis" (Barakhel Son and Co., Shipping House in Tanis)[14] in which he drew attention to the fact that a late Hebrew source contains a reference to the same shipping company. The Testament of Naphtali of the *Testaments of Twelve Patriarchs* (twelve sons of Jacob) tells of a shipping company called Berakhel's Son. The Testament of Naphtali is a pseudepigraphic work the composition of which is placed in about −148, the year Johnathan of the House of Hashmanaim (Maccabees) conquered Jaffa and thus opened an access to sea and maritime trade.

In the Testament, a vision is narrated of a ship that passes near the shore of Jaffa with no crew or passengers. But on the mast of the ship is written the name of the owner, son of Berakhel.

The name Berakhel, like Birkath-El, means God's blessing and is a slightly different construction of the possessive (like the English, "God's blessing" and "blessing of God").

Eisler wondered: Could it be that the shipping house existed still, as late as −150? This would mean that its ships navigated along the Syrian coast for over nine hundred years, since Wenamon's travel took place "in about −1100." But such a span of time is "three times as long as the duration of the most durable of the English or Hanseatic companies." An assumption that the author of the Testament of Naphtali could have gathered his knowledge from a copy of the Wenamon narrative must be rejected, claimed Eisler, on general grounds, but also because the two references to the shipping company spell the name slightly differently.

In our estimate, Wenamon went on his travels not "about −1100" but close to −400 and therefore there are not nine hundred and fifty years between the times of origin of these two sources. Further,

[13] M. Burchhardt, *Die Altkanaanaeischen Fremdworte und Eigennamen im Aegyptischen* (Leipzig, 1909–10).
[14] *Zeitschrift der Morgenlaendischen Gesellschaft*, Vol. 78 (Vol. 3 of the New Series) (1924), 61–63.

it is conceivable that the Testament of Naphtali was composed before the Hashmanaim asserted independence from the Seleucid domination, possibly still in the Persian period; if, however, the Testament is properly attributed to the middle of the second century, the shipping firm could still be in existence or its existence one or two centuries earlier could have been known to the author of the Testament. But not if almost a millennium lies between.

W. F. Albright disagreed with Erman and assumed that the name, read by him as Warkar, is "neither Egyptian nor Semitic but probably Asianic (Anatolian or Aegean)" and belonged to some man who participated in the movements of the Peoples of the Sea and then settled in Egypt.[15] Albright's argument is built on the time attributed to the raid of the Sea Peoples. Nevertheless, most Egyptologists elect to follow Erman's reading, as witnessed by J. A. Wilson.[16]

"Repetition-of-Births"

Wenamon went on his travels sometime during the later part of the Persian domination of Egypt. Could we identify the time with greater precision?

In the opening part of the Papyrus Wenamon it is said that Wenamon started his journey in "year 5, 3rd month of the 3rd season." But of what era was it year 5? Usually in Egyptian documents the year in the opening of a text refers to the ruling year of a monarch. Then who was the monarch at the time Wenamon went on his errand? His name is not given. It is, however, said that when Wenamon reached Tanis in the Delta, before embarking, he gave letters of mandate written by Herihor to Nesubanebded. Again, in Dor, when robbed of gold and silver, Wenamon spoke to Bedel, the prince of the locality: "It [gold and silver] belongs to Amon-Re,

---

[15] "Some Oriental Glosses on the Homeric Problem," *American Journal of Archaeology*, LIV (1950), 174.

[16] "Werket-El (= Birkath-El?) was apparently a Phoenician merchant resident in Egypt, trading particularly with Sidon." *Ancient Near Eastern Texts* (1950), p. 27.

king of gods, the lord of the lands; it belongs to Nesubanebded; it belongs to Heri-Hor, my lord, and the other great men of Egypt." No king is mentioned, nor is either of these two referred to as a king.

Herihor, the priest who sent Wenamon, and Nesubanebded, the governor in the Delta, are regarded as potentates under Ramses XI, the supposedly last ephemeral Ramesside king; with him, the Twentieth Dynasty expired. It is assumed that Ramses XI was no longer in power since the robbed messenger, in his complaint to the Syrian prince of Dor, invokes only the authority of the high priest of Thebes and of the governor of the Delta; and later, when detained by Zakar-Baal, prince of Byblos, he again mentions only these men, but no king of Egypt, whose protection he should have invoked if there had been royal power in Egypt. Therefore it was assumed that the fifth year may refer to "the kingless period following the Twentieth Dynasty."[1] This, however, seems implausible. A kingless time would not be stated in terms of year and month at the opening of a document. The Egyptians designated the time by the ruling year of the monarch *in power*. In Egypt at the time there was no monarch and yet the document was dated "year 5."

In other documents of the same time, similarly, in the opening sentences, certain years are mentioned, but the king is not named; however, occasionally a reference is made to "the Repetition-of-Births." A. H. Gardiner, in his *Egypt of the Pharaohs*, writes concerning the time of the high priest Herihor: "Instead of dates continuing to be expressed, as normally, in terms of the regnal years of the monarch, a mysterious new era named the Repetition-of-Births makes its appearance."[2]

The Papyrus Mayer A is headed "Year 1 in the Repetition-of-Births." In this papyrus the same tomb robbers are named as in the Papyrus Abbott, which has the date "Year 1, first month of the Inundation season, day 2, corresponding to Year 19." Obviously two methods of dating an event were in use. Year 19 could, for instance,

[1] J. Wilson in Pritchard, *Ancient Near Eastern Texts* (1950), p. 25.
[2] P. 304.

refer to the pontificate of a high priest, but what would "Year 1 in the Repetition-of-Births" mean? Was it some sort of Renaissance?

Sometimes it is assumed that Herihor claimed a new Renaissance era for Egypt with his assumption of the pontificate or the throne (occasionally, but not always, his name was placed in an oval, or cartouche, the distinguishing mark of the kings). But why should the time of Herihor be glorified as the beginning of a Renaissance? From the story of Wenamon and his journey made under the mandate of Herihor, no impression can be gained that Herihor was about to claim the dawn of a new era or even a royal title.

Besides, "Repetition-of-Births" and dating by this mysterious era are known already from the time of Ramses XI, a number of years before Herihor: thus "Year 7 of the Repetition-of-Births" under Menmare-setpenptah Ramesse (Ramses XI) is found in a document relating how the appointment of a certain Nesamun to the post of scribe at the storehouse of Karnak was decided by the oracle.[3]

After some deliberation, the "year 5" at the beginning of the Wenamon Papyrus was interpreted as relating to the "Repetition-of-Births" era initiated by Herihor.

But it appears to us that "year 5" refers to the reigning year of the Persian overlord, either Darius II Nothus (−424 to −404), in which case the travel took place in −419, or Artaxerxes II, who started his reign in −404, in which case the travel occurred in −399.

Our surmise as to the meaning of the date, and the Repetition-of-Births in general, receives support from a custom instituted in the reigns of Persian kings. We need only open a book on the history of the ancient Persian Empire, such as *The Medes and Persians* by W. Culican,[4] to read on the first page:

"Persepolis . . . begun by Darius in −518, it was completed by Xerxes. . . . In it each New Year's Day the Achaemenid kingship was renewed and men from every part of the empire came to offer their tokens of obeisance."

[3] The phrase "Repetition-of-Births" seems to have been used in the days of Amenemhet I and in the days of Seti the Great. Cf. Gardiner, *Egypt of the Pharaohs*, pp. 127 and 249.

[4] W. Culican, *The Medes and Persians* (London, 1965).

Wenamon Builds a Shrine

Wenamon, it can be taken for granted, reached Egyptian soil and at home, upon the successful completion of the adventurous itinerary, wrote the story of his mission to Byblos.

As an emissary of the high priest Herihor, Wenamon must have had some prominence in the priestly hierarchy and, possibly, it would be worth while to look for traces of him in Karnak or, even better, in the el-Khargeh or Siwa oases, the places where the worship of Amon was cultivated in the Persian period of Egyptian history. Such a search, as we shall immediately see, will not be fruitless.

The temple of the oracle of Zeus-Ammon in the Siwa oasis is known today as the temple of Aghurmi and is in a ruinous state. Even less is left of the temple of Umm-Ebeida in the same oasis. Diodorus, relying on Cleitarchus, a biographer of Alexander, mentions, at a distance from the acropolis with the temple of the oracle, "a second temple of Ammon in the shade of many large trees. In its vicinity, there is a spring which is called 'Spring of the Sun.' . . ."

As in the time of Alexander, Umm-Ebeida is surrounded by groves of trees. Today, the remains of a single wall, with bas-reliefs and hieroglyphics chiseled on it, still stand; around are slabs of stone, some with written signs on them. Before the end of the nineteenth century there were more of the walls and also a ceiling capping them but then they were dynamited by some local potentate to obtain stones for building purposes.

In 1900, G. Steindorff visited the Siwa oasis, examined the remaining wall, and read the name of the builder: Wenamon. The text on the wall identifies him as "The real master, the great chief of the foreign lands, Wenamon. . . ." A bas-relief shows him kneeling before the god Amon: the god of the temple of the oracle was worshiped also in the shrine erected by Wenamon.

Steindorff was not prepared to connect Wenamon of the travel to Byblos with Wenamon who erected a shrine to the god Amon:

none of the buildings of Siwa dates farther back in time than the beginning of the Persian domination in Egypt[1]; Wenamon's travel to Byblos, however, is placed in the eleventh century.

It is significant that Wenamon identified himself on the wall of the temple he built as "chief" or "master" of—or authority on—foreign lands. A lay citizen or a priest could not conceivably be a "chief of foreign lands." But in view of what we learned of Wenamon's travels to foreign countries he could have claimed the distinction of being an authority on foreign lands. We also learn from the inscription that Wenamon's father was Nakht-tit and his mother Nefer-renpet. The Wenamon Papyrus did not mention (in the surviving text) the names of the author's parents.

Is it possible to determine more closely when Wenamon built the shrine to his god Amon?

Over a hundred and fifty years ago Minutoli visited and described the oasis and its temples.[2] He noticed on one of the fallen slabs at Umm-Ebeida two cartouches and he reproduced them in a drawing in his book. The cartouches are no longer found on what is left of the ruins but "in spite of the inexactness of the letters, there is no doubt that they belong to Nectanebo II," writes Ahmed Fakhri in his volume, Siwa Oasis.[3] "The name of Nectanebo II was written on the facade but in the inner chamber we find the name of the builder of the temple [Wenamon] repeated several times." We have shown already that Nekt-hor-heb, whose cartouches were found here and elsewhere, was not Nectanebo II of the Greek authors but a potentate under Darius II.

Now it is quite certain that "year 5" in the opening of Wenamon's travelogue refers to the fifth year of Darius II or −419.

Since it was Herihor who sent Wenamon on his mission and Nekt-hor-heb appears to have been associated with Wenamon in the building of the shrine at Umm-Ebeida in the oasis, it follows that Herihor also lived under Darius II; he was vested with the

---

[1] A. Fakhri claims the origin of the oracle temple under Amasis II was shortly before the conquest of Egypt by the Persians.

[2] H. C. Minutoli, Reise zum Tempel des Jupiter Ammon in der Libyschen Wüste (Berlin, 1824).

[3] P. 100.

religious rank of a high priest but in the oases, the southern (el-Kargeh) and the northern (Siwa), he had also a secular rank, that of a commander of the army.

We could establish on good grounds that the traveler on "miserable journeys," whose manuscript came to us without its end portion, safely reached Egypt and, what is more important, that he lived in the Persian period of Egyptian history, more precisely, under Darius II. The manuscript and the building were creations of one and the same person, here reunited from two existences seven hundred years apart.

As we shall see shortly, the high priest in the Zeus-Ammon (Amon) temple at Siwa who met and blessed Alexander the Great was a third-generation descendant of Herihor. These generations cover the period from the travel of Wenamon in −419 to the advent of Alexander in Egypt (−332), or eighty-seven years.

The Royal Cache

For about ten years prior to 1881, antiquities from some clandestine source were reaching tourists and dealers in Luxor, Cairo, and Paris; these antiquities were obviously coming from a cache or from tombs unknown to archaeologists. When the illegal traffic reached an alarming scale, inquiries and detective work led to a certain family of Arabs of Gournah village on the western plain across the Nile from Luxor. When interrogated, the members of the clan steadfastly denied any part in illicit digging or even any knowledge of such things. The Khedive of Egypt himself took a close interest in the affair, being kept informed by Gaston Maspero, a noted Egyptologist in charge of antiquities. One member of the clan was put into prison on mere suspicion; he spent two months there without revealing anything. But when released for lack of clear evidence, he quarreled with his accomplices, among them his elder brother, demanding a half instead of a fifth of the proceeds from the future sale of the antiquities, to compensate him for the time spent in prison; denied this and injured by the injustice, he was about to disclose the secret to the authorities when he was preceded by his elder brother.

Close to the temple of Deir el Bahari built by Queen Hatshepsut of the Eighteenth Dynasty, under the cliffs, a covered hole in the rock concealed a well twelve meters deep that led to a corridor about sixty-five meters (over two hundred feet) long; at its end there was a chamber seven meters by four and five meters high. A smaller chamber or niche was located halfway along the corridor. In the chamber and in the niche were coffins and mummies of many of the great pharaohs of the past and some of the names were read by the light of a candle by Maspero and his assistant, Emil Brugsch.

In the cache were the mummies of Ahmose I, who founded the Eighteenth Dynasty upon the expulsion of the Hyksos from their fortress Avaris; of Amenhotep I, the most venerated of all kings and thought holy; of Thutmose I and of his son Thutmose III, the great conqueror; of Seti the Great of the Nineteenth Dynasty and of Ramses II, his son, and also of Ramses III of the Twentieth. It was almost unbelievable. Maspero admitted having expected to find a tomb cache of some obscure king or princeling but he found kings known to every student of history; they were found not one by one but all collected together, a real Valhalla. The names of the kings were written on wrappings accompanied by statements as to who rewrapped each one of them. The work of rewrapping was begun by the high priest Herihor; other mummies were rewrapped under the supervision of his son Paiankh, still others under Peinuzem I, son of Paiankh, and some under his sons Mesahert and Menkheperre, then a few under Peinuzem II, son of the latter, and the entire work was completed by Si-Amon.

The cache dates from the Twenty-first Dynasty, the succession of princely priests, and many mummies of the period were included, some of the rewrappers themselves, like that of Peinuzem II. Originally the tomb had been built for a little-known Queen Inhapy, and it appears that Si-Amon collected there and rewrapped for the last time the royal mummies rewrapped earlier by the princely priests of the Twenty-first Dynasty.

But before all this was learned, the contents of the tomb were removed.

The removal was performed in a hurry. Maspero intimates in his account of the find[1] that he had to count even on the possibility of an armed incursion by some Bedouins, who upon hearing that treasures of ancient kings of Egypt had been found were not averse to raiding the treasures, supposedly all gold and diamonds. But anyone familiar with the resolute way government officials used to act in Egypt under the khedives would think that the true motive for the speedy removal of the mummies was excitement over the find, which made the Egyptologists desirous of satisfying their curiosity and meeting without delay and in the light of day the famous kings of the past.

"Two hundred Arabs were quickly assembled and put to work. The museum-owned ship, summoned in haste, had not yet arrived but there was 'chief' Mohammed Abdessalem [who revealed the secret] on whom we could rely. He descended into the hole and took charge of removing the contents." Two assistants in the antiquities service received the objects as soon as they emerged from under the ground and had them carried down the hill and placed there side by side "without relenting their surveillance for an instant." Maspero continues: "Forty-eight hours of energetic work sufficed to exhume all but the task was only half complete." It took seven or eight hours to transport the large coffins, carried by men, from the foot of the cliffs to the river in the heat of July and in the raised dust. The number of objects was so considerable that it was hardly possible to watch over their safety and some disappeared but were retrieved, with the exception of some fifty figurines covered with blue enamel. "By eleven at night, the mummies, the coffins, the furniture, reached Luxor. Three days later the museum's ship arrived, was loaded and departed to Boulaq [the site of the Museum of Cairo] under full steam with its freight of kings."

Some of the mummies, which had been preserved for thousands of years, started to emit an odor of decay and were opened; some

---

[1] G. Maspero, *Les Momies royales de Déir el-Bahari*, published as the first volume of *Mémoires de la Mission Archéologique Française au Caire* (Paris, 1889).

others were opened by Emil Brugsch, most impatient to learn their content, in the absence of Maspero and without his authorization; but the mummies of Seti the Great, of Ramses II, and some others were not opened until two years later in the presence of the Khedive.

No real treasures were found between the wrappings of the mummies. If the story of Herodotus is true, it is quite probable that when Cambyses ordered some of the ancient tombs to be opened their treasures were confiscated and thus an example was set. Numerous cases of tomb robberies and records of court proceedings fill much of the surviving literature of the period that we recognized as the second half of the fifth century and the beginning of the fourth—all through the time of Herihor and his successors. They are often adjudged as pious priests for the acts of reburial. But it appears that the priests themselves were most eager to detect and appropriate to themselves the riches that could be found in tombs; jewels in gold and precious stones inserted between the wrappings were looked for when everything in costly furnishing had already been removed. And did not the priests of the so-called Twenty-first Dynasty, as we shall learn from other burials, appropriate for their own funerals the sarcophagi, furnishing, and jewels destined originally for royal persons of earlier times?

The mummies of ancient kings and those of the priestly succession were assembled from different hiding places by Si-Amon, who sealed the cache in the "tenth year."

A decade after Maspero removed the royal and other mummies from the cache south of Deir el Bahari to Cairo, the same Arab who had led the archaeologist to the find called the attention of E. Grebaut, Maspero's successor in the post of director of antiquities, to another cache, not far from the same place, this time north of Deir el Bahari. A shaft led to a long narrow passage (about a hundred meters on one level and almost sixty on a level below the first) lined with coffins: it was a real catacomb. G. Daressy, in charge of the operation, found there one hundred and fifty-three coffins; the occupants were all members of priestly families, usually people of some distinction but not of high hierarchy.[2] Many mummies were female, "concubines of Amon" and temple singers. A room had been prepared for the family of the high priest Menkheperre and his wives. (We shall soon meet this person as the priest who received Alexander the Great in the Zeus-Ammon temple in the Siwa oasis.)

Before this second cache was emptied of its contents, Daressy spent a few nights in a tent near the opening of the shaft to protect it from modern tomb violators. When the coffins were brought to Cairo, it was found that the museum could not play host to all these coffins and mummies; after a while sixteen groups, each of four or five mummies with their coffins, were sent as gifts to various governments of Europe from Portugal to Russia with no control retained by the Cairo Museum as to their future fate; as Daressy discovered, one of the mummies reached Irkutsk in Siberia, a trip never anticipated by the owner of the body when alive.

The dockets on the mummies of both caches provided much material for a clarification of the dynastic order of kings and high priests of the Twenty-first Dynasty; but the "dark period" is still regarded as dark and much conflicting and confusing evidence is continuously being debated.[3]

For our purposes it is important to learn that Peinuzem, son of Paiankh, son of Herihor, rewrapped the mummy of Ramses III, or even originally wrapped it. This leads us to the conclusion that Paiankh and also Psusennes (whom Peinuzem called his father but who was probably his father-in-law) were contemporaries of Ramses III (Nectanebo I). Herihor, having started on his priestly career under Darius II, in the last quarter of the fifth century, preceded Ramses III.

The royal cache was closed and sealed by the Tanite prince-priest

[2] G. Daressy, "Les Sépultures des prêtres d'Ammun à Deir El-Bahari" in *Annales du Service des Antiquités de l'Égypte,* I (1900); idem, "Les Cercueils des Prêtres d'Ammun," ibid., VIII (1907).

[3] Cf. "Some Notes on the Chronology and Genealogy of the Twenty-First Dynasty," by Eric Young in *Journal of the American Research Center in Egypt,* II (1963), 99–111; Černý, *Cambridge Ancient History,* Vol. II, Chap. XXXV; "On the Chronology of the Twenty-first Dynasty," by E. F. Wente in *Journal of Near Eastern Studies,* XXVI, 3 (July 1967).

Si-Amon, regarded as the last in the Twenty-first Dynasty, in the "Year 10." It could not, on the accepted time scale, contain the mummy of a person who lived under the Twenty-second (Libyan) Dynasty. But the mummy of a priest of Amon, Djetptah-efonkh, of the Twenty-second Dynasty, was among the mummies in the cache.[4] It was, therefore, assumed that the cache had been re-opened under the Libyan kings to insert there the body of the priest.[5] This conjecture is obviously very weak. But from the view of this reconstruction, we should have expected that, besides mummies of the Seventeenth, Eighteenth, and Nineteenth Dynasties, a mummy dating from the Libyan Dynasty of the ninth–eighth centuries would have been interred in the cache. The absence of a mummy dating from the Libyan Dynasty would be a fact requiring explanation; its presence confronts the accepted timetable with a disturbing fact.

Theocratic States in Judah and in Egypt

Under the Persians, Jerusalem was a dependent city and, with the area under its jurisdiction, a commonwealth dominated by a theocracy. With Nehemiah at the head of the commonwealth and then Ezra, the theocratic form grew ever more pronounced.

It is instructive to compare the theocratic regime in Thebes, Tanis, and in the oases under the so-called Twenty-first Dynasty with the regime of the contemporaneous Jerusalem. Priests, high priests, prophets in the service of the temples and their oracles, temple singers, temple porters, hereditary temple slaves—all have counterparts in Jerusalem and in Thebes, Tanis, and the oases. In many cases we can better understand an Egyptian text or situation by studying biblical post-Exilic texts or referring to the Temple

---

[4] Maspero, *Les Momies royales* (Paris, 1889), pp. 572–73. B. Porter and R. Moss, *The Theban Necropolis* (Oxford, 1964), p. 666.

[5] Gardiner, *Egypt of the Pharaohs*, p. 320. H. Gauthier, in *Annales du Service des Antiquités de l'Egypte*, Vol. 18 (1919), pp. 252ff.

9. Pylon (Portal) of the Temple of Ramses III at Medinet-Habu. *From L'Architecture et la Décoration dans l'Ancienne Egypte; Les Temples Ramessides et Saïtes by G. Jéquier, Plates Courtesy Morancé-Paris.*

10. The pylon of the Khonsu Temple erected during the Twenty-first Dynasty. *From* l'Architecture et la Décoration dans l'Ancienne Egypte; Les Temples Ramessides et Saïtes *by G. Jéquier, Plates Courtesy Morancé-Paris.*

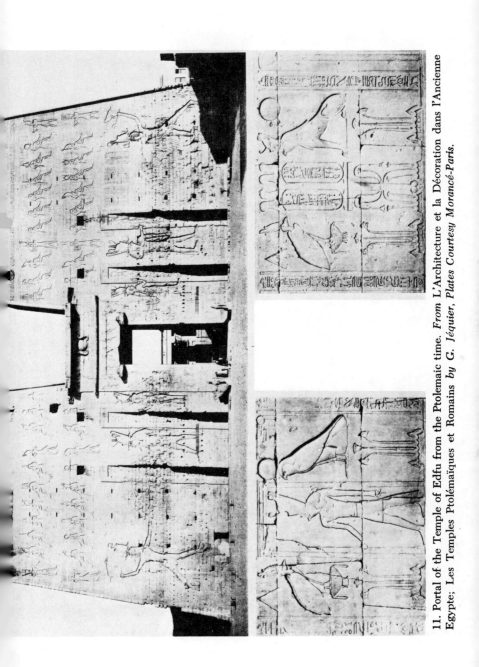

11. Portal of the Temple of Edfu from the Ptolemaic time. *From* L'Architecture et la Décoration dans l'Ancienne Egypte; Les Temples Ptolémaïques et Romains *by G. Jéquier, Plates Courtesy Morancé-Paris.*

12. Leather canopy of the funeral tent of Peinuzem II. The leather canopy used by Si-Amon to put to grave Peinuzem II, one of the last priest-princes of the Twenty-first Dynasty, supposedly of the first half of the tenth century. *From Egypt After the War by H. W. Villiers-Stuart.*

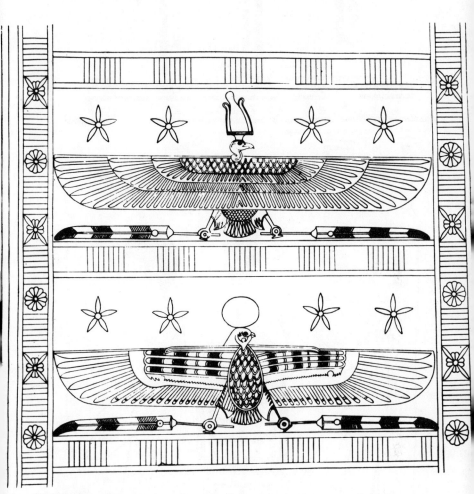

13. Hawks and vultures on the ceiling of the tomb of Si-Amon. *From* Siwa
Oasis *by Ahmed Fakhri.*

14. Si-Amon in the presence of deities. A vulture hovers over his head—a sign of royal status. *From* Siwa Oasis *by Ahmed Fakhri.*

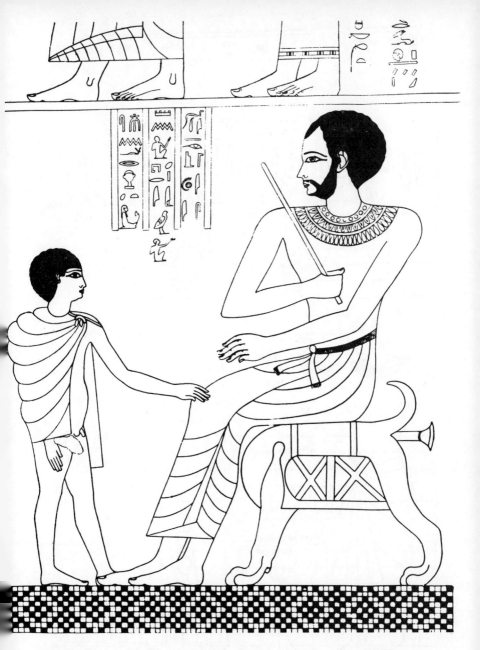

15. Si-Amon and his son. Si-Amon has black curly hair and his body is colored light yellow. His son is a red-brown color and wears a short cloak of Greek style. *From* Siwa Oasis *by Ahmed Fakhri.*

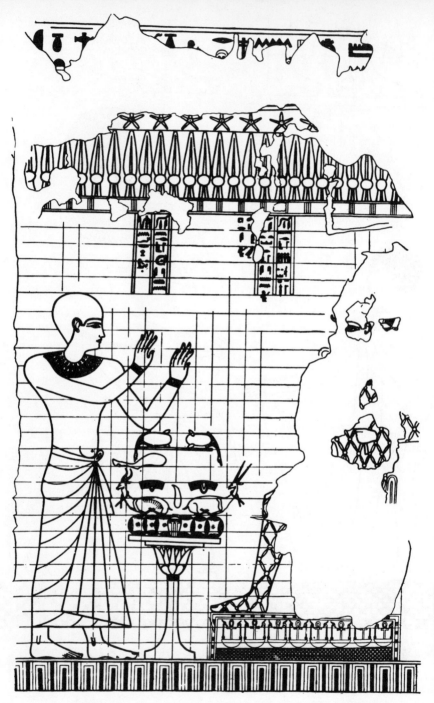

16. Si-Amon adoring Osiris. *From* Siwa Oasis *by Ahmed Fakhri.*

service in Jerusalem in the Persian period. For instance when a "porter" by the name of Ahautinofer, accused of having taken part in stealing a gilded chest from a temple, testifies before the Egyptian court and refers to the removal of the high priest (by unidentified authority), we can, with the help of verse 73 in Chapter 7 of the Book of Nehemiah, understand that "porter" was a temple employee of some rank. The Hebrew text speaks of "the priests, and the Levites, and the porters, and the singers. . . ." The very removal of the high priest Amenhotep from his position as referred to in that testimony has its counterpart in the attempt to remove the high priest Jonathan of Jerusalem by the satrap Bagoas, an event described by Josephus Flavius.[1]

The temple areas had living quarters for the priests—in Jerusalem and in Egypt. Udjeharresne asked Cambyses to order the removal of unauthorized persons, among them soldiers of occupation, from the living quarters of the temple of Neith in Sais and an order was given to remove the squatters with all their belongings. "All their superfluities which were in the temple should be thrown down, all their baggage should be carried for them outside the wall of the temple. And his majesty commanded that the temple of Neith should be cleansed. . . ." A not dissimilar procedure took place in Jerusalem when Nehemiah "cast forth all the household stuff of Tobiah out of the chamber" that the high priest Eliashib had given Tobiah "in the courts" of the temple precincts; Tobiah was an adversary of Nehemiah. "Then I commanded, and they cleansed the chambers" (Nehemiah 13:7–9).

Taxes in money and victuals were imposed on the population of Jerusalem and the surrounding towns for the benefit of the Temple, its priests and Levites; cattle, fowl, wine, bread, and oil were among the victuals. A taxation of the population for the treasures of the temples was a much more pronounced institution in Egypt under the Twenty-first Dynasty and hieroglyphic and demotic texts dealing with such taxation are abundant. Cattle and fowl and wine and bread and oil were tribute that the state and its population had to deliver to the temples and their priests.

[1] *Jewish Antiquities*, XI, VII.

The Temple of Jerusalem under the Persians had in its organization involuntary servants or hereditary slaves attached to the Temple. Nehemiah (11:3) refers to them: "The priests, and the Levites, and the Nethinim," the latter being these hereditary slaves. Hereditary slaves were attached in great numbers to the temples of Egypt; also large land possessions or fiefs of the temples were worked by peasants in dependence, actually serfs.

The books of the prophets Haggai and Zechariah (who spoke in the days of Darius the Great) and of Malachi, like the books of Nehemiah and Ezra, present a picture of a theocracy governing the Temple and the country. The main difference between Jerusalem and Egypt is in the worship of a Supreme Deity in Jerusalem with no partner or challenger to his supremacy and the worship of a supreme god Amon who has partners and challengers in the Egyptian pantheon. The ethos of the Mosaic law and the ethical heritage of the pre-Exile prophets had nothing to compare with in the temples of Egypt, where the Apis cult, a legacy of earlier ages, colored all services.

Oracular pronouncements were an institution that dominated other priestly functions and even took precedence over other considerations in decision making in the state affairs of Egypt. In the days of the Persian hegemony the Temple of Jerusalem also had an oracle—"a priest with Urim and with Thummim" (Ezra 2:63).

The post of high priest was hereditary in Judah and in Egypt alike. Whereas we are not well acquainted with the genealogy of high priests under the Persians before the installation of Herihor, a man of no distinction in priestly circles in this post, we are familiar with the order of succession that starts with him—Psusennes, Peinuzem, Menkheperre, Peinuzem II.

In Judah the entire line of the high priests from the days of Cyrus to the time of Alexander is known from the entry in the book of Nehemiah (12:10–11): Jeshua, Joiakim, Eliashib, Joiada, Jonathan, and Jaddua; the line is also known from Josephus Flavius.

Books with genealogies of priests were kept in temples and were often consulted in Jerusalem as well as in Egypt. Ezra, though of a priestly line, was not descended from a high priest. Nevertheless, he succeeded in molding the Jewish religion into forms that were unbreakable through the Persian, Greek, and Roman times, and through the nineteen centuries of Diaspora. The Egyptian priests of his time supplemented their income from taxations and donations with raids on ancient tombs with their treasures, disrobing the mummies of their ancestors in search of anything of value. Accordingly, the religions of Egypt and of Israel fared very differently in the centuries to come.

Ezra

The role of Ezra in creating rabbinical Judaism cannot be overestimated. He was the editor of the Pentateuch and possibly the author of those parts of it that are known as the Priestly Codex; it is conceivable that he edited the books of Kings and Chronicles and it is also assumed by some biblical scholars that he had his hand in composing the books that go under the names of Nehemiah and Ezra and that could have been originally a single book. He was guided by the vision of the past—the misty time of the patriarchs, the days and years when the nation, led by Moses, went through its most sublime period rich in tribulations, the seven centuries of settled life under judges, prophets, and kings, that ended for the Northern Kingdom of Israel when crushed by the Assyrians, and left Judah to continue for one hundred and thirty-five years in its struggle against the overwhelming odds of Babylon and Egypt until it was crushed, too. Closer to Ezra's own time was the life of the exiles in the Babylonian captivity from which, following the fall of Babylon, stormed by the Persians in −538, small groups returned, one of them led, a hundred or more years later, by Ezra himself. He also carried with him from exile the vision of the future role of Israel—the name to be taken over by Judah. He introduced the reading of the Torah (Pentateuch) in public; he instituted the feast of Tabernacles (Succoth) adopting some of its pageantry, like the use of palm branches, from a Persian festival; but he was ferociously dedicated to the idea of not sharing the priestly mission

of the Jewish people with the Gentiles and thus influenced this
nation not to seek proselytes—thus, in centuries to come leaving to
a Jewish sect, the Christians, the role of "conquering the conquerors," the Romans who brought an end to the Bait Sheni, or
Second Commonwealth, the period that extended from the time
of the Persian conquest, through the centuries of Hellenistic domination, and to the year 70 of the present era.

Ezra exalted the role of Moses, who lived over a thousand years
before his own time, and lifted him above all other authority and
above what Moses' authority had been during the existence of the
First Commonwealth. Pure monotheism, not yet discernible as such
even among most of the prophets prior to Jeremiah, crystallized
in the Exile and the learned scribe, no prophet and not of royal
origin, not even of a distinguished ancestral line, was its codifier.
He endowed the Sabbath with supreme holiness and thus became
a great social reformer and benefactor of the working man down
to our own age. More than any other prophet, priest, or scribe, he
carries the responsibility for the form that Judaism took and preserved through the days of the Second Commonwealth—Persian,
Hellenistic, and Roman times, and upon the destruction of the state
by the Romans, through the nineteen centuries of dispersion (Diaspora) among the nations. In the rabbinical tradition Ezra is second only to Moses. He performed his task not amidst peals of
thunder or from a cloud-shrouded mountain, but on the streets of
Jerusalem, still in ruins since its destruction by Nebuchadnezzar,
a depopulated city that had not yet risen from the ashes.

A historical problem that has never ceased to vex biblical scholars
is whether Ezra preceded Nehemiah, each of whom has a book
named for him in the Scriptures,[1] or followed him. The canon has
Ezra preceding Nehemiah: Ezra came from Babylon in the seventh
year of Artaxerxes, Nehemiah, however, from Susa in the twentieth
year of the king. Yet strong arguments were presented to show that
Ezra followed Nehemiah, not preceded him. Among these arguments is that in Ezra's time the high priest in Jerusalem appears
to have been Jonathan, son or grandson of Eliashib, whereas in the

---

[1] In early times the books of Nehemiah and Ezra constituted a single book.

days of Nehemiah the office of the high priest belonged to Eliashib. A reference to Ezra and Nehemiah acting in common (Nehemiah 7:9) is regarded as a corrupt text and the corrupt grammar of the verse supports this judgment.[2] Much has been written on the subject of the sequence and the preferred but not uncontested view has it that Nehemiah came to Jerusalem in the twentieth year of Artaxerxes I (−445) and stayed there for a number of years, returning to Persia and coming once more for a short stay in the thirty-second year of the same king (Nehemiah 13:6). Ezra came to Jerusalem not in the seventh year of Artaxerxes I (−458) but in the seventh year of Artaxerxes II (−398), sixty years later. The absence of any reference to Ezra in the Elephantine papyri, the last of which was written in −399, tends to support the view that he arrived in Jerusalem the following year, −398.

A conciliatory school among biblical scholars places Ezra's journey halfway between these dates by considering "seventh year" as corruption of "thirty-seventh year" of the first Artaxerxes, or −328. This view was offered by W. F. Albright. It would signify that Ezra continued his stay in Jerusalem when Darius II Nothus mounted the throne.

An argument could be construed for changing not the year but the name of the king, and to read "in the seventh year of Darius," meaning Darius II, the son of the first Artaxerxes and father of the second. For placing Ezra's sojourn in Jerusalem under Darius II, some hint can be derived from Ezra 10:16, a verse the grammatical form of which requires amending. When Ezra decreed that the Jews should divorce non-Jewish wives, the elders of the congregation "have sat down on the first day [day one] of the tenth month *l'drosh* the matter." The word *l'drosh* ("to study" or "to discuss") is not written as it should but with a letter *yod*, making the word look exactly like the name of the king Darius in Hebrew: in the same book of Ezra (4:24; 6:16; 7:13) the name Darius (the Great) is written the way the misspelled "to study" is written. In

---

[2] The verb (*va'yomar*) is employed in the singular, whereas it is said of Nehemiah, Ezra, and the Levites. See, however, Nehemiah 12:36.

view of the many examples in the same book and in that of Nehemiah, where the day, the month, and the regnal year of the Persian king are given as the date of an event, the impression is strengthened that in the verse we are discussing Darius was meant, the day and the month being given but the year having been dropped when the text became corrupt, possibly at the hand of a later scribe who failed to understand how Darius the Great could be referred to in this context, himself being unaware of the existence of Darius II (−424 to −404). That the scribe-copyists were confused as to the order of succession of the Persian kings can be seen in Ezra 4:24 where Darius II is confused with Darius I (cf. also Ezra 6:15).

If Ezra came to Jerusalem in the thirty-seventh year of Artaxerxes (−428) he must have been a contemporary of Wenamon, sent by Herihor to Byblos to obtain cedarwood for the barque of Amon. However, if Ezra left Babylon for Jerusalem in the seventh year of Artaxerxes II, then Wenamon's travel in the days of Darius II preceded that of Ezra's coming from Babylon by twenty-two years (from the fifth year of Darius II to the seventh year of Artaxerxes II). Yet, what is less probable, if Wenamon traveled to Byblos in the fifth year of Artaxerxes II, Ezra and Wenamon might have started on their respective journeys only two years apart.

Priest-Prince Psusennes

Psusennes, son of the Nesubanebded who figured in the travels of Wenamon as the military prince with a residence in Tanis, inherited from his father the residence and the title, and added to it those of high priest and first prophet of Amon, the titles of his father-in-law Herihor, and on a number of occasions used the title "king." In this northern capital, in the compound of the great temple area, Psusennes built an enclave of his own surrounded by a massive wall of bricks. The temple area was explored by Pierre Montet; the identity of the builder of the enclave was immediately obvious to him: in the northeast corner of it there was a foundation bearing the name of Psusennes; that name was also on many bricks of the walls of the enclosure.[1]

In a corner between the temple and the brick wall Montet discovered the tomb of the same priest-prince. But instead of being strengthened in his first expressed view that the enclave was erected by Psusennes, Montet found himself obliged to revoke it:

"This view expressed in our recent publications is not correct. Now we know that the great temple in its final form dates from a much later date because under the northeastern and southwestern corners we have found deposits of Osorkon II and in the southeastern corner a deposit of Nectanebo I [Nekht-nebef]."[2]

Of course, a pharaoh of the eleventh century before the present era could not have built on foundations from under which comes a deposit made by a king of the ninth or eighth century; he could not continue a building started by a king of the fourth century—unless he himself is counted as an eleventh-century king only through error and actually belongs in the fourth century at the earliest. This thought did not occur to Montet but the problem was not resolved by a mere revocation of the assessment made in his earlier publications: it must be shown how Psusennes of the eleventh century could build on foundations laid down in the fourth century. If the following *is* an explanation, let us set it down for the record:

"The temples of Tanis were rebuilt so many times and so mishandled in modern times that not one stone of the Old, Middle, and New Kingdoms occupies its original place."[3]

Temples were rebuilt, old material was reused, but what Montet continues to call in his later publications "The Temple of Psusennes" could not contain deposits of later centuries under its foundations.

The apparently conflicting evidence, with deposits of the eighth and fourth centuries under a structure presumably of the eleventh

---

[1] P. Montet, *Tanis* (Paris, 1942), pp. 43, 55–56.

[2] Montet, *Les Constructions et le tombeau de Psousennès à Tanis* (Paris, 1951), p. 10.

[3] "*Les temples de Tanis ont été tant de fois reconstruits et si maltraités dans les temps modernes que pas une pierre de l'Ancien, du Moyen et du Nouvel Empire ne se trouve plus à sa place originale.*"

century, is not conflicting at all if we realize that Psusennes flourished one generation after Nekht-nebef: it was the first half of the
fourth century.

The fragmented foundation stone found by Montet which carries
the name of Psusennes has next to it a "barbarian name," Shahedet,
inserted in a cartouche. Montet reproduced the fragment and wondered at the meaning of the name next to that of Psusennes. He
concluded or assumed that Shahedet could be the name of a little-
known female deity, presumably a Libyan goddess.[4] This appears
to be a very strained solution: why should Psusennes place in a
cartouche next to his own name the name of some little-known
Libyan deity in this form never met elsewhere?[5] The name certainly sounded barbaric to the Egyptian ear.

It seems more in accord with the purpose of cartouches, which
give the name and titles of a royal person, that Shahedet is nothing
but a title and, in agreement with the revised chronology, a Persian
title, the first part of it meaning "king."[6] Upon being asked whether
the word could mean "king-priest," "hereditary ruler," "vice-king,"
or the like, Professor George G. Cameron of the University of Michi-
gan answered that the word "*could* have a respectable [Persian]
etymology."[7]

Osorkon II, who placed foundation deposits under two corners
of the temple enclave, also built himself a tomb inside the enclosure.
Very little was found of funerary equipment—the tomb had already
been violated by tomb robbers and left rather empty in antiquity.
The laborers who worked for Montet in clearing this tomb passed
"without noticing" ("*sans s'en apercevoir*") to the tomb of Psu-

[4] Montet, *Psousennès* (Paris, 1951), p. 184.
[5] In an effort to explain the occurrence of the word or name Shahdidit (with
a *d* in the second syllable) in some other texts of the period, Legrain hypothesized a Libyan goddess of that name ("La Déesse Shahdidit"), *Annales
du Service des Antiquités d'Égypte*, XV, 284–86. However, Shahdidit in
Persian signifies "king's retainer" or "king's official." But, Didit being the
Egyptian name for Mendes in the Delta, Shah Didit could mean King of
Mendes.
[6] Thus "shahzada" signifies "a son of a king or shah; used as a title" (Web-
ster's New International Dictionary of the English Language, Merriam Publication, 1948).
[7] From a letter dated January 30, 1967.

sennes, thus making a discovery. This tomb had not been emptied of its treasures: violators had not discovered it. Montet wrote: "The thieves who pillaged the tomb of Osorkon II, adjacent to that of Psusennes, having made numerous trial diggings all around and having found nothing, abandoned their search."[8]

How could it happen that with many trial diggings the tomb thieves of antiquity missed the adjacent tomb whereas the fellahin working for Montet, even without perception of a discovery, moved from one subterranean tomb to the other? Yet signs of search and tunneling around the tomb of Osorkon were still in evidence.

Apparently Osorkon's tomb was pillaged before Psusennes was put to rest and possibly by Psusennes himself. Furthermore, as we shall immediately learn, Psusennes' tomb was also originally built for a king or prince of the Libyan Dynasty. Psusennes appropriated it for himself.

When the tomb was first opened it was thought to have been built for the king or prince whose coffin—without a sarcophagus— was found in the room that later proved to be but a vestibule. Montet describes the scene—it was in 1939. As soon as the news reached the royal palace in Cairo that a tomb of an ancient king had been opened and a coffin found in it, King Farouk, accompanied by Canon Etienne Drioton, director of the Antiquities Service of Egypt, arrived to participate "with his own hands in archaeological work." Montet proceeds: "I helped him to place the [silver] lid alongside the coffin that contained the mummy and its jewels in a gilded cartonnage. At this moment it was observed that the coffin was of an unknown king, Heqa-kheper-rê Chéchanq [Sheshonk], who could not have reigned less than a century after Psusennes."[9]

This, of course, on the assumption that Psusennes reigned in the eleventh century and that the Libyan Dynasty followed the priestly dynasty misnamed Twenty-first.

From the vestibule there were blocked entrances to four mortuary chambers.[10] These were not immediately entered; huge

[8] Montet, *Psousennès*, p. 8.

[9] Ibid., p. 20.

[10] J. Černý mistakenly says that only two mortuary chambers were found in Psusennes' tomb (rev. ed., *Cambridge Ancient History*, Vol. II, Chap. XXXV, p. 654.).

monoliths were found to have been inserted into the passages, seal-
ing them almost hermetically. That season of 1939, before leaving
Tanis, Montet opened only one chamber. It contained a huge sarcophagus. "It was empty. The name and the titles of the person
who occupied it were obliterated from the walls [of the chamber
and of the sarcophagus]. We were completely mystified. In a tomb
constructed for Psusennes, showing no sign of any breach we
[previously] found [in the vestibule] the coffin and the rich adornments of an unknown king of a much more recent date and [now]
we find a sepulchral annex that was violated, the name of the original owner having been erased."

The next season two well-protected chambers connected with
the vestibule but closed by monoliths were opened—actually the
roof blocks were lifted. One of the chambers was occupied by the
sarcophagus of Psusennes. Of rose granite, it was originally made
for Merneptah-Hotephirma (or Hophra-Maat) of the Nineteenth
Dynasty. The name had been chiseled out but in one single instance
remained intact. "All the Twenty-first Dynasty usually did was to
change cartouches" (Montet). Inside the rose sarcophagus there
was another one, of black granite, "borrowed" from an unknown
owner since his name was made illegible. Inside the black sarcophagus was a coffin of silver. The face of the king was covered
by a mask of gold.

Psusennes was entombed splendidly. But almost everything was
appropriated from mortuary endowments of earlier kings; the tomb
itself was also "adopted."

It is difficult to understand the mentality of those who arranged
that their mummies should be nestled in tombs built for others, in
sarcophagi not their own, and expected in this way to enjoy the
bliss of the life thereafter. It was therefore a "consideration" that,
in occupying a mortuary chamber, Psusennes did not completely
evict the original owner of the tomb, Sosenk (spelled by Montet,
Chéchanq or Sheshonk), one of the less well known princes of the
Libyan Dynasty.

Among many silver and gold objects entombed with Psusennes
were numerous necklaces and also a bead from a necklace incised

with cuneiform signs; specialists in cuneiform tried hard to make a reading of three short lines and came up with a not too meaningful text. If the text is not Persian (written in cuneiform) but Akkadian (Assyro-Babylonian), it is quite probable that the bead came also from an older tomb, possibly of the same Sosenk: in his coffin there was found an heirloom cylinder with cuneiform signs on it too.

There were twenty-eight bracelets in Psusennes' funeral equipment. One of them attracted special attention on the part of its finder. It is of gold with decorative inlays and has an inscription in hieroglyphs: "The king, master of two lands [of Upper and Lower Egypt], master of the sword, first prophet of Amen-re-sonter (Psousennes Miamoun), given life." What drew Montet's attention was the way the word "king" (n-s-w) was spelled: it was written not in a regular way but in a very peculiar form: it was spelled by designing a baboon (cynocephalus) holding an eye (oudja). "The word n-s-w or 'king' is written here as in the Ptolemaic period. . . ." The baboon and the eye between its hands was a sophisticated way, actually a pun on words, to express the word "king" and appeared only very late in Egyptian texts.[11]

Montet observed another peculiarity in the same sentence: "n-t-r" (accompanying the name Amon-re) "is written with a hawk as often found in the Ptolemaic period."

Such discoveries need not only be registered and described; conclusions must be drawn from them.

One more find: on a wall of the chamber occupied by Psusennes an inscription tells of "Psusennes, speaking truth" as he appeals in adoration to goddess Mut, "the heavenly lady, suzerain of Two Lands, mistress of the Hellenic coast. . . ."

Of this Montet writes: "The sea of the Hellenes (*Helou-nebout*) was for the Egyptians the Mediterranean from Alexandria to Rosetta. The seaboard of the Hellenes was the portion of the Egyptian coast west of Damietta."[12]

Since in inscriptions of much earlier times there occurred a refer-

[11] Montet, *Psousennès*, p. 149. Cf. Émile Chassinat, "Le Mot *seten* 'Roi'" in *Revue de l'Égypte Ancienne*, II (Paris, 1929), 5 f.
[12] Montet, *Psousennès*, p. 92.

ence to Helou-nebout, Montet assumes that it was at first applied to the shores of the Aegean Sea and then to the Egyptian coast as well, a fact that, in his opinion, is proof that rather early, and certainly before the accepted dates of the first appearance of Greeks in Egypt under Psammetich in the seventh century,[13] Greeks had already firmly established themselves along the coast from one end of the Delta to the other.[14]

But from Herodotus we learn that the "Hellenic coast" was the area along the coast of the Delta that was the possession of many Greek cities, a kind of colonial enclave, with Hellenic temple services permitted by Amasis, whose long reign preceded the Persian occupation of the land. Herodotus wrote (II, 178):

> Amasis was partial to the Greeks, and among other favours which he granted them, gave to such as liked to settle in Egypt the city of Naucratis for their residence. To those who only wished to trade upon the coast, and did not want to fix their abode in the country, he granted certain lands where they might set up altars and erect temples to the gods. Of these temples the grandest and most famous, which is also the most frequented, is that called the Hellenium. It was built conjointly by the Ionians, Dorians, and Aeolians, the following cities taking part in the work, the Ionian states of Chios, Teos, Phocaea, and Clazomenae; Rhodes, Cnidus, Halicarnassus, and Phaselis of the Dorians; and Mytilene of the Aeolians. These are the states to whom the temple belongs, and they have the right of appointing the governors of the port; the other cities which claim a share in the building, claim what in no sense belongs to them. Three nations, however, consecrated for themselves separate temples, the Aeginetans one to Zeus, the Samians to Hera, and the Milesians to Apollo.

The "Hellenic coast" referred to in the tomb of Psusennes had its beginning in the days of Amasis, and with Psusennes belonging in the fourth century before the present era, it is natural to find in his tomb a reference to the goddess Mut, as "suzerain of Two Lands, mistress of the Hellenic coast." With Psusennes, together with the entire so-called Twenty-first Dynasty, removed to the time preced-

[13] Herodotus, II, 152.
[14] Montet, in *Revue archéologique*, 6ᵉ série, XXXIV, 138–40.

ing Amasis by five hundred years, the anachronism of the reference to the Hellenic coast in Egypt is an unsolvable problem.

Thus in the chamber containing the mummy of Psusennes, the son-in-law of Herihor, several indices, everything else aside, point to this member of the military princely family as belonging to a time much closer to the Ptolemaic period than the eleventh century. His writing the title "king" in a manner in use in the Ptolemaic period and his referring to the coast west of Damietta as Hellenic point in the same direction as his use of a Persian title in his cartouche.

The chamber next to that of Psusennes was opened the same season—it also had a sarcophagus; it was occupied by "King" Amenemope; it has been concluded that he was a descendant of Psusennes, possibly his great-grandson. Archaeologists observed that his funeral place and equipment did not look at all like that of a king. If the entire structure did not measure up to the royal tombs of the Eighteenth Dynasty near Thebes, the impoverished state of Amenemope's chamber could not but surprise the excavators. The sarcophagus had once been occupied by Moutnedjemi, either the mother or the wife of Psusennes.[15] Her body was removed to make room for that of Amenemope; her name was changed to his but the erasures and substitutions were not made carefully.

In the fourth chamber was entombed a son of Psusennes; finally, the chamber that was opened in the first season and was found to be unoccupied had been, as it was subsequently realized, once occupied by a comrade-in-arms and probably a relative of Psusennes. He was removed to prepare room for somebody of a subsequent generation but the project was not carried out.

It is quite certain that the latest arrangements in the tomb and its chambers were the work of Si-Amon; an inscribed scarab with his name was found in the vestibule.[16]

The tomb with its vestibule and four chambers is far smaller than the royal tombs of Thebes: Psusennes, most certainly, looked for an unobtrusive but well-protected place to hide his mortal remains,

[15] Montet, in various parts of his book on the tomb of Psusennes, refers to Moutnedjemi as Psusennes' mother and in other instances as his wife without explaining this inconsistency.

[16] Montet, *Psousennès*, p. 186.

knowing from his own practice that his body, in the days to come, might be subjected to the fate that he himself had inflicted on others.

The Last Persian Occupation
of Egypt

Artaxerxes III, by his character and his planning of state affairs, augured a restoration of the empire to its former greatness. When Tachos (Ramses IV) fled to him, he was not yet prepared to reduce Egypt to the vassalage from which it had freed itself almost forty years earlier, at the beginning of his father's (Artaxerxes II's) reign. Nectanebo II (Ramses VI) reigned, with the help of Greek mercenaries, for over a decade; he built and patronized temples and hewed for himself a large tomb, but when Artaxerxes III moved on Egypt and overcame the resistance offered at Pelusium, Nectanebo made no further stand: this last native pharaoh forsook everything, his palace, his country, and his people, and fled to the Sudan, never to be heard of again except in the so-called Alexander romance—a rather late composition: it was he who, as the earthly personification of the god Amon, visited Olympia, Philip's queen, in her bedroom in the palace, to sire Alexander. Another version of the divine origin of Alexander has Amon-Zeus coming to Olympia in the form of a python.[1]

During the short period—less than ten years—of the last Persian domination over Egypt, a certain Petosiris, a dignitary or curate of the temple of the god Thoth at Hermopolis, became known for his learning. He was probably the same Petosiris who, according to Servius, a Roman writer of the late fourth century of the present era, was one of the important sources of ancient knowledge of the

[1] From the Sudan Nectanebo II tried to re-establish his domination in southern Egypt (Diodorus, XVI, 51); therefore it is quite possible that, with the advent of Alexander, Nectanebo II returned as a private citizen to Egypt and died there. See also Hermann Bengston, *The Greeks and the Persians from the Sixth to the Fourth Centuries* (New York, 1965), p. 351. (Tachos, who earlier fled to Persia, could also have been among the repatriates with Alexander's conquest.)

catastrophic events precipitated by an "immense globe" of fire, of "bloody redness," referred to as the Typhon comet, that caused destruction "in rising and setting."[2]

The tradition of the unusual natural events of earlier ages, learned by Pythagoras and Solon on their travels to Egypt (Solon's informant was Sonchis, a priest in Sais), was not yet extinguished about the time closely preceding the collapse of the Persian Empire. The tomb of Ramses VI in the Valley of the Kings near Thebes has an astronomical ceiling in the tradition of the earlier tombs of Senmut, an architect under Queen Hatshepsut,[3] and Seti, one of the great kings of the Nineteenth Dynasty, a subject of discussion left for an intermediary volume. These ceilings preserve rich material for the inquiry into the celestial order in the centuries discussed in *Worlds in Collision*.

For the purpose of our reconstruction of the history of Egypt under the Persians, a certain passage in the epitaph on Petosiris' tomb is relevant:

"I passed seven years as administrator of this god Thoth . . . men of foreign land ruled Egypt. . . . No work was done (in the temple) since the foreigners had come and had invaded Egypt."[4]

In this designation of the Persians as "foreigners" who "had come and had invaded Egypt" we find the very words and expressions we read in the papyri of the Twenty-first Dynasty, namely in the letter of Ourmai, whom we recognized as a contemporary of Cambyses, and then in the court records with the testimony of Ahautinofer, a temple porter who spoke of "foreigners" who occupied the temple and removed the high priest.

Occasionally, documents of the Persian period refer to P-r-s, or Persia; and in a document dating from the third of the Ptolemies (the Canopus Decree), the Persians are referred to as Pereset (P-r-s-tt), a matter mentioned on an earlier page: this reference to Pereset as the people who carried the statues of gods from Egypt

---

[2] See *Worlds in Collision*, Section "The Comet of Typhon."

[3] *Worlds in Collision*, Section "Poles Uprooted."

[4] G. Lefebvre, *Le Tombeau de Petosiris* (1924), I, 3 f. Olmstead, *History of Persia* (Chicago, 1948), p. 441.

to Persia, to be brought back by Ptolemy III and restored to their temples a few score years after the collapse of the Persian Empire, is of such consequence for the revision of ancient history that it cannot be sufficiently emphasized.

It is sometimes said that it was not Alexander who brought the Persian Empire to its downfall but the eunuch and royal confidant, Bogoaz, who poisoned Artaxerxes III (−338), in order to place the latter's son on the throne, but after a while, observing a spirit of independence in the youth, poisoned him, too, thus nearly terminating the Achaemenid Dynasty. A distant relative of the last king was searched out by the eunuch and placed on the throne as Darius III (−336). To secure his own life, Darius quickly poisoned the man who had made him king. But the three years of his reign were insufficient to consolidate the empire, establish his own authority, and bring the satraps to obedience. From the Ionian shore of Asia Minor to Turkestan in Central Asia, from the river Indus to the cataracts on the Nile, the empire was reeling: its entire structure had always converged on the person of the Great King, and the wave of palace assassinations undermined the coherence of the whole.

The less than ten-year-long last domination of Egypt by Persia is counted as the Thirty-first Dynasty, Artaxerxes III to Darius III being its pharaohs.

The epic of Alexander's war against Darius III, with the famous battles at Granicus (−334) and Issus (−333), is well known and there is nothing that the present reconstruction can add or needs to alter; but with the coming of Alexander to Egypt one of the best gems of this synchronized history comes to light. The reader should bear in mind that the Prince-Priest Menkheperre, son of Peinuzem, who soon will greet an august visitor to the temple of the oracle of Amon, lived, in conventional history, in the eleventh century before the present era.

Chapter III

ALEXANDER

Alexander Before the Oracle of Amon
in the Oasis

IN THE FALL of −332 Alexander crossed the desert and came to
Egypt. The Persian satrap, who could not depend on the people of Egypt, offered no resistance. The population received
Alexander jubilantly. "The Egyptian people hailed him with joy as
their deliverer from the Persian yoke."[1] He sacrificed to Apis and
brought royal offerings; this implies that he was crowned king of
Egypt where "the Pharaoh was regarded as the incarnation of the
greatest god."[2] He arranged athletic and literary contests and took
care also that the customs of Egypt and its religious services be
held in honor.

During Alexander's stay in Egypt a large group of captured rebels
were brought to him from the islands of the Aegean, and he banished the rebels of Chios—Appolonides and his followers—to Yeb
in southern Egypt. First he went some distance south; then he proceeded to the western mouth of the Delta and had surveyors plan
a large city—the future Alexandria. From there he visited the oracle
of Amon in the oasis of Siwa, where he was pronounced a son of
Amon (Zeus) and the incarnation of the god himself. Returning
from the desert, he organized the administration of the country and
then, pressed by military considerations (at Tyre he rejected a peace
offer by Darius), left Egypt in the early spring of −331.

The most famous incident—his visit to the oracle of Amon—is de-

[1] U. Wilcken, *Alexander the Great* (London, 1932), p. 113.
[2] Ibid., p. 115.

scribed by a number of authors; some of them used the no longer extant record of Callisthenes, who accompanied Alexander on many marches and liked to boast that Alexander was famous not for what he did but for what Callisthenes wrote about him. Ptolemaeus and Aristobulus and other contemporaries of Alexander—their records are not extant—as well as Cleitarchus, a resident of Alexandria, who collected material from eyewitnesses of Alexander's exploits, served as sources for the Greek and Roman authors of following centuries who wrote about Alexander in Egypt.[3]

Egyptian sources are supposedly silent on Alexander's visit to the oracle of Amon in the desert. But Alexander was not one of Egypt's regular visitors, and the oracle of Amon was the chief sanctuary for the people of Egypt in the fourth century; therefore this silence on the subject of Alexander's pilgrimage is enigmatic.

One of the most prominent documents of the period of the Twenty-first Dynasty is the so-called Stele of the Banished, or Maunier Stele, found in Luxor, now in the Louvre. The stele is in a poor state of preservation ("very difficult to read"[4]). Its text deals with the oracle of Amon and the affairs of the oasis. It was composed by a high priest of Amon, Menkheperre, son of Peinuzem. Peinuzem was one of the priest-princes who rewrapped the royal mummies.

The text begins with the date: "Year 25, Third month of the Third season, day 29." After some broken lines this follows: "The majesty of this august god was [again broken lines]. Then he took his ways to the scribes, surveyors,[5] people." The high priest, described on the stele also as "commander in chief of the army," is named: "Menkheperre, triumphant, son of King Peinuzem-Meriamon . . . companion of his footsteps."

The text proceeds:

MAUNIER STELE: Their hearts rejoiced because he had desired to

---

[3] Arrian, *Anabasis of Alexander*, III; Diodorus; Plutarch.

[4] Breasted, *Ancient Records*, Vol. IV, Sec. 650, note.

[5] Breasted translates this as "inspectors." Brugsch translates the sentence: "*Da legte er den Weg zurück zu den Schreibern, den Vermessern und zu den Leuten.*" H. Brugsch, *Reise nach der Grossen Oase* (1878), p. 86.

come to the South in might and victory, in order to make satisfied the heart of the land, and to expel his enemies.

The victor who expelled his enemies was received with rejoicing. In the first month of the third season the following took place:

> MAUNIER STELE: He arrived at the city with a glad heart; the youth of Thebes received him, making jubilee, with an embassy before him. The majesty of this august god . . . establish[ed] him [the high priest of Amon] upon the throne of his father, as High Priest of Amon-Re, king of gods.

The victorious god—or the divine victor—accorded him honors and presents and confirmed him in his office.

In the fourth month of the third season, on the fifth day of the feast of the "Birth of Isis,"

> MAUNIER STELE: The majesty of this august god, lord of gods, Amon-Re, king of gods, appeared [in procession], came to the great halls of the house of Amon, and rested before the inclosure wall of Amon. The High Priest of Amon-Re, king of gods, commander in chief of the army, Menkheperre, triumphant, went to him and praised him exceedingly, exceedingly, many times, and he founded [for him] his offering, even [every] good thing.

Modern scholars assume that there are two actors in the story: the high priest and his god-oracle. These scholars wonder about the procedure: "It appears as if he had long been absent from Thebes, and needed to secure the recognition of the god; it is by no means the condition of a resident head of the priesthood."[6]

"His majesty" who arrived in the south as a victor is clearly not Menkheperre because he is referred to in the same text as one whom his majesty confirmed in the office of high priest.

After the high priest of Amon had praised his divine visitor "exceedingly," and brought offerings "for him," he started to interrogate the oracle.

> MAUNIER STELE: Then the High Priest of Amon, Menkheperre, triumphant, recounted to him, saying:

[6] Petrie, *History of Egypt from the XIXth to the XXXth Dynasties*, Vol. III, p. 211.

"O my good lord, (when) there is a matter, shall one recount it?"

Then the great god nodded exceedingly, exceedingly.[7]

The high priest asked about

MAUNIER STELE: . . . the matter of these servants, against whom thou art wroth, who are in the oasis, whither they are banished. Then the great god nodded exceedingly, while this commander of the army [the high priest] with his hands uplifted, was praising his lord, as a father talks with his own son.[8]

The end of the last sentence is most unexpected. A priest would speak to the god Amon as a son to a father, but not as a father to a son. Nevertheless, the text of the stele says that the priest spoke to the god as a father speaks to a son. The baffled translator of the text remarked: "The inversion of the members of the comparison is in the original."[9]

By repeating and developing his question, the priest succeeded in obtaining the answer that the exiles who were in the oasis should be removed, and in the future no exiles should be banished there. It was obviously important to the priest to make sure that this oracle of the god was made known and observed. He said:

MAUNIER STELE: "O my good lord, thou shalt make a great decree in thy name, that no people of the land shall be banished to the distant region of the oasis——from this day on." Then the great god nodded exceedingly.——"It shall be made into a decree upon a stele and be set up in thy cities."

Making decrees and writing them on steles was the prerogative of kings.

The second question put by the priest to the oracle of Amon refers in some way to murderers, whether they should be punished by execution.

MAUNIER STELE: Then the High Priest of Amon, Menkheperre, triumphant, went to the great god, saying: "As for any person, of whom they shall report before thee, A slayer of living——thou shalt

[7] Breasted, *Records*, Vol. IV, Sec. 655.
[8] Ibid.
[9] Ibid., note.

destroy him, thou shalt slay him." Then the great god nodded exceedingly, exceedingly.

The combination of words in the question referred by the high priest to the oracle of Amon, concerning the "slayer of living," appeared strange, and its meaning was asserted to be obscure; it caused difficulty to its first (Brugsch) and later (Breasted) translators and resulted in the strained passage just quoted.

Before the last question and the answer of the oracle to it, the text contains a sentence that appears to be unrelated to the context: "While I was in the womb, when thou didst form [me] in the egg," as if to the god Amon was attributed the physical creation of the divine lord while in a womb.

The stele contains also a request for benediction or for a prophecy of good fortune and benevolence on the part of the gods: "Grant that I may spend a happy life. . . ." It was accompanied by a question: "Will all achievement be my portion?"[10] The request is granted and the oracle announces: "There is purity and health wherever thou tarriest."

The entire stele is regarded as cryptic. "The remarkable errand" of the priest "is intentionally narrated in such veiled language that it is impossible to determine exactly what its nature was."[11] But we shall find the text clear.

The following circumstance must not be overlooked: the text discloses the fact that the priest asked that a decree based upon the answers of the oracle should be placed in the cities of Egypt, and the present stele, found in Luxor (Thebes), indicates that his request was carried out. Therefore the oracle need not necessarily have been that of the Amon of the place where the stele was discovered. The preoccupation with an oasis makes it apparent that the stele deals with the oracle of Amon of the oasis. But we shall proceed best if we follow Alexander on his famous journey to the oracle of Amon.

[10] Brugsch's translation: *"Wird mir aller Lohn zu Theil?"* Brugsch, *Recueil de monuments égyptiens* (Leipzig, 1862–85), I, 39 ff., and his *Reise nach der Grossen Oase.*
[11] Breasted, *Ancient Records,* Vol. IV, Sec. 650.

He came from the north as victor and liberator of the country from its Persian enemies, whom he expelled; he arranged festivals in the cities of Egypt and was joyfully acclaimed by the youth of the country. He acknowledged and confirmed the civil and religious officials of the country, "permitted the district governors to govern their own districts as had been their way all along."[12] "From Memphis, ascending the river, the king penetrated to the interior of Egypt,"[13] and then "he sailed downstream towards the sea" and "himself marked out the ground plan of the city [Alexandria]."[14] There he directed the surveyors of the land, who measured the site and "ordered those in charge of the work to proceed with it, while he himself set out for the temple of Amon."[15] He made his journey to the oasis in the rainy season, for it is told that a rainfall helped him in the desert.

The castle in the middle of the oasis was surrounded by a triple wall. Quintus Curtius Rufus wrote of it:

> The first rampart encloses the ancient palace of their kings; within the second are lodged the prince's wives, children, and concubines —here, likewise, is the oracle of the god; in the outward circle of bastions were posted the royal armed attendants and bodyguards.[16]

This teaches us that the high priests of the oracle in the oasis claimed royal titles. Herodotus (II, 32), who in the mid-fifth century wrote about the northern oasis in his description of Libya and Egypt, said that a king ruled in the oasis of "the oracular shrine of Ammon."

Diodorus of Sicily gave a few more details about this home army:

> Within the third wall were the lodgings of the archers and darters, and guard-houses of those who attend as guards upon the prince when he walks abroad.[17]

From these descriptions we see that the priest of the oracle of

---

[12] Arrian, *Anabasis of Alexander*, III, 1.

[13] Quintus Curtius Rufus, *The History of the Life and Reign of Alexander the Great*, trans. P. Pratt (London, 1809), IV, VII.

[14] Arrian, *Anabasis of Alexander*, III, 1.

[15] Plutarch, *Lives*, "Alexander," trans. B. Perrin (Loeb Classical Library, 1919), XXVI.

[16] Curtius Rufus, *The History of the Life and Reign of Alexander the Great*, IV, VII.

[17] Diodorus, *The Historical Library*, XVII, 5.

Amon in the oasis was a prince who had an army of his own, which fact explains the titles used in the stele: prince, priest, commander of the army.

When Alexander and his guard arrived at the outer wall surrounding the castle, the chief priest came out and saluted the king. In the language of Plutarch:

> When Alexander had passed through the desert and was come to the place of the oracle, the prophet of Amon gave him salutation from the god as from a father.[18]

Strabo, who cited Callisthenes, wrote:

> The priest permitted the king alone to pass into the temple in his usual dress, but the rest changed their clothes; . . . all heard the oracles from outside except Alexander, but he inside.[19]

The flattery with which the priest addressed Alexander on meeting him before the wall is mentioned by several authors: so Curtius Rufus speaks of "concerted adulation" accorded by the priest to Alexander. The stele says:

> MAUNIER STELE: The majesty of this august god, lord of gods, Amon-Re . . . came to the great halls of the house of Amon, and rested before the inclosure wall of Amon. The High Priest . . . Menkheperre, triumphant, went to him and praised him exceedingly, exceedingly, many times, and he founded [for him] his offering, even [every] good thing.[20]

The offering is mentioned by Plutarch: "Alexander made splendid offerings to the god." All the authors who described this visit told about the way the priest addressed Alexander. Diodorus says:

> When Alexander was introduced by the priests into the temple, and saw the god, one of the old prophets addressed himself to him, and said: "God save thee, my son, and this title take along with thee from the god himself."

Alexander answered, "Your son I will ever be called."

Now we see that the words on the stele about the priest "praising his lord, as a father talks with his own son," are not an "inversion of a comparison."

---

[18] Plutarch, *Lives*, "Alexander," XXVII.
[19] Strabo, *The Geography*, XVII, i, 43.
[20] Breasted, *Ancient Records*, Vol. IV, Sec. 654.

Curtius Rufus, too, wrote (IV, vii):

> As the king was approaching, the senior priest saluted him "son," affirming, "that his father, Jupiter [Amon], bestowed that title."

This application of the term "son" to Alexander by the priest of Amon which is stressed by Diodorus, Plutarch, and Curtius Rufus is important because of its singularity and because it makes clear and verifies the otherwise absurd sentence of the stele.

The way in which this oracle answered questions was peculiar. On the stele it is repeatedly said: "The great god nodded exceedingly, exceedingly." Diodorus said the same of the oracle of Amon visited by Alexander: "The god by a nod of his head directs them." Strabo, too, dwelt on this peculiarity:

> The oracular responses were not, as at Delphi and among the Branchidae, given in words, but mostly by nods and tokens, as in Homer, "Cronion spoke and nodded assent with his dark brows," the prophet having assumed the role of Zeus; however, the fellow expressly told the king that he, Alexander, was son of Zeus.

Here is a further reason why the priest spoke to his idol and to Alexander in similar fashion (calling both god Amon): Alexander was proclaimed an incarnation of the god Amon (Zeus) himself. Moreover, he was assured of being a physical son of Amon. The words on the stele telling the divine victor that Amon formed him in the egg gain in meaning.

Alexander "not only suffered himself to be called Jupiter's son, but required it." "When fortune has induced men to confide entirely in herself, she commonly makes them more avaricious of glory than able to sustain it."[21]

From the Great Harris Papyrus dating from the reign of Ramses III or IV, it is known that exiles were regularly sent to the southern oasis to do forced labor in the gardens belonging to the temple. From antiquity to Christian times the southern oasis was a deportation place for offenders. Before Alexander came to the oasis of the oracle of Amon he sent some of his enemies, brought to him from Chios, to Heb, misunderstood by Greek authors as Yeb, which was

---

[21] Curtius Rufus, *The History of the Life and Reign of Alexander the Great*, IV, Chap. vii.

Elephantine on the Nile; but Heb was the name of the southern oasis.[22]

The priest of the oracle of Amon was very anxious for the king to decree that no exiles should be sent to the oases.

The question that interested Alexander was, according to Diodorus:

> "Whether I have executed justice upon all my father's murderers, or whether any have escaped?" At which the oracle cried out, "Express thyself better, for no mortal can kill thy father, but all the murderers of Philip have suffered just punishment."[23]

Curtius Rufus tells it this way (IV, vii):

> The king proceeded to inquire, "Whether all who conspired the death of his father had been punished?" The response was that "the crime of no one could hurt his father, but that all the murderers of Philip had suffered punishment."

Plutarch's version is similar (XXVII of "Alexander"):

> The prophet of Ammon gave him salutation from the god as from a father; whereupon Alexander asked him whether any of the murderers of his father had escaped him. To this the prophet answered by bidding him to be guarded in his speech, since his was not a mortal father. Alexander therefore changed the form of his question and asked whether the murderers of Philip had all been punished. . . . The god gave answer that . . . Philip was fully avenged.

Now we have the real meaning of the awkwardly translated sentence on the stele about the punishment of the murderers. There is no sense in a question about whether murderers must be punished; even without an oracle everyone knows that they must. The question actually was whether all the murderers of Alexander's father had been punished, and the answer was: None of the murderers (of Philip) escaped punishment.

The hieroglyphics on the stele, where the question was asked and the words "murderer" and "living" were found in one sentence, were speaking not of the "murderer of the living" but whether any assas-

---

[22] "*Der Name des Tempels, oder vielmehr der Örtlichkeit, dessen Cultusmittelpunkt er bildete, wird unzählige Male in den Texten genannt: er lautete Heb oder Hib.*" Brugsch, *Reise nach der Grossen Oase*, pp. 19 and 25 ff. Cf. also the chapter "The Great Oasis as a Place of Exile in Antiquity," ibid., p. 83.

[23] Diodorus, *The Historical Library*, XVII, 5.

sin was still among the living. And the answer was not, "Thou shalt destroy him, thou shalt slay him," but "Thou hast not failed to destroy him, to kill him."

Alexander also asked whether he would enjoy good fortune and whether the god would give the entire world to his dominion, or in Plutarch's words, "Whether it was given to him to become lord and master of all mankind?" To this the priest answered that "the god would certainly bestow upon him what he had desired," and that "his wonderful successes and prosperous achievements were evidences of his divine birth" (Diodorus); we remember the words on the stele, "Grant that I may spend a happy life . . ." and "Will all achievement be my portion?"

Alexander "bestowed many rich and stately gifts upon the oracle"[24] and gave the priest "large gifts of money,"[25] or, in the words of the stele, "his majesty decreed to him many gracious wonders."

The twenty-fifth year, the royal date of the stele, is a date connected with Alexander. He was born in −356. On his visit to Egypt from the late fall of −332 to the spring of −331, he was in his twenty-fifth year. The royal years of Alexander must have begun with his birth, as he was pronounced by the oracle the son of a god and not of a mortal.

The twenty-fifth year of the stele; the arrival of the victor who came to the south and freed the country by expelling the enemies; the acclaim by the population of the country; the jubilation and festivals; the confirmation of the priests; the work of surveying the land (for the new city); the royal visit to the oracle of Amon with every little detail including the king's arrival before the walled enclosure, the coming of the priest with blessings and flattery, the fact that the priest was a hereditary prince and a commander of archers and darters, his addressing "the majesty the king" by the name of Amon and the title "son" that he gave to the royal guest and the assertion that he was bodily formed by the god while in "an egg"; the curious way the oracle had of nodding answers, the question about the exiles and the request for a royal decree, the question about the murderers and whether any escaped punishment and

---

[24] Ibid.
[25] Plutarch, *Lives*, "Alexander," XXVII, 4.

were still among the living; the gifts to the priest and the offerings
to the god—all these are described by the Greek and Latin authors
in the story of Alexander's visit to the oracle of Amon in the oasis,
as well as by the priest of the oracle himself. Also the order of the
questions and of the responses is exactly the same on the Stele of
the Banished and in Alexander's Greek and Latin biographies.

The stele dates from the fourth century; more precisely, from
the early spring of −331.

Once again the so-called Twenty-first Dynasty reveals itself as
that of the princes of the oases, where they were established by the
Persians to command the outposts on the Libyan front. The stele of
a priest-prince, Menkheperre, of the oracle of Amon of the Siwa
oasis describes Alexander's visit to that place; the accounts of the
Greek authors agree with that of the priest-prince even in small
details.

It has often been said that no Egyptian record of the visit of Alexander to the oracle of Zeus-Amon in the oasis exists.[26] But this is not
the case: the Stele of the Banished is such a record.

It is also said that we shall never know what answer Alexander
received from the oracle in the oasis, beyond what was reported by
those who accompanied him, but who were not inside the temple
at the oracle's delivery. They reported that he promised to tell the
secret to his mother upon his return to Macedonia. Alexander "in
a letter to his mother says that he received certain secret responses
which he would tell to her and to her alone" (Plutarch)—but he
never returned home. "What questions he [Alexander] put to the
oracle, what answers he received—these are problems which historians have debated ever since and to which we shall never know
the correct answer for Alexander kept his own counsel. He wrote
to his mother telling her that he would communicate his secret to
her alone after his return; but since he did not go back to Macedonia it died with him."[27] This regret at our ignorance of the oracle's pronouncements and the resignation as to the chance ever to

[26] J. Grafton Milne, "Alexander at the Oasis of Ammon" in *Miscellanea
Gregoriana* (Vatican, 1941), p. 148.
[27] Harold Idris Bell, *Egypt from Alexander the Great to the Arab Conquest*
(Oxford, 1948), p. 30.

learn of what went on between the king and the priest are also unwarranted since we have the oracle's answers to Alexander's questions incised in stone of the Stele of the Banished, prepared by the priest, the other person who participated in that famous but secret session.

Did Alexander Visit the Egyptian Thebes?

Alexander remained in Egypt from the fall of −332 to the spring of −331. Of his activities in Egypt, his founding of Alexandria and his visit to the Siwa oasis are best known because they are described by all his late Greek and Latin biographers; they, however, selected their material from no longer extant writings of Alexander's companions on his campaign of conquest of Asia and Egypt in Africa. Cleitarchus, a resident of Alexandria soon after its founding, collected written and oral information about Alexander in order to compose a biography. His work is known mainly through quotes and references in later writers.

The problem that we shall raise now is a minor one: did or did not Alexander visit Thebes, the capital of Upper Egypt? In the descriptions of his sojourn in Egypt, as found in late biographies, such information is absent and it seems as if he limited his itinerary to the Delta or Lower Egypt, its old capital Memphis being named, and the future site of Alexandria, and the desert road to the northern oasis. As to this journey, the testimonies of Ptolemy and Callisthenes contradict—whereas one has it that Alexander returned by the same route he went, namely, along the coast and then southward, the other gives a return route by an entirely inland route. From among the late authors, Curtius Rufus injects a sentence quoted by me on an earlier page; "From Memphis, ascending the river, the king penetrated to the interior of Egypt," but in a passage close to the end of his narrative the same author states: "Alexander felt a strong inclination . . . to visit the interior of Egypt, and even Ethiopia. The celebrated palace of Memnon and Tithonus was about to draw him, eager to explore antiquity, almost as far as the Tropic of Cancer. But the impending war . . . denied time."

By the palace of Memnon, Curtius Rufus must have meant the temple of Luxor built by Amenhotep III since his colossal seated statues on the western plain of Thebes, across the Nile from Luxor, were known in the Greek world as representing the legendary Memnon.[1] Thus it appears that Curtius Rufus made Alexander penetrate the interior of Egypt up the river, but not as far as Aswan, close to the Tropic of Cancer, not even as far as Thebes.

The nature of Alexander, curious, exploring, and also vain, would hardly let him omit a visit to the temples of the ancient capital known to him from reading Homer: Achilles, Alexander's foremost hero, speaks of the unexcelled riches of the hundred-gated Thebes with two hundred chariots to each gate; to the Greeks it was the most splendid city in the entire world. Even today Thebes yearly draws many tourists. As the son of the god Amon, Alexander must have felt a strong inclination to visit the majestic temple of Amon in Karnak—the eastern Thebes: he did not spare himself the discomfort of the desert travel to Siwa, a journey of many days, and a comfortable boat could take him to Thebes in a shorter time. He spent full half a year tarrying in Egypt and was not prevented by considerations of shortness of time from sailing up the stream to Thebes. Also it is proper to suppose that in order to be crowned king of Upper and Lower Egypt, the title he assumed, he would have had to appear for a ceremony at Thebes as well as Memphis.

In the Luxor and Karnak temples of Amon, Alexander built votive chambers, and some of the bas-reliefs with Alexander on them are still preserved and shown to tourists. These votive chambers strongly convey the idea that Alexander visited Thebes and sacrificed there to Amon, the supreme deity of the Egyptian pantheon.

From the Stele of the Banished (Maunier Stele) the same conclusion can be drawn. "Their [people's] hearts rejoiced because [his majesty] had desired to come to the South in might and victory, in order to make satisfied the heart of the land, and to expel his enemies. . . ." The reference to "South" could conceivably mean merely that the king arrived in Egypt from the north—he came from

[1] See my *Oedipus and Akhnaton*, p. 38.

Macedonia via Anatolia, Syria, and Palestine—but the next passage reads: "He arrived at the city with a glad heart; the youth of Thebes received him, making jubilee, with an embassy before him." The damaged stele, in the next sentence, has a reference to his majesty establishing Menkheperre "upon the throne of his father, as High Priest of Amon-Re, king of gods, commander in chief of the armies of the South and North." It would be an extremely strained supposition to assume that the "jubilee" was all for the high priest who arrived at Thebes, upon his appointment, and not for "his majesty" who appointed or confirmed him in his hereditary post.

The votive inscription of Alexander in the Amon temple at Karnak deserves some renewed attention on the part of archaeologists. Thutmose III was known by the royal nomen Menkheperre. This was, as we learned, also the name of the prince-priest who received Alexander in the oasis. Therefore, it would be worth while to re-examine the extant parts of the inscription in order to decide whether it is correct to say that "Alexander built a votive chamber for Thutmose III." It could be so, since Thutmose III was the greatest military hero of Egyptian history, who lived and warred six hundred years before Alexander[2]; but could it not be that the name Menkheperre there refers to the high priest and would not Menkheperre himself be the one to take care that Alexander's name or figure should be carved in Karnak in some relation to himself? A son of Menkheperre, as we shall see, wrote a long inscription about some trivial matter on the walls of Karnak and would a much more important event be omitted from mention there by his father? The Stele of the Banished was actually found in Luxor, the other temple compound of Thebes. Yet there are strong indices that the chapel Alexander built was, as is usually thought, in honor of the famous ancient pharaoh.

"The Oracle of Amun at Siwa was a branch of that of Thebes."[3] This also explains why Menkheperre should be active in both places. Either before his pilgrimage to the oasis or upon his return from there, Alexander visited Thebes.

---

[2] *Ages in Chaos*, I, p. 143–77.
[3] Fakhri, *Siwa Oasis*, p. 42.

Chapter IV

SI-AMON

Peinuzem II

As Alexander, after his exploits in Central Asia and in the Indus Valley, lay dying in Babylon he was asked what his last wishes were; he requested one thing only—to be entombed in the Siwa oasis where eight years earlier he had heard the oracle declare him son of god. A cortege brought Alexander's body to Egypt but Ptolemy was against giving the body to the priests of the oasis and selected for him a tomb in Alexandria. It has never been discovered. A marble sarcophagus of unexcelled beauty was found in Sidon. It is adorned by figures at war and hunting. It is now in the Museum of Istanbul and is known as Alexander's sarcophagus, but no inscription and no proof, except its excellence, subscribe to this identification.

When the empire created by Alexander broke up following his death, Ptolemy, son of Lagus, who had accompanied Alexander on his marches of conquest as far as India, secured Egypt for himself and fought on land and sea for a greater share in the inheritance. Some formal tokens of loyalty were accorded to Philip Arrhidaeus, the half-witted half brother of Alexander, and after his death, to the boy Alexander, Alexander's posthumous son by Roxana, until she and her son were murdered (−310). Only thereafter did Ptolemy proclaim himself king over Egypt and Palestine and initiate a dynasty that endured (in Egypt) for almost three hundred years and expired with Cleopatra in −30.

Menkheperre, son of Peinuzem, who received Alexander in the oasis, was followed in the office of high priest by a son Peinuzem, named for his grandfather. From him there remain several inscriptions, one of them rather extensive, carved on a wall of the Amon temple at Karnak. Peinuzem II figures as a high priest or prophet but not as a king; neither does he refer to his deceased father, Menkheperre, as a king or late king. Peinuzem dates his inscriptions in the years 2, 3, 5, and 6 of some king who is not named. "It is desirable to know the identity of the unnamed king," wrote Naville.[1] As a son and successor of Menkheperre, Peinuzem must have lived and functioned in the days of Ptolemy I. The years 2, 3, 5, and 6 would, then, apply to the royal years of Ptolemy I, though they may refer to the time when Ptolemy, after Alexander's death, virtually in supreme authority over Egypt, had not yet proclaimed himself king.[2] We assume that Peinuzem II exercised the functions of the prophet of Amon in the last two decades before the year −300.

In the large Karnak inscription Peinuzem functions before "the great god," which, as Naville observed, stands for "the king." As in the Stele of the Banished, the "great god" appoints scribes, inspectors, and overseers. Some of them committed fraudulent acts; Peinuzem inquires of the oracle of Amon whether a certain Thutmose, a son of Soua-Amon and a temple attendant, is guilty of appropriating to himself some of the temple property. The oracle answers with violent movements of his brow, as in the Stele of the Banished. The long text amounts to a rehabilitation of the suspect. How true was the verdict of the oracle we cannot know but this chiseling on the ancient walls of the Karnak temple with such a trifling issue at such great length is a sign of decadence.

It is assumed that Peinuzem II had a son Psusennes; this Psusennes II is sometimes counted as the last "king" of the Twenty-first Dynasty. There exists no inscription that with certainty could be ascribed to him or about him. It is further assumed that this Psusennes had a daughter named Makare. Why are these assump-

[1] E. Naville, *Inscription historique de Pinodjem III* (Paris, 1883). In more recent publications, this Peinuzem is referred to as II.

[2] H. Gauthier, *Le Livre des rois d'Egypte*, V (1917), 213: *"La chronologie de Ptolémée I-er nous offre, du reste, une curieuse particularité, en ce qu'elle fait usage d'un double mode de datation."*

tions made? In order to create a link between the dynasty of priest-kings that goes under the name of Twenty-first and the Libyan Dynasty, counted as Twenty-second, that ruled in the ninth–eighth centuries.

A statuette of the Nile god, a votive dedication by a pilgrim, would not attract much attention on the part of archaeologists. But one such statue, when its inscription was read, was found to have been dedicated by High Priest Meriamun-Sosenk, who describes himself as son of King Osorkon and of his wife Makare, daughter of King Pesibkenno (Psusennes). The surmise was made that a link had been found between the two dynasties, one expiring, the other taking over.[3] It was also assumed that the high priest Sosenk later mounted the throne as King Sosenk, although the monumental inscriptions have this Sosenk preceding, not following, Osorkon.

It is not known with any degree of certainty that Peinuzem II had a son Psusennes (II), nor is there any evidence that, if there was such a scion in the priestly succession, he had a daughter Makare. But a surmise that a Psusennes II followed Peinuzem II, further, that he had a daughter Makare, and finally that she married Osorkon I and bore a son Sosenk, led to a confusion in which descendants changed roles and times with their ancestors. It is thus that the order of dynasties is thought to be established. Actually, on this *sole* link the Libyan Dynasty and the Ethiopian, which followed the Libyan, are made subsequent to the dynasty of priest-princes whom we recognized as having flourished under the Persians and even under the first Ptolemies. Since Peinuzem II officiated under Ptolemy I, a son of his could not be the father-in-law of a monarch who reigned more than six hundred years earlier.

Si-Amon

We have reached the terminal figure in this work of reconstruction of ancient history. In various modern efforts to establish the succession of the kings and high priests of the Twenty-first Dynasty,

[3] Breasted, *Ancient Records,* Vol. IV, Secs. 738–40.

King Si-Amon is regularly placed at the end of the list of the kings.[1]

It was Si-Amon who closed and sealed the royal cache at Deir el Bahari, but not before he had placed among the mummies of ancient pharaohs the remains of Peinuzem II, who himself had rewrapped some of the mummies of ancient kings. It was probably again Si-Amon who replaced the remains of Psusennes' queen with those of "King" Amenemope in the tomb in the temple precinct in Tanis. A scarab of green stone with Si-Amon's name was found in the tomb's vestibule and it "amounts to a signature" (Montet).

Peinuzem II, son of Menkheperre, flourished under Ptolemy I (Soter), and Si-Amon must have lived under the same king or, more probably, under his successor, Ptolemy II Philadelphus (−285 to −246). Whereas Ptolemy I was a warrior king, his younger son, in whose favor he abdicated the throne two years before his death, was a splendor-loving king and an enthusiast for Hellenic culture. Philadelphus married his sister, in this taking license from Egyptian royal usage, but otherwise he abhorred the mysterious atmosphere of the native religious cults, and a gay religious cult of Serapis, to a great extent, supplanted the ancient cults of Amon, of Ptah, and of other deities. The library of Alexandria, founded by Ptolemy I, became a great center of learning under Ptolemy II. Alexandria, now the capital of Egypt, obscured Sais, Memphis, and other cities in the Delta. Ptolemy II was a patron of arts.

Living under the Ptolemies, Si-Amon must have witnessed the change of scene. The Egyptian culture that, though affected, survived the impact of the Hyksos invasion, of the Libyan, Ethiopian, Assyrian, and Persian dominations, was now exposed to a spirit and mode not even oriental; whereas in the past Greek mercenaries had settled and merchants frequented Egypt and philosophers had come —since Solon, Pythagoras, Herodotus, and Plato—to seek knowledge, the new trend was bringing changes not only in fashion but in wisdom, too, from Hellas to Egypt, and especially to Alexandria, destined soon to become the cultural capital of the world, supplanting

---

[1] J. Černý, *Cambridge Ancient History*, Vol. II, Chap. XXXV. E. F. Wente, *Journal of Near Eastern Studies*, XXVI, 3 (July 1967). Eric Young, *Journal of the American Research Center in Egypt*, II (1963), 99 ff.

Athens. It was not a pure Greek culture that descended on the lands conquered by Alexander: the Macedonian conquest resulted in the emergence of what is called Hellenistic culture, quite different from the Hellenic; it was an amalgam of the latter with oriental cultures. If, however, there was one place in the entire area bequeathed by Alexander to his comrades-in-arms that inherited from the spirit of Athens, it was Alexandria.

The Egyptian priesthood continued to enjoy the patronage of the kings; temples were built in Kom Ombo, in Esneh, and in other places that in architectural style did not differ from the temples of the Twentieth Dynasty; the temples and their hierarchy enjoyed large incomes from their fiefs, from royal munificence, and from donations of the laity. But the ancient rites were subject to the impact of the spirit of Hellenism; and the new deity, Serapis, soon became supreme.

Even though in the oases there was more of a chance for the time-honored creed and superstitions to survive, Hellenism could not fail to send its cleansing wind across the desert too. To some extent, the cultural change in the Delta could be compared to the change that the age of enlightenment brought to eighteenth-century Europe; but under Ptolemy there was also much of seventeenth-century Versailles, a mood of indifference to religion, and this despite the prevalence of the people of the cloth in politics and cultural affairs. The court was "magnificent and dissolute, intellectual and artificial."

To embellish Alexandria, the Ptolemies ordered several obelisks to be transferred and erected in public places. The two obelisks that in our days stand, one on the Thames Embankment in London and the other in Central Park in New York, were erected before the Caesarion in Alexandria by Octavian Augustus; but it is not known for certain when they were transferred to Alexandria from Heliopolis, north of Memphis, where they were originally erected by Thutmose III of the Eighteenth Dynasty. It is supposed that Octavian Augustus transferred them; for this there is no testimony.

It is conceivable that the removal of the obelisks from Heliopolis (the On of the Egyptians) required an authorization by the priesthood. The texts on them date from the time of Thutmose III but close to the base there are hieroglyphics with the name of Si-Amon added at a later time.[2] If the lines, not too well preserved, were added at the time of the transfer, then they are probably to the effect that it was he, Si-Amon, who authorized this act.

Quite a number of other instances are known of Si-Amon having left his name or signature—on objects found in Memphis, Tanis, and in some other places in Upper Egypt. He was quite active in his efforts to preserve and restore temples and monuments of earlier centuries. He also felt it his duty to preserve the pitiful remains left from the sumptuous royal entombments of the great pharaohs and from the interment of the members of his own clan.

When converting the tombs of two ancient and little-known queens into receptacles for the mummies of great kings, high priests, and lesser hierarchy, Si-Amon made these places appear so inconspicuous that through the entire Greek, Roman, Byzantine, Arab, Mameluke, and Turkish rules, until the end of the nineteenth century, they remained undiscovered. He did not betray these repositories by erecting monuments; most probably the funerary arrangements, assembling and transferring the coffins, were made under the protection of darkness.

No tomb, and especially no tomb of a prominent man of military nobility or clergy, was ever safe from violation after the end of the sixth century in Egypt. Even if under the Ptolemies there must have been more order, supervision, and safety than before, it was natural for Si-Amon, scion of a line of military princes and priests, in his desire to build for himself a mortuary chamber after his own plan and design, to select a site in the Siwa oasis, in the shadow of the temple of the oracle of Zeus-Amon, hallowed ground, and we shall follow him there. Alexander aspired to be entombed there but he was not.

In the side of a hill called Gabal el-Mota in the oasis, there are a few tomb chambers now lying open. One tomb was built for Ni-per-pa-Thoth, described in a brief text on the wall as "prophet of

---

[2] Maspero, *Les Momies royales,* p. 674; K. A. Wiedeman, *Aegyptische Geschichte* (1884–88), p. 532.

Osiris, scribe of the divine books, the priest"; he is also eulogized
as "the great one of his town," "the follower of his god," and "excellent man." The god Amon was not mentioned and it appears that
Ni-per-pa-Thoth, a prophet of Osiris, a pious man, selected the oasis
as sacred and pure ground, in preference to Abydos or to the
Serapeum in Memphis, long connected with the Osirian traditions,
now become a cult center of Serapis.

"Daressy dated it [the tomb of Ni-per-pa-Thoth] to the XXth
Dynasty when he first examined the drawing, but later on preferred
a later date thinking that it was from the time of Alexander the
Great."[3] This, of course, is a reduction of eight hundred years in
the estimate based on the accepted chronology.

In the northwest side of the hill is the tomb of Si-Amon, which
was found in November 1940. "This tomb is by far the best that
has yet been found in the Western Desert and rivals any work of
the period in the tombs of the Nile Valley."[4]

"When this tomb was found it caused a great sensation among
the Siwans, everybody went to see it, and the most fantastic explanations of the scenes [in murals] were made. . . . Some of the
Siwans even claimed that in the hieroglyphic texts they could read
warnings of the catastrophe that had befallen them [due to World
War II]. One of the magicians pretended that from the number
of the stars in the ceiling he could calculate when the Last Day
of mankind would come."

Soon after its discovery the tomb became living quarters for a
large family with its pet animals, sheep, and hens; they cooked inside it and baked their bread and "consequently many parts of the
coloured walls were covered with soot or lost [their] brightness. . . ." But "still worse was the cutting out of many pieces of
the scenes by the troops who were at Siwa [during World War II]
and who used to come to see the newly found monuments." The
tomb, preserved from before the beginning of the Christian Era,
was exposed to rapid destruction. "The man who was living in the

[3] Fakhri, *Siwa Oasis*, p. 127.
[4] Ibid., p. 132.

tomb permitted every visitor to step in and do what he liked expecting a gratuity."[5]

The sepulcher consists of a hall about thirty feet long and eight feet wide, and of an unfinished burial chamber about ten feet long and five feet wide. As the hieroglyphics next to the painted figure of the tomb owner repeatedly state, the tomb was built by and for Si-Amon. The walls and the ceiling of the hall are adorned with colorful paintings, some of them of exquisite quality: such is the mural showing the goddess Nut beside a tree all in bloom, herself offering food, water, and incense to the tomb owner. On another mural Si-Amon is adoring Isis, who is followed by a Bennu bird. In still another painting a vulture is spreading its wings over Si-Amon.

In none of the preserved paintings has Si-Amon a uraeus or cobra, the sign of royal power, over his brow, but a vulture with spread wings over him *is* a royal sign. In the inscriptions that are still preserved—many of them are defaced—his name is written without encircling it in a cartouche. But the frieze along the walls is made of cartouches not filled in—a design rather unusual for the tomb of a private man. A person, however rich or prominent in communal affairs, would not decorate his mortuary chamber with scores of cartouches, a trademark of royalty. The cartouches are arranged in groups of two blues and two yellows.

The ceiling of the hall is decorated with royal symbols: hawks and vultures with spread wings and with royal insignia held by the talons. Coming so close to claiming royal status, why didn't Si-Amon write his name in the designed cartouches or attach a uraeus to the brow of any of his portraits?

The answer is at hand: under the Ptolemies—and certainly under Ptolemy II—it would have been a grave state offense for anyone, except Ptolemies themselves, to claim royal titles. Si-Amon made the closest approach permissible: he had royal symbols adorning the walls and the ceiling but he restrained himself from ordering the artist to add a compromising claim to a royal title and thus to the

[5] Ibid.

throne. Already Peinuzem, son of Menkheperre, did not dare to apply to his father's name or to his own the title "king."[6]

Not feeling free to write next to his name and figure, "king," Si-Amon preferred to write nothing. Whereas the other tomb, that of Ni-per-pa-Thoth, has the offices once held by the deceased written on the walls ("prophet of Osiris," "Scribe of the divine documents," "the great one in his town," "priest"), the name Si-Amon and his figure are left without any qualification as to the position or offices he held in his lifetime. The tomb was not finished and possibly the ovals of the cartouches were designed to have, at a later time, the name of the deceased written in, should the political situation change, but even so the appearance of the tomb is in many respects comparable to the royal tombs of the Valley of the Kings near Thebes.

Discussing these details, we neglected to describe the two ways Si-Amon wished to be portrayed. In the majority of scenes he is depicted in traditional Egyptian attire—his face and head are shaven; but in a few of the murals he is shown with a mane of black hair and a black curly beard. Furthermore, in a picture where he is presented with his younger son—he sits and the boy stands before him—the boy "wears a short cloak of Greek style." "He has curly black hair and puts over his shoulders a cloak of pure Greek style" (Fakhri).

It is unquestionable: the tomb of Si-Amon dates from the Hellenistic period of Egyptian history. Si-Amon, living in Hellenistic times, could not escape the influence of the prevailing spirit and mode.

At the time Si-Amon died his mortuary chamber was not yet finished. Soon after his death a series of niches were cut into the walls of the large hall and mummies were placed there. These mummies were recovered by Fakhri and ascribed by him to the Ptolemaic period. This period lasted until the death of Cleopatra in −30.

Since the Twenty-first Dynasty has been misplaced in the eleventh–tenth centuries and, in some estimates, Si-Amon's regnal years are placed between −969 and −950,[7] he is made a contem-

[6] Cf. Černý, Gardiner.
[7] Young, *Journal of the American Research Center in Egypt*, II (1963), 109.

porary of King Solomon. A prominent Egyptologist who wrote the chapter "From the Death of Ramesses III to the End of the Twenty-first Dynasty" for the revised edition of the *Cambridge Ancient History* admitted that it is "uncertain which king of the Twenty-first Dynasty was on such friendly terms with Solomon that he sent his daughter to Jerusalem to become one of Solomon's wives."[8] A suggestion follows that Si-Amon could have been the father-in-law of Solomon since Solomon reigned in the first part of the tenth century.

Si-Amon lived and died under the Ptolemies, seven hundred years after Solomon. He entombed Peinuzem II, son of Menkheperre; Menkheperre, as we demonstrated, received Alexander in the temple of the oracle in the oasis in the year −331. Thus we arrived at the conclusion that Si-Amon lived under the Ptolemies.

We have also complementary and compelling evidence for equating Si-Amon, owner of the tomb in the oasis, with Si-Amon who closed in "year 10" the royal cache at Deir el Bahari.

When first entering the cache, E. Brugsch lifted at the beginning of the long passage a thick package of rolled hide.[9] It must have been left in the tomb by the Egyptian priest before he sealed it. When unrolled, the hide was identified as a leather canopy for use over a coffin during the funeral ceremony for Peinuzem II. All painted and decorated, it has a design of rosettes, alternately yellow and red, of eight petals each, surrounding rectangular spaces occupied by vultures that spread their wings and hold in their talons round grips with ostrich feathers spread widely. The two side strips of the canopy are decorated by a frieze composed of a row of lances (lance tips set on circles) and under the frieze are designs of animals (ducks and antelopes prepared for offering); each antelope is painted as standing on a checkered board of small green and

---

[8] J. Černý, *Cambridge Ancient History,* Chap. XXXV, p. 656. G. Maspero hypothesized that Si-Amon could have been Solomon's father-in-law.

[9] Maspero, *Les Momies royales de Déir el-Bahari,* pp. 584 ff.; Maspero and Brugsch, *La Trouvaille de Déir-el-Bahari* (Cairo, 1881), plate 17 (photograph); H. W. Villiers Stuart, *The Funeral Tent of an Egyptian Queen* (1882) (the canopy is reproduced as a large spread in colors); E. Brugsch, *La Tente funéraire de la Princesse Ismikheb;* Maspero, in *L'Archéologie égyptienne* (1887), fig. 264; idem. (1907), fig. 287.

red squares depicting a carpet or a mosaic floor. Between the animal designs are cartouches inscribed with the name of Peinuzem II.

The ceiling in the tomb of Si-Amon in the oasis has a very similar design: again in rectangular spaces with heads crowned with royal headgear, vultures are painted, spreading their wings (alternating with falcons in the same postures): in their talons, as on the leather canopy, are rounded grips with flat plates holding ostrich feathers widely spread; the feathers, as on the canopy, are designed with three alternating dark and three bright portions. The headgear, the grips, the feathers, the confines of the wings (semi-oval from below, straight at the upper edge)—all present very similar peculiar designs that are found also on the canopy used by Si-Amon in the funeral of Peinuzem II. As on the canopy, the royal birds are designed in colors one under another in long rectangular spaces likewise surrounded by rosettes; a frieze of lance heads set on circles and carpet motifs of checkered squares complete the unusual similarity of design and motifs between the canopy used in the cache where Si-Amon left his signature on many royal mummies and the tomb that Si-Amon built for his own occupancy.

Ahmed Fakhri, who described the tomb of Si-Amon in the Siwa oasis, did not associate it with the prince Si-Amon of the Twenty-first Dynasty assigned to the first half of the tenth century. In the tomb in the oasis the Egyptologist saw indisputable evidence of Greek style—even elements of "pure Greek style." Not finding in the tomb next to the name of Si-Amon any description of the offices held by him in his lifetime, Fakhri decided that Si-Amon could not have been a priest or an official; therefore a hypothesis was offered by him to the effect that Si-Amon must have been a Greek immigrant who married into an Egyptian family, adopted the Egyptian faith, but did not abandon his Greek way of life, and, having grown rich as a merchant or landowner, built himself a sumptuous sepulcher, unequaled in the Western Desert.

On one hand, the tomb of Si-Amon was built and decorated in the Hellenistic period of Egyptian history—the Greek chiton on Si-Amon's young son and some of his own portraits permit no other date. On the other hand, the canopy used in the funeral cortege of Peinuzem II was placed in the royal cache in Deir el Bahari by Si-Amon of the so-called Twenty-first Dynasty; he also left his signature on the swathing of the mummy of Peinuzem II and sealed the cache.

The murals of the tomb in the oasis and the canopy found in the cache were made in the very same age and possibly by one and the same artist working for Si-Amon. If we had no other evidence for bringing the Twenty-first Dynasty so much closer to our age, this evidence alone would have outweighed every argument, if such were in existence, for the accepted dates for Si-Amon, Peinuzem, Menkheperre, and the entire dynasty of the priestly princes. But this is only the last bit of evidence in a long line of other unambiguous testimony coming from each and every generation of the priestly succession.

Conclusions

In the opening section of this second part of this volume, two versions of the period known as Twenty-first Dynasty were put before the reader, both contending for the title of true history. One claimant contended that the dynasty belongs to the eleventh–tenth centuries but was unable to produce a single synchronical point of contact between Egypt under this dynasty and the foreign countries of those centuries: this despite the fact that neighboring Palestine, as attested by the Scriptures, during this entire time was a state very active militarily under Saul and David and commercially and culturally under Solomon. In Solomon's days Egypt also became the center of a plot against Israel. The claimant was found mute when asked to produce witness or evidence yet insistent as to the claim.

The other version produced evidence—and how compelling it is any peruser of these pages can evaluate—to the effect that the entire dynasty belongs in the Persian time and in the beginning of the Greek period in Egypt. Witnesses filed by, were interrogated, and cross-examined.

From the letter of Ourmai one learns that Egypt was on all sides surrounded by foreign troops, and that an army of occupation was oppressing the population, children were sold into slavery, sacred places were violated, tombs were opened; the narrator, a member of the former aristocracy of the land, wandered afoot and begged bread from the soldiers of occupation—all and everything as in the story of Herodotus about the conquest of Egypt by the Persians under Cambyses. For the conventional scheme, however, such events learned upon the publication of Ourmai's letter in 1960 were not in agreement with the plan. The Twenty-first Dynasty was supposed to have taken over the reins of government without any foreign intervention.

However, some political disturbance was suspected to have taken place during the Twenty-first Dynasty and, actually, it could have been deduced that a foreign power was involved. The temple servant Ahautinofer testified at a court hearing on temple robberies that a high priest, Amenhotep, was removed ("suppressed") and that the accused himself was arrested by a foreigner and carried away. From this testimony and from the records of other processes the fact of occupation of the land by foreign troops commanded by captains came to light. A number of persons had non-Egyptian and often Persian names.

The "mysterious" counting by the "renewal" or "renaissance" years on the documents of the high priest Herihor was found by us to have a parallel in the usage established under the Persian kings in the ceremony of the "renewal of the kingdom" on the days of the Mazdaic New Year: ambassadors from all subdued nations used to arrive at Persepolis for the festivals of "renewal," or "renaissance."

Wenamon, who under Herihor sailed to Byblos to purchase cedarwood, refers to the shipping house of Birkath-El that engaged in commerce between Tanis and the Syrian harbors; the same shipping company, now under the firm name of Berakhel's Son, was known to the author of the Testament of Naphtali, a literary work composed in Persian or Hellenistic times. The same Wenamon, "master of foreign lands," built a shrine in the Siwa oasis; the shrine is attributed to the fifth or fourth century. Actually it was built when Nekht-hor-heb was the administrator of Egypt under Darius II.

The king-priest Psusennes who followed Herihor had his name written in one cartouche and the Persian title—Shahedet—in the other next to the first. In an inscription in his tomb Psusennes refers to the Mediterranean coast of Egypt from Damietta to Rosetta as the Hellenic coast, though the Greeks did not settle in Egypt before −663. The title "king" is written by him in the fashion known from Ptolemaic times.

A grandson of Psusennes, Menkheperre, received Alexander in the temple of Amon's oracle in the oasis, and the details of this visit with parallel texts in the biographers of Alexander and on the Stele of the Banished were scrutinized by us sentence by sentence.

Peinuzem, son of Menkheperre, rewrapped mummies removed from the violated tombs of ancient kings and was himself buried in the royal cache at Deir el Bahari before it was sealed by Si-Amon; Peinuzem's funeral canopy, left in the sealed cache, was compared by us with the murals and the ceiling paintings of the tomb of Si-Amon in the Siwa oasis and left no doubt that it was the same Si-Amon who sealed the cache and who built for himself the tomb; in it, on some of the murals, his son is shown clad in Greek attire and he has a Greek hairdo.

There is no room left for even a slightest chance that the Twenty-first Dynasty can be removed from the Persian and early Ptolemaic times. And if we recall the findings we made and the conclusions we were led to draw concerning the Twentieth Dynasty, discussed in the first part of this volume, the chances to retain these dynasties, the Twentieth and Twenty-first, in the twelfth–tenth centuries can be estimated as nil.

And this compelling conclusion is arrived at independently of the fact that, as was demonstrated in *Ages in Chaos* (Vol. I), the twelfth–tenth-century period in Egypt has no vacancy to accommodate any stray dynasty: the Hyksos domination of Egypt continued till the mid-eleventh century and from then on, for two centuries, the Eighteenth Dynasty ruled over Egypt in one of her most glorious periods, Ahmose, Amenhotep I, Thutmose I, Hatshepsut, Thutmose III, Amenhotep II, Thutmose IV, Amenhotep III, Akhnaton, Smenkhkare, and Tutankhamen successively occupying the throne.

Retrospect and Prospect

It is not without design that this volume of *Ages in Chaos*, dealing with the Persian period, and thus with the last two centuries of the history under reconstruction, follows the first volume. In the first volume of this attempt at rewriting ancient history, the narrative was carried from the downfall of the Middle Kingdom in Egypt to the el-Amarna period, near the end of the Eighteenth Dynasty (an illumination of the concluding years of that dynasty is found in my *Oedipus and Akhnaton*). But in Hebrew history, it was shown, the discussed period comprises the time from the Exodus from Egypt to the kings Jehoshaphat in Jerusalem and Ahab in Samaria: the heretical pharaoh was their contemporary and they exchanged letters with him which are still in existence.

In the conventional version of history, the end of the Eighteenth Dynasty is placed in the second half of the fourteenth century, ca. −1340. The synchronical version, however, places the terminal years of this dynasty in about −830. There is a difference of over five hundred years.

The Persian conquest of Egypt took place in −525. In the conventional scheme there are a little more than eight hundred years between the end of the Eighteenth Dynasty and the Persian conquest, but only a little over three hundred years for the same period in the synchronical history.

The question, then, arises, how could eight hundred years of composed history find room in a period of time so much shorter? There are at our disposal only three centuries to complete the story. This stretch of time must seem inadequate to accommodate the Nineteenth Dynasty (that of Seti, Ramses II, and Merneptah), the Twentieth (that of Ramses III and the later Ramessides), the Twenty-first (of priest-kings), the Twenty-second to Twenty-fifth (the Libyan and Ethiopian Dynasties), and the Twenty-sixth, the so-called Saitic Dynasty of Psammetich, Necho, Apries, and Amasis that was terminated by the Persian conquest. All these dynasties lay claim on room in a time span that appears utterly inadequate to accommodate all of them. The criticism expressed by workers in ancient history upon the publication of the first volume of *Ages in Chaos* was directed not against any specific subject but regularly against what appeared to them the impossibility of completing the work of reconstruction. Also those who read carefully the first part of this work and felt compelled to accept the documented synchronical version of ancient history from the fifteenth to the ninth century inquired, But how could centuries of history be eliminated, or, Which are the ghost years or spurious dynasties?

In the present volume, two of the "pretenders" among the dynasties, the Twentieth and the Twenty-first, are shown not to belong to the time before the conquest of Egypt by the Persians. They are exposed as "impostors": the kings of the Twentieth Dynasty are but alter egos of the kings of the Twenty-ninth to Thirtieth Dynasties of the fourth century, and the kings who go under the name of the Twenty-first Dynasty are but princely priests of the oases, established there by Darius II and his successors. Not only does the Twenty-first Dynasty not belong within the time conventionally allotted to it—the eleventh century and the first half of the tenth—but it also preceded, was contemporaneous with, and survived the Twentieth. Actually, the last "kings" of the Twenty-first Dynasty continued their combined tasks as commanders of the frontier outposts and as priests of the oracles into Ptolemaic times.

With the removal of the "ghost" dynasties, the Twentieth and the Twenty-first, from the list of rightful claimants to a historical place prior to the subjugation of Egypt by the Persians, the above-mentioned problem of five centuries' difference between the two versions of history is cut in two: on the conventional timetable these two dynasties occupy the period from ca. −1200 to −945 or over two hundred and fifty years. Thus the problem is already half solved.

Could the dynasties not yet discussed, the Nineteenth and

Twenty-second to Twenty-sixth, all be fitted into the space of three centuries?

We shall tackle the remaining problem in several volumes about the Dark Age of Greece, the Assyrian conquest, and Ramses II and his time.[1] In these volumes I intend to show that the Dark Ages in Greece and Asia Minor are spurious; that the "Hittite Empire" was but a Chaldean kingdom; and we shall be able to align the entire period from −830 to −525.

From the point of view of the complete reconstruction, *Peoples of the Sea* should count as Volume IV of the series, because it narrates the events from the Persian conquest to the Hellenistic (Ptolemaic) age.

As was said in the Introduction, with the Eighteenth Dynasty moved down the scale of time by more than five centuries (*Ages in Chaos*, Vol. I, *From the Exodus to King Akhnaton*), we removed one abutment from conventional history and erected instead an abutment for the reconstruction; with the removal of the Twentieth and Twenty-first Dynasties to the age of Persian domination over Egypt, anchoring them centuries away from their putative places, a second such abutment is erected. On these two abutments now rests the span of ancient history.

Ancient history shown to be misplaced and distorted at both ends cannot plead for the salvaging of the mid-part intact.

The reader, unless he was following with great care the development of this reconstruction of ancient history, could easily be bewildered: the Manethonian Eighteenth (Theban) Dynasty is followed not by the Nineteenth (Tanitic) but by the Twenty-second to Twenty-third (Libyan) Dynasties; after the Ethiopian or Twenty-fifth comes the Nineteenth, which is the same as the Twenty-sixth; it is succeeded by the Twenty-seventh (Persian), and the Twentieth Dynasty of native kings who wrested some independence is the same as the Twenty-ninth and Thirtieth; the Twenty-first runs, for the most part, parallel with the Twentieth but starts earlier (under Darius II) and continues into Ptolemaic

---

[1] The Dark Age of Greece and the Assyrian conquest may be dealt with in a single volume, *In the Time of Isaiah and Homer*.

time. Under the Thirty-first Dynasty goes the restoration of Persian rule in Egypt before the conquest by Alexander, followed by the Ptolemies.

In order to bring clarity to history and rid it from the Manethonian numbering of dynasties that contributes only to chaos, I introduce a different nomenclature for the Egyptian dynasties.

The *Middle Kingdom* of Egypt (the division into Eleventh and Twelfth Dynasties is unnecessary) came to its end in a natural catastrophe in the mid-fifteenth century before the present era; the land was invaded by the Arabs (Amalekites, known as Amu to the Egyptians, or as Hyksos to Greek authors). The *Arab Dynasty* ruled for over four hundred years, till about −1020. Already before that date there were vassal princes in Thebes. The Arab domination of Egypt was terminated by the united efforts of Saul of Israel and Kamose and Ahmose of Thebes. For the next (almost) two hundred years (ca. −1020 to ca. −830) the land was ruled by the *Theban Dynasty* (known as the Eighteenth) of Thutmoses and Amenhoteps. Close to the end of that period, Akhnaton moved the capital to Akhet-Aton (el-Amarna) but Thebes was soon restored as the capital under Smenkhkare and Ay.

The Theban period was followed by the *Libyan domination* of Sosenks and Osorkons for over one hundred years (ca. −830 to ca. −720). Next came the *Ethiopian rule* that endured for fifty or sixty years; however, at the same time the Assyrians pressed from the north and the land was occupied repeatedly by Sennacherib (who crowned Haremhab), Esarhaddon, and Assurbanipal (who elevated Necho I-Ramses I to be a vassal king). When Necho was killed by invading Ethiopians, Assurbanipal once more occupied Thebes (−663).

The period of the *Tanitic Dynasty* follows: Seti (Psammetich of the Greek authors), son of Ramses I (Necho I), obtained independence from Assurbanipal and acted as his ally in his wars against the Chaldeans and Medes. Seti's capital was in Tanis in the Delta. The Tanitic Dynasty endured from −663 to −525. After Seti reigned Ramses II (Necho II), his son, who for a lengthy period had been Seti's co-ruler. He carried on a prolonged war with Nebuchadnezzar, the Chaldean. Ramses' heir Merneptah (Hophra of Jeremiah and Apries of Herodotus) lost the throne to a rebel, General Amasis; the latter reigned in peace for over forty years and died when Cambyses the Persian was already on his march of conquest toward Egypt.

From −525 to −332, for close to two hundred years, Egypt was dominated by the *Persian kings* (Cambyses, Darius, Xerxes, Artaxerxes I, Darius II, Artaxerxes II and III); some of them were crowned also as Egyptian pharaohs; they kept native governors in Egypt like Psamshek or Nekht-hor.

In the fourth century, during the reigns of Artaxerxes II and Artaxerxes III, Egypt achieved a measure of independence comparable to the independence the Greek states maintained during the time of the Great Kings of Persia. Nepherites, Acoris, Nectanebo I (Ramses III), Tachos, and Nectanebo II were the indigenous kings of that period and they could be termed *Native Kings* or, if preferred, *Sebennytic Dynasty,* for the place of origin of the most famous of them. At the same time a *Priestly Dynasty* established already by Darius II (about −420) ruled in the military outposts— the oases of the Libyan desert. They continued there till past −300.

The Persians succeeded in −343 in reconquering Egypt, Nectanebo II escaping to the Sudan, but ten years later Egypt received Alexander as its liberator (−332). The *Macedonian Dynasty* endured three hundred years, with the Ptolemies on the throne till Cleopatra's suicide in −30. Thereafter the Roman caesars ruled Egypt.

This order of dynastic succession, relieved of the numbered dynasties, is simple to comprehend: Arab, Theban, Libyan, Ethiopian (repeatedly interrupted by Assyrian conquests), Tanitic, Persian (partly Sebennytic), and Macedonian Dynasties in this sequence. As can readily be seen, for most of the fourteen hundred years (ca. −1450 to −30), Egypt was ruled by foreigners: the three periods when it was ruled by native kings were under the Theban (−1020 to −830), the Tanitic (−663 to −525), and the Sebennytic (ca. −391 to −341) Dynasties, altogether something like 380 years out of 1420.

CHRONOLOGICAL CHARTS

	PERSIA	PALESTINE and SYRIA
550		
545	Cyrus conquers Lydia, captures Croesus	
540		
535	Cyrus conquers Babylon with Nabonides or his son co-ruler. Belshazzar comes. The end of the Neo-Babylonian (Chaldean) Empire	Cyrus' edict concerning the return of Jewish exiles
530		
525	Cambyses (529–521) conquers Egypt	
520	Darius I (521–485) the Great	Zerubbabel (fl. 520)
515	Darius visits Egypt (517)	Haggai, Zechariah, prophets. Beginning of the period known as "Second Commonwealth" ending in the year 70 of present era
510		
505		
500		
495		
490		
485	Xerxes (485–465)	
480	Esther romance	
475	Wars, founding of Persepolis	
470		
465	Artaxerxes I (465–424)	
460		
455		
450		
445		Nehemiah arrives in Jerusalem (445). Opposition: Eliashib, high priest; Malachi, prophet
440		

	PERSIA	PALESTINE and SYRIA
435		
430		Second visit of Nehemiah (433)
425		
420	Darius II Nothus (424–404) helped by Arsames to the throne	
415		Ezra, the Scribe, arrives in Jerusalem (417)
410		
405		
400	Artaxerxes II (404–358) Anabasis; Cyrus the Younger	
395		
390		
385		
380		
375		
370		
365		
360		
355	Artaxerxes III (355–338)	
350		
345		
340	Artaxerxes III defeats Nectanebo II	
335	Darius III (336–330)	
330	End of Persian Empire (–331)	
325	Alexander in Central Asia and Indus Valley	
320	Alexander dies in Babylon (–323)	
315		
310	Berosus composes history of Assyria-Babylonia	
305		
300		
295		
290		
285		
280		
275		

	PERSIA	PALESTINE and SYRIA
270		
265		
260		
255		
250		
245		

	GREEK WORLD	EGYPT
550	Solon (640–558)	
545		
540		
535		
530		
525		Amasis dies (525); followed by Psammetich; Cambyses conquers Egypt (525)
520		Ourmai's letter of lament
515		
510		Darius I builds canal to Suez Gulf, codifies Egyptian laws, builds military-religious outposts in Western oases and a Jewish military outpost in Elephantine
505	Pythagoras dies (ca. 507)	
500		
495		
490	Battle at Marathon	
485		Xerxes rules over Egypt and Sudan; High Priest Amenhotep
480		
475		
470		Court procedures in tomb robberies; government of western Thebes invested
465	Athenians send troops to help Inaros	Inaros' rebellion against Persia (–460); Amyrtaeus I
460	Age of Pericles (460–429) begins	Arsames appointed satrap over Egypt; High Priest Amenhotep, for supporting Inaros, removed by Pinehas, military commander

GREEK WORLD	EGYPT
455 Aeschylus (b. 525) dies (456)	Arsames makes Ah-hapi his administrator
450	Arsames appoints Psamtek to govern southern Egypt and
445 Sacred War (449–448): Athens vs. Sparta; thirty-year peace signed (445)	Nekht-nebef to govern northern Egypt; Psamtek sends corn to Athens; Greek and Carian mercenaries at Abu Simbel
440	Nekht-nebef governor of northern Egypt; Herihor appointed high priest (438)
435	
430 Peloponnesian War (431–404)	Nesunebded appointed governor at Tanis
425	
420	Nekht-hor-heb appointed by Arsames governor of Egypt (424)
415	Wenamon sent by Herihor to Byblos (419)
410	Jewish Temple at Elephantine destroyed
405 Sophocles (b. 496) Euripides (b. 489)	Wenamon builds Aghurmi temple in Siwa oasis; Nekht-hor-heb mourns Arsames
400 Xenophon in Cyrus the Younger's march	Amyrtaeus II seizes power
Thucydides (ca. 460–ca. 400)	High Priest Peinuzem I
395 Socrates' trial and death (399)	Nepherites establishes native rule
390 Corinthian War (394–387)	
385	Acoris (393–380); High Priest Psusennes
380	
375	Nectanebo I (Ramses III-Nekht-a-Neb) on the throne (379)
370	Pharnabazus brings his troops from Asia Minor, is opposed by Chabrias, then helped by Iphicrates
365	
360 Agesilaus leaves for Egypt (361)	Tachos (Ramses IV)

	GREEK WORLD	EGYPT
355		Nectanebo II (Ramses VI) starts sixteen-year reign
350	Demosthenes against Philip (351)	High Priest Peinuzem rewraps the mummy of Nectanebo I (Ramses III)
345		
340	Aristotle in Macedonia (342–332)	Nectanebo flees from victorious Artaxerxes III
335	Alexander succeeds Philip (336)	Second Persian domination of Egypt (342–332); Petosiris
330		Alexander in Egypt, founded Alexandria, received by High Priest Menkheperre in Siwa oasis
325		
	Philip Arrhidaeus	Ptolemy, son of Lagus, ruler of Egypt
320	Hellenistic period of Greek history starts	Ptolemy I (Soter) crowned king (308–285)
315		Ptolemy I in war with Seleucus
310	Seleucus I builds Antioch	
305		
300		Euclid (fl. 300)
295		Peinuzem II high priest
290		
285		Ptolemy II (Philadelphus (285–246)
280		Manetho composes history of Egypt
275		High Priest Si-amon builds in Memphis, seals the cache with royal mummies, supervises the transfer of Thutmose I obelisks from Heliopolis to Alexandria, builds himself a tomb in Siwa oasis
270	Aristarchus of Samos	
265		
260		

	GREEK WORLD	EGYPT
255		Eratosthenes, librarian of Alexandria library
250		
245	Archimedes of Syracuse	Archimedes in Alexandria; Septuagint translation of the Bible
240		
235	First Punic War	Ptolemy III (Euergetes) (246–221); Canopus Decree (238)

SUPPLEMENT

Astronomy and Chronology

Chapter I

THE FOUNDATIONS OF EGYPTIAN
CHRONOLOGY

A Mighty Tree

THE STUDENT of ancient history, especially the history of the
second millennium before the present era, is accustomed to
relate the chronology of the entire ancient East to Egyptian
reckoning. "A system of relative chronology can be established by
excavation in any country that has been long inhabited, but it is
left hanging in the air until linked up with Egypt, whether directly
or indirectly through a third region."[1] Kings and dynasties, law-
giving and building activity, wars and peace treaties of empires and
kingdoms are allocated to centuries according to the rule of Egyptian chronology. When a document is unearthed which records the
relations of some king with a pharaoh of a certain dynasty, the time
of the king becomes fixed because the date of the pharaoh is known.
The succession of the Assyrian and Babylonian kings with the dates
of their reigns is studied with the help of the so-called king-lists
but is constantly being adjusted to comply with Egyptian dates
wherever a synchronism is assumed. Thus the lawmaker king Ham-
murabi of the First Babylonian Dynasty, who for a long time was
placed in about −2100, in recent decades has been transferred to
about −1700, in order to synchronize the Egyptian Middle Kingdom
with the First Dynasty of Babylon, on the basis of material from
both places found in a common deposit on Crete. The past of the
Minoan culture on Crete and the past of Mycenae on the mainland

[1] O. G. S. Crawford, *Man and His Past* (London, 1921), p. 72.

of Hellas are likewise divided and apportioned among the centuries, with Egypt playing the defining role.

Egyptian chronology must be a mighty trunk to support branches of the history of many kingdoms and cultures of the past. Is Egyptian chronology itself really rooted in strong evidence? It would seem that it is now too late to raise the question: not only the entire scientific literature in Egyptology but also complete libraries dealing with man's past have been composed according to the scheme set up by Egyptologists for all other branches of ancient history.

Everyone is agreed that Egyptian chronology is so well devised, century by century, decade by decade, and often year by year, that no new evidence could break down this massive growth. What, then, is the foundation of this system, which the Egyptologists have concluded is absolutely firm and from which scholars in other fields have confidently borrowed their data and standards?

The Egyptians are not known to have had any continuous system of counting years by eras. Events were dated according to the ruling years of the current monarch. Hatshepsut's visit to the Divine Land took place in the ninth year of the queen; the battle of Kadesh occurred in the fifth year of Ramses II. Sometimes, however, a king and his son ruled together; in that case the chronology of the dynasty cannot be built merely by adding the years of the monarchs, since it is not always clear whether the years of the ruler on the throne must be reduced by the number of years of coregency. Then, too, the length of the reigns can be established only approximately from the documents: the highest year number mentioned in a king's monumental inscription is accepted as a tentative terminal date, but it is not necessarily the last year of his rule. In many instances it is impossible to establish, from the data on the monumental documents, the succession of kings in a given dynasty. Nor—what is far more important and decisive, and I wish to stress it—is the sequence of the dynasties by any means definitely determined. In only a few individual cases is there historical evidence to indicate the order of two dynasties that ruled consecutively.

The monumental evidence, it is admitted, does not provide material sufficient by itself to construct a chronological system. If such a system can be built by other means, the monumental inscriptions may help here and there in fixing more precisely the dates of events in the reigns of individual kings.

A few documents, like the Torino Papyrus, broken into innumerable fragments and reassembled by painstaking yet not faultless efforts, and the Palermo Stone, both starting the genealogy of kings from the earliest times, do not really reach the age of the New Kingdom, which together with the Late Kingdom comprises the period of this reconstruction. Yet for the periods these documents cover, startling lines of succession are named, such as over one hundred kings for the Thirteenth Dynasty, the last of the Middle Kingdom. An exaggerated effort to make the earlier history of Egypt seem of great duration renders these documents of very limited value.

"A Skeleton Clothed with Flesh"

"It is no exaggeration to say that we continue to arrange the history of Egypt and to place the facts of this history in the very same order that is a legacy of Julius Africanus who wrote in the third Christian century."[1] Africanus, one of the Fathers of the Church, preserved the legacy of Manetho of the third pre-Christian century. Manetho was an Egyptian writer, historian, polemicist, and anti-Semite, inventor of a baseless identification of Moses with Typhon, the evil spirit, and the Israelites with the Hyksos; also, contradicting himself, he identified Moses with the rebellious priest Osarsiph, of much later times, who called on the lepers of Jerusalem to help him in his war with his own country.

In composing his history of Egypt and putting together a register of its dynasties, Manetho was guided by the desire to prove to the Greeks, the masters of his land, that the Egyptian people and culture were much older than theirs or than the Babylonian nation and civilization. Berosus, a Chaldean priest and a contemporary of

[1] R. Weill, *Bases, méthodes et résultats de la chronologie égyptienne* (Paris, 1926), p. 1.

Manetho, tried to prove to the Greeks under the Seleucid rulers the antiquity of Assyro-Babylonian history and therefore he extended that history into tens of thousands of years. Similarly, Eratosthenes, a learned Greek from Cyrenaica, chief librarian at the Alexandrian library under Ptolemy II and III, and a younger contemporary of both Manetho and Berosus, tried to prove the excellence of his Greek nation by claiming for it a great antiquity reaching back into mythical times. It is to his reckoning that we owe the still much-accepted date −1183 for the fall of Troy (or 871 years before the beginning of the Seleucid era in −312).

This tendency similarly displayed by these three men must be kept in mind when we deal with the chronology of the ancient world.

Manetho's list of dynasties is preserved in two versions. Those of Eusebius and Africanus differ especially with respect to the duration of the dynasties; they are both at variance with the royal successions as quoted by Josephus from Manetho.[2] Besides these discrepancies, the main confusion arises from the fact that it is not easy to determine which of the kings known from monumental inscriptions are meant by Manetho. The list is "so terribly mangled by copyists that it would be most unsafe to trust its data" unless it is confirmed by other evidence.[3]

Sequences of kings with strange names never found on monuments fill the various versions of Manetho. There is reason to think that the copyists mutilated a list that had come from the hand of its author in an already chaotic and untrustworthy state.

"The chronology of Manetho" is "a late, careless and uncritical compilation, which can be proven wrong from the contemporary monuments in the vast majority of cases, where such monuments have survived."[4]

What we have of Manetho is "only a garbled abridgement in the works of the Christian chronographers [Africanus, Eusebius, and Syncellus]. . . . In spite of all defects this division into dynasties

[2] Compiled in *Manetho*, trans. Waddell (Loeb Classical Library).
[3] H. R. Hall, "Egyptian Chronology," *Cambridge Ancient History*, I, 167.
[4] Breasted, *A History of Egypt* (2nd ed.), p. 23.

has taken so firm a root . . . that there is but little chance of its ever being abandoned. In the forms in which the book has reached us there are inaccuracies of the most glaring kind. . . . Africanus and Eusebius often do not agree. . . . The royal names are apt to be incredibly distorted. . . . The lengths of reigns frequently differ in the two versions, as well as often showing wide departures from the definitely ascertained figures. When textual and other critics have done their best or worst, the reconstructed Manetho remains full of imperfections. . . . None the less, his book still dominates our studies. . . ."[5]

Despite the fact that Manetho's lists were discredited by the documentary evidence of the Eighteenth and Nineteenth Dynasties, the best known of all and rich in documents, the dynasties for which there is no documentary evidence were preserved in accordance with Manetho's scheme, since there were no extant monuments to refute those parts of the lists. The fact that in many cases no documents were found to substantiate the existence of such dynasties was not always regarded as an obstacle sufficient by itself. There are almost no tangible clues even to the existence of Manetho's Seventh to Tenth Dynasties or some other, later dynasties.

The totals of the years of Manetho's dynasties were earnestly debated; they were stretched or contracted according to the convenience of the historiographers. This could be done without fear of challenge as no one in modern times credits Manetho with numerical exactness.

Efforts to identify the kings known from contemporary inscriptions with the kings in Manetho's lists are often reduced to mere choosing. To illuminate this, let us consider the following example. When rich monumental material was found regarding the reign of a pharaoh for whom historiographers selected the name of Ramses III, he was not identified with any king in the lists of Manetho. Not being found in these lists, he was assigned to the Twentieth Dynasty, probably because the kings of that dynasty are unnamed in the dynastic lists of Africanus and Eusebius, though Georgius Syncellus, a Byzantine monk and copyist, preserved a list of kings

[5] Gardiner, *Egypt of the Pharaohs*, pp. 46–47.

of that dynasty, but none with the regal name of Ramses III. The twelve (unnamed) kings of Diospolis of the Twentieth Dynasty reigned 135 years (Africanus) or 178 years (Eusebius), and it seemed safe to place Ramses III and succeeding Ramseses in this dynasty. Actually, as I tried to show in this volume, Ramses III was Nectanebo of Manetho's lists, and he belonged to the last dynasty of Egyptian kings, the Thirtieth. To put ten dynasties after him—the Twenty-first to the Thirtieth—is to create a distortion for which Manetho can be made to bear only a small share of the responsibility, if any, for he did not assign Ramses III to the Twentieth Dynasty. Consequently this king is represented by a fictitious Ramses III in the twelfth century and by Nectanebo I in the fourth century.

The transition from the Twenty-first to the Twenty-second Dynasty is generally admitted to be a hazy chronological affair. As this reconstruction discloses, the Twenty-first Dynasty reigned in the oases before, during, and after the Twentieth Dynasty (the same as the Twenty-ninth and the Thirtieth) in the valley of the Nile. The Twenty-second or Libyan Dynasty, however, reigned after the Eighteenth Dynasty, as is left to be demonstrated in one of the intermediary volumes of the present work.

About the Twenty-fourth Dynasty, Syncellus, copying Africanus' version of Manetho's list, wrote: "The twenty-fourth dynasty. Bochoris of Sais, for 6 years: in his reign a lamb spoke [here is a short lacuna in the manuscript] 990 years." Eusebius wrote similarly, but he differs greatly regarding the duration of this dynasty: "Bochoris of Sais for 44 years: in his reign a lamb spoke. Total, 44 years." Such information, in lieu of historical material, about the Twenty-fourth Dynasty is entirely useless. We have to guess whether 6 years or 44 or 990 is correct.

Notwithstanding the fact that the chronology of Manetho is branded as a "careless and uncritical compilation" which monumental evidence has shown to be wrong in the vast majority of cases, it serves as the framework of the history of Egypt. The division into dynasties, as given by Manetho, has remained in use to this day. His work is regarded as presenting the continuity of the historical traditions of Egypt, while the sequence of events in the past of peoples lacking such continuous tradition remains speculative since there is no framework in which to order the archaeological data.

"Absolute certainty in these matters is only possible where a continuous literary tradition has always existed. The modern study of European and American prehistoric archaeology, for instance, which has no literary tradition by its side, must always remain largely guesswork. The main scheme of the history of ancient Egypt is now a certainty, not a mere hypothesis; but it is very doubtful if it would ever have become a certainty if its construction had depended entirely on the archaeologists. The complete skeleton of the scheme was provided by the continuous literary tradition preserved by the Egyptian priest Manetho; this has been clothed with flesh by the archaeologists."[6]

These sentences were written by the same author (H. R. Hall) who was quoted on a previous page concerning the mangled condition and untrustworthiness of the extant texts of Manetho.

But actually it was not the archaeologists who originally filled out the scheme of Manetho with data derived from hieroglyphic texts chiseled on monuments or written on papyri. The strange fact is that *long before the hieroglyphics were read for the first time* the kings of Egypt were placed in the centuries in which conventional chronology still keeps them prisoner.

Who First Placed Ramses III in the Twelfth Century?

In 1799, four miles from Rosetta at the western mouth of the Delta, Monsieur Boussart, a French officer in General Bonaparte's army, found a stone inscribed three ways: in Greek, in hieroglyphics, and in an unknown cursive writing occasionally put on papyri, later called "Demotic" script. Thomas Young, English physician and physicist, who was first to explain color sensation as due to the pres-

[6] H. R. Hall, *The Oldest Civilization of Greece* (1901), pp. 18–19.

ence of specific nerve endings for red, green, and violet in the retina of the eye, first to understand and measure astigmatism and to discover the phenomenon of light interference, the strongest argument in favor of the wave theory of light, for which he was much derided, was also the first to read a few words in hieroglyphics, the name Ptolemy in the Rosetta Stone—the name was circled in an oval (cartouche)—having been the first clue. The story of his efforts and successes and tragic relations with Champollion is an engrossing one. It appears that Young achieved much more in reading hieroglyphics than is generally credited to him.

Jean François Champollion (1790–1832) at the age of eleven heard of the Rosetta Stone and determined to dedicate himself to the task of deciphering the hieroglyphics; the precocious boy studied Coptic and became engrossed in the philology of oriental languages. Only twenty years later, on December 21, 1821, the simple thought came to his mind that since there were about three times as many hieroglyphic signs on the Rosetta Stone as there were Greek words in the parallel text, the hieroglyphics, or pictures of men in various positions, and parts of the human body, flowers and birds, do not stand for ideas—a centuries-old conviction—and are not symbols in this sense, but are phonetic signs or letters (almost exclusively consonants, similar in this respect to the Hebrew script). On September 22, 1822, he announced his success to the Académie in Paris. In 1825 he was able to translate an inscription of Amenhotep III. Yet "for three more decades, even scientists were not willing to admit anything more than the fact that at best a few royal names could be deciphered, but they insisted that everything else was pure phantasy."[1] Not until 1866 did the discovery of another three-script text—the Canopus Decree, of which the reader will find more on a later page—completely confirm Champollion's reading. By then he had been dead for thirty-four years.

Then how soon after Champollion's first reading of the hieroglyphics did the deciphering of monumental inscriptions or papyri texts supply the clue to the problem we are interested in, namely, the dating of Ramses III's reign? One would surmise it must have

[1] Johannes Friedrich, *Extinct Languages* (1957), p. 25.

been in the days of Lepsius (1810–84) or Chabas (1817–82) or H. Brugsch (1827–94), the men who advanced Egyptology to the level of an exact science—but this is not the case. The fact is that Ramses III was placed in the twelfth century before Champollion's reading of hieroglyphics and, thus, before any monumental inscription would justify such allocation.

In a book by a Scottish psychiatrist, J. C. Prichard, published in 1819, or two years before that memorable day in Champollion's life, on p. 61 it is stated that Ramses III started his reign in −1147. Obviously this estimate could not be based on any hieroglyphic text. Prichard apparently took his dates from some earlier chronologist. Then is there any reference to Ramses III in classical authors that permitted this conclusion? Neither Herodotus nor Thucydides nor any other classical author-historian mentions Ramses III—at least, no such reference is known to exist.

The bas-reliefs of Medinet Habu, a very impressive group of battle scenes, had of course not been unnoticed—since antiquity every inquisitive traveler to Thebes who crossed the Nile to look at the Colossi of Memnon (statues of Amenhotep III), or the mortuary temple of Queen Hatshepsut at Deir el Bahari, or the Ramesseum, the mortuary temple of Ramses II, and the broken colossus of that king, lying in the dust, visited also the temple of Medinet Habu. The king who built this mortuary temple received from modern scholars the name of Ramses III.

It appears that the French chronologist Joseph Justus Scaliger (1540–1609) made the earliest attempt to date the Egyptian dynasties of Manetho in his *Thesaurus temporum* (1606). "Sothic period" calculation, an astronomical clue to Egyptian chronology, seemed to give some promise. In the seventeenth and eighteenth centuries no new attempts to date the kings of Egypt were made. Prichard's date for Ramses III's mounting the throne was changed by Rosellini (1841) to −1477 with no explanation; Champollion-Figeac (1778–1867), the brother of the decipherer, in 1839 placed Ramses III in −1279, but, again, without giving any ground or authority.

When the texts accompanying the bas-reliefs of Medinet Habu

were read it was found that the king fought the Philistines and this
fitted well with his dating in the twelfth century, the time of the
biblical Judges: in the book of Judges Philistines play an important
role. Then was there any ground for revising the estimate of pre-
Champollion days?

But did Ramses III battle the Philistines?

Chapter II

SIRIUS

THE DYNASTIES OF Manetho were made the framework of Egyptian history; only his mathematical figures are not respected because they are considered "absurdly high."[1] Historians, however, believe they have astronomical evidence to determine the numerical values for the basic plan.

No records of solar and lunar eclipses were found in Egypt, as they were in Babylonia.[2] The Sothic period, a computation based on the rising of the star Sothis (Spdt in Egyptian), or Sirius, became the alpha and omega for the numerical construction of Egyptian chronology.

The Egyptian year, for a considerably long period of history, consisted of 360 days; at some date in history, in a calendar reform, five days were added to the year. Under the Ptolemies another reform was contemplated—introducing a leap year every four years. In −238, in the ninth year of Ptolemy III Euergetes, a priestly decree was published in the Delta. In the last century it was found in Tanis and is known as the Canopus Decree for the place where the conclave to reform the calendar had taken place. Like the Rosetta Stone, it was composed in Greek, in hieroglyphic Egyptian, and in demotic Egyptian—and if it had been found before the Rosetta Stone it would have been the key to deciphering the hieroglyphics.

In order that the feast of the star Isis and other festivals "should not wander around the seasons," it was decreed at Canopus that

---

[1] Breasted, *A History of Egypt* (2nd ed.), p. 23.

[2] "Heaven not[?] devoured the moon" is recorded in the time of one of the Libyan kings (Takelot II) and is usually interpreted as a reference to a lunar eclipse.

one day every four years should be added and the calendar freed from dependence on observation of the star Isis.

This reform did not take root because of the opposition of dominant groups among the priests who would not agree to make the feast of Isis stationary with respect to the seasons. The introduction of a leap year is connected with the name of Julius Caesar. Octavianus Augustus made the calendar with leap years the legal calendar in Rome, and a few years later, in −26 or by other calculations in −29, introduced it in Alexandria in Egypt.

The Egyptians of the Hellenistic and Roman periods knew that the length of the year is 365¼ days: the Canopus Decree and the writings of Diodorus of Sicily[3] prove it. It is possible that Caesar borrowed this knowledge from the Egyptians, but they themselves were reluctant to make their religious year equal to their astronomical year.

The Roman authors of the first pre-Christian and following centuries, who felt themselves privileged to have a better calendar, were familiar with the simple computation that a quarter of a day each year accumulates to a full year in 1461 years of 365 days.

In the year +238, or four hundred and seventy-five years after the Canopus Decree (−238), Censorinus, a Roman author, wrote: "The Egyptians, in forming their great year, do not take the moon into consideration; the Greeks call it [this great year] *cynic*, the Latins call it *canicularis*, because it begins at the rising of the Dog Star on the first day of the month which is called by the Egyptians Thot. . . . Also the span of four of their years is shorter than the span of four natural years by, approximately, one day; this reestablishes correspondence on the one thousand four hundred and sixty-first year. This [great] year is also called by some the heliacal year, and by others, 'the year of the God.' "[4] Censorinus then went

---

[3] "They add five and a quarter days to the twelve months and in this way fill out the cycle of the year. But they do not intercalate months or subtract days, as most of the Greeks do. They appear to have made carefully observations of the eclipses both of the sun and of the moon, and predict them, foretelling without error all the events which actually occur." Book I, 50 (trans. Oldfather).

[4] *Liber de Die Natali*, XVIII.

on to explain the "supreme year" of Aristotle, which lasts until sun, moon, and planets return to the position from which they started, and the cataclysmic year, comprising the period between two successive world catastrophes, whether by deluge or fire, which, according to Aristarchus of Samos, is 2484 solar years.

Censorinus explained Sothis as the Egyptian name for Sirius, the Dog Star of the southern constellation Canis Major. For part of the year this star is not visible in the Northern Hemisphere, where Egypt is, and every solar year, at the same time in the summer, it returns to its initial position in the sky of Egypt.

Besides the 365¼ rotations of the earth during the year, its revolution around the sun produces one additional rotation of the earth with respect to the stars. Because of this the stars cross the horizon about four minutes earlier every night.

Starting with the vernal equinox, the Northern Hemisphere is inclined with its illuminated part to the south (so that the Arctic is illuminated) and its shadowed part to the north. After the summer solstice the night side of the Northern Hemisphere slowly turns southward and the stars of the south begin to appear. It is in the second half of the summer that Sirius emerges in the sky of Egypt from the brightness of the daybreak, a short time before the sunrise.

At first the star comes up only a little over the horizon before the rising sun blots out its light and that of other stars. Each succeeding night it rises a few minutes earlier and mounts higher in the sky before daybreak. The heliacal rising of a star is on the morning it is seen for the first time preceding the rising sun.

The heliacal morning appearance of Sirius announced the flooding of the Nile, which swelled when the tropical rains fell in torrents in Ethiopia and the snow in the mountains melted. The dog days (from the Dog Star) in ancient Egypt comprised the end of July and the greater part of August, the hottest season of the year.

On a calendar that has only 365 days to the year and is short one day every four years, the heliacal rising of any star, including Sirius, would occur one day later every four years.[5]

---

[5] This calculation is far from being exact, as the Julian year of 365¼ days is not the true (sidereal) year; 1460 Julian years of 365¼ days (or

As explained by Censorinus, the "great year" begins with the year when the heliacal (morning) rising of Sirius is on the first of the month Thot. After four years it would rise on the second of Thot. After 1461 years of 365 days, or 1460 years of 365¼ days, Sirius would again rise heliacally on the first of Thot. This span of time comprises one Sothic period. This means that the first of Thot, or the New Year, and all the days of the year move through the four seasons during the Sothic period. Sirius rises heliacally each summer but on the first of Thot only once (for four consecutive years) in 1460 years; this date, nevertheless, is assumed by modern scholars to have been celebrated yearly as the day of the symbolic rising of Sirius or the day of the Opening of the Year.

Censorinus added that in the one hundredth year before he wrote his work (*Liber de Die Natali*) a new Sothic period had begun. He wrote this book in the year 238 of the present era, and indicated that the new Sothic period had begun in the year 139; the previous period, it is easily computed, started in 1322 before this era.[6] The date 1322 B.C. (or −1321) forms the very foundation of Egyptian chronology.

Theon of Alexandria in Egypt, an author of the fourth century of this era, wrote that the apocatastasis of the Egyptian year—the pe-

---

1461 years of 365 days) differ from 1460 sidereal years by about nine days, making a difference of about thirty-six years in the Sothic period. How, then, could the Egyptians have acquired their knowledge of the Sothic period by direct observations? In search of an answer to this question it was argued that, by an exceedingly rare chance, in relation to Sirius, Egypt had a natural Julian year and not a sidereal year because of two phenomena: the precession of the equinoxes, or the spinning of the terrestrial axis with a period of about 26,000 years, and the orientation of Sirius in relation to other stars, worked together, in the time from the fourth to the first millennium before the present era, to make, with respect to Sirius, the Julian and not the sidereal year more representative of the motion of the earth at the latitudes of Egypt.

[6] It should be noted that between the first of Thot of the first year of the present era and the first of Thot of the first year before this era, there are actually not two years, but only one. Between a certain date in the year 139 of this era and the corresponding date of the year 1322 before this era, there are 1460 and not 1461 years. Therefore the year 1322 B.C. is but −1321 in astronomical computations. (Unless otherwise indicated, all dates that are mentioned in this book are "historical" rather than "astronomical." The difference is that "astronomical" dating assumes that there was a year 0, while "historical" dating assumes that there was not any year 0.)

riod in which a disregard of the Julian reform as introduced in Alexandria by Augustus causes an accumulated error of an entire year
—came to its close in the fifth year of Augustus or the year 26 before
the present era, the same year in which, according to some authorities, the calendar reform was enforced in Alexandria. As mentioned
previously, Censorinus placed the beginning of a new Sothic
period in the year +139.

On a manuscript of Theon an annotation was discovered written
in "barbarian Greek,"[7] which says that "since Menophres and till the
end of the era of Augustus, or the beginning of the era of Diocle-
tian, there were 1605 years." The last year of the era of Augustus
was the year +283 to +284. Reducing this by 1605 years, one arrives
at —1321, the same year when a Sothic period started, according to
Censorinus.

In order to create a chronological table, the first step was to identify Menophres. It is usually maintained that Theon's Menophres
was Ramses I, the founder of the Nineteenth Dynasty.[8] Thus the
year —1321 is fixed as the year that Ramses I mounted the throne,
and as only one year is allotted to his reign, the year —1321 must
have been the year of his reign.

It would have been an easy task to construct the chronology
with this one fixed date had the Egyptians computed the ruling
years of their kings or other events by the years of Sothic periods,
but they did not: there is no known instance of an event being recorded by the serial year of a Sothic period. There is no Egyptian
document known to mention the Sothic period or to state, "In such
or such year of the Sothic era." According to the view predominant
at present, the Sothic period is not regarded as an era by which the
ancients reckoned the years; it is employed by moderns only as a
device to calculate chronological dates. But for that purpose vanish-
ingly few references in ancient texts are available: the entire heritage of ancient Egypt was searched for any possible reference to the

[7] T. H. Martin, "Mémoire sur la date historique d'un renouvellement de la
période sothiaque," in *Mémoires présentés par divers savants à l'Académie
des Inscriptions et Belles-Lettres*, Série I, Vol. 8, Pt. 1 (Paris, 1869).

[8] L. Borchardt prefers to see in Menophres King Seti the Great, son of Ramses
I and father of Ramses II.

rising of Sothis, even if not on the first of Thot, but with very meager results.

In a papyrus found in the precinct of the Illahun temple at Faiyum it is said that Sothis rose on the first of the month Pharmouti in the seventh year of an unnamed king, apparently of the Middle Kingdom. Upon deliberation, L. Borchardt limited the choice to Senwosret III and Amenemhet III, and upon further consideration concluded that in this alternative, Senwosret should be given the preference. The month Pharmouti being defined as the fourth month of the second, or winter, season, its displacement to the summer season, when the Dog Star rises heliacally, indicates that the seventh year of Senwosret was over 900 years after the beginning of a Sothic period or 555 years before the end of the Sothic period in −1321, four years being allowed for every day of retreat of the first day of Thot from the night of the heliacal rising of the Dog Star. The seventh year of Senwosret is computed to have been −1876.

The time of one king of the Twelfth Dynasty being established, the dates of other kings of the same dynasty can also be calculated, if not precisely, at least approximately. Accordingly the Twelfth Dynasty expired in or about −1788.

On a stone found in Elephantine there is a reference to a rising of Sothis in the days of Thutmose III of the Eighteenth Dynasty, and it is interpreted as a heliacal rising[9]; the month and the day are given but the year of Thutmose's reign when the event took place is not given; this makes calculations vague, besides the incertitude as to whether a heliacal rising was meant.

The so-called Ebers Papyrus is known for its calendar of twelve months of thirty days each, with no epagomenal days at the end or at the beginning of the year, thus of a year of 360 days; the papyrus contains certain data that, upon revision and much text emendation and guesswork, connect the festival of the Opening of the Year to a certain date under Amenhotep I of the Eighteenth Dynasty. But, besides much emendation, the very fact that the Ebers calendar is

---

[9] L. Borchardt, *Quellen und Forschungen zur Zeitbestimmung der Aegyptischen Geschichte*, 2 (Cairo, 1935), 18–19.

not of 365 but of 360 days confounds every computation in which
a quarter of a day difference in a year is the basis for the chronological use of the heliacal rise of Sothis (Sirius).

Therefore only the Illahun reference in the papyrus of the Middle
Kingdom and the other reference, of the Theon manuscript, to the
era of Menophres can be counted on for the work of erecting a
chronology based on astronomy, or on Sirius' heliacal rising, or a
Sothic period of 1460 years.

Between the end of the Twelfth Dynasty and the beginning of
the Nineteenth Dynasty of Ramses I time must be reserved for the
Thirteenth Dynasty, the last one of the Middle Kingdom, for the
three or four dynasties of the Hyksos who ruled during the long
period of transition from the Middle Kingdom to the New Kingdom,
and for the glorious Eighteenth Dynasty with which the New Kingdom began. Also the presumably dark period following the end of
the Eighteenth Dynasty and preceding the beginning of the Nineteenth Dynasty must be inserted between −1788 and −1321.

The time of the Eighteenth Dynasty was computed with the
help of astronomy too. "The dates of certain new moon festivals
which were celebrated on certain days of the month in certain years
of the kings Thutmose III and Amenhotep I [of the Eighteenth
Dynasty] can, by computing back from the epoch of Menophres,
be fixed to the years 1474 and 1550."[10] This is not at all simple: the
computations of the stations of the moon were combined with the
calculation of the heliacal risings of Sirius. A certain new-moon
festival of Amenhotep I was fixed at −1550, and another of Thutmose III at −1474. Amenhotep I was the successor to Ahmose, the
founder of the Eighteenth Dynasty, and so the date of the beginning of the New Kingdom is fixed, too, at −1580.

The last step—to establish the dates of individual events mentioned in inscriptions—seemed to be a simple matter after the dates
of the festivals were fixed. So we read that Thutmose III left Egypt
on his first campaign to Palestine on April 19, −1483.[11]

10 Hall, "Egyptian Chronology," *Cambridge Ancient History* (1st ed.), I, 170.
11 A. T. Olmstead, *History of Palestine and Syria* (1931), p. 132. Breasted
places the event at April 19, −1479.

Two Hundred Years Are Too Few
and 1660 Are Too Many

The first difficulty arises with the number of years remaining for the period between the Twelfth and the Eighteenth Dynasties, which, for historical reasons, seems inadequate to embrace the Thirteenth Dynasty and all the Hyksos dynasties. Several of the kings of the Thirteenth Dynasty, as well as of the Hyksos dynasties, had long reigns. "It will be admitted by all who have studied the material for the history of the time that to allow only two centuries for the period between the Twelfth and the Eighteenth Dynasties is difficult."[1] How could these two centuries (−1788 to −1580) embrace the historical succession of reigns and especially the wide span of cultural development?

There appeared to be two avenues of escape, which have been outlined in *Ages in Chaos,* Volume I. One could attempt to show that if one hundred years were assigned to the Thirteenth Dynasty the second hundred years would suffice for the time of the Hyksos, although Josephus, who used Manetho, wrote that the Hyksos had ruled for 511 years. This was the way chosen by Eduard Meyer, who found that one hundred years was enough for the Hyksos. Despite the argument against it expressed above, the "one hundred years for the Hyksos" view prevailed.

The other method of reconciling history with chronology, constructed with the aid of astronomy, is even more extreme. In order to reconcile the reference to Sothis in the papyrus of Illahun of the Middle Kingdom and the date (−1580) established for the beginning of the New Kingdom, another Sothic period of 1460 Julian years must be inserted. Thus, instead of two hundred years, 1660 years must be allotted to this interval; the history of the Middle Kingdom and of the Old Kingdom must be pushed back by an additional Sothic period; and the history of Egypt must be extended by the same number of years. This point of view was propounded

[1] Hall, "Egyptian Chronology," *Cambridge Ancient History* (1st ed.), I, 168.

and defended by Flinders Petrie, but its supporters remained in a small minority.

From the viewpoint of the historical material, two hundred years appear insufficient to include the ruling years of the kings of the Thirteenth and the Fourteenth to the Seventeenth (Hyksos) Dynasties, and to allow for the cultural changes that Egypt underwent. On the other hand, 1600-odd years for the same period seem excessive.

"Were the Sothic date unknown, our evidence would not require more than 400 or at most 500 years between the two [from the end of the Twelfth to the beginning of the Eighteenth] Dynasties."[2] And this is the stretch of time allotted to the period in question in *Ages in Chaos,* Volume I ("The Length of the Hyksos Period").

It was not proposed to remove the beginning of the New Kingdom to a later date; all agreed that the New Kingdom is definitely established in time. If the dates of the Middle Kingdom or the Old Kingdom are at all open to discussion, historical dates starting with the New Kingdom are regarded as almost as firmly fixed as the order of the stellar sky. Because of this the fixed and established chronology of the world begins with −1580, the year of the expulsion of the Hyksos and the beginning of the Eighteenth Dynasty. This "is the earliest date," it is said, "of which we can be absolutely certain within the margin of a few years either way."[3]

Historiography divides the past of the world into two great parts: the period before the New Kingdom in Egypt in which chronological hypotheses are not forbidden, and the period from the New

[2] Ibid., p. 169. Maspero, von Bissing, and a number of other scholars refused to accept either view and rejected the Sothic calculations. *"Les périodes sothiaques, au lieu de simplifier les calculs chronologiques, n'ont d'autre résultat pour nous que d'y introduire une nouvelle inconnue et peut-être une nouvelle chance d'erreur."* G. Jéquier, *Histoire de la civilisation égyptienne des origines à la conquête d'Alexandre* (Paris, 1913), pp. 26–27.

[3] Hall, "Egyptian Chronology," op. cit., p. 170. See also Albright, *From the Stone Age to Christianity,* p. 166; Breasted, *A History of Egypt,* p. 22. Also, T. Säve-Söderbergh, "C-14 Dating and Egyptian Chronology" in *Radiocarbon Variations and Absolute Chronology,* ed. I. U. Olsson (Stockholm, 1970), p. 38: "The beginning of the XVIIIth Dynasty is dated to one of two alternatives separated by not more than twenty years," the rest of the reigns "between the 16th and 11th century" having "margins of a few years only."

Kingdom to the present, in which the historians have no great changes to propose, no greater than a few years for one or another event. All the histories of the various peoples are geared firmly together from −1580 on.

Statements of Censorinus and Theon Combined

The established chronological system depends entirely on the accuracy of the statements of Censorinus and Theon and on the correctness of the interpretation of these statements. The first of them told when a Sothic period ended, and by a simple subtraction of 1460 Julian years we can determine when it started. The second, or his annotator, gave the name of, presumably, a king who lived at the beginning of this period. Learning from Theon the name of the king who inaugurated the era, and placing this king in the time indicated by Censorinus as the beginning of the Sothic period, the historians have a fixed point on which to build Egyptian chronology and the history of the ancient world.

Censorinus and Theon, like many other authors of the third and fourth centuries of the present era, were epigoni of a great age in science and literature, compilers and commentators with little access to the original sources of ancient wisdom.

Censorinus' *Liber de Die Natali* is generally regarded as the work of an author who did not mingle acquired knowledge with fancies of his own. The sources of his information, however, are often in the writings of his predecessors, not all of them conscious of the importance of separating fact and supposition.

Theon of Alexandria was a prolific compiler of scholia and commentaries, but in the opinion of some modern scholars his work reveals neither a profound thinker nor an exact writer. Here and there copyists have added to his works; the "barbarous" language of the remark about the Egyptian calendar, attributed to him, provoked the suspicion that it was an addition.[1]

[1] Martin, *Mémoires, Académie des Inscriptions et Belles-Lettres*, Série 1, Vol. 8, Pt. 1, pp. 232 ff.

It is a very hazardous undertaking to build the history of the ancient world with a chronology constructed on a combination of statements by two authors of the third and fourth centuries, even if these statements are in harmony with each other. We know how many erroneous assertions, even sheer inventions and gross absurdities, were stored in Latin authors who wrote about Egypt. Here, for example, are some of Tacitus' statements: "In the consulate of Paulus Fabius and Lucius Vitellius [+34, under Tiberius], after a long period of ages, the bird known as the phoenix visited Egypt, and supplied the learned of that country and of Greece with the material for long disquisitions on the miracle. . . . As to the term of years [between two visits of the bird], the tradition varies. The generally received number is five hundred; but there are some who assert that its visits fall at intervals of 1461 years, and that it was in the reigns, first of Sesostris, then of Amasis, and finally of Ptolemy (third of the Macedonian Dynasty), that the three earlier phoenixes flew to the city called Heliopolis with a great escort of common birds. . . ."[2] Pointing out that between Ptolemy III and Tiberius less than two hundred and fifty years elapsed, Tacitus expressed the opinion that one of the phoenixes was spurious, "but that the bird occasionally appears in Egypt is unquestioned." Not differently wrote Pliny, who cited Manilius to the effect "that the period of the Great Year coincides with the life of the bird, and the same indications of the seasons and stars return again."[3] Naming his authorities, Pliny gave the year of the consulship of Quintus Plautius and Sextus Papinius (+36) as the date when a phoenix flew to Egypt.

Censorinus and Theon are among those writers of late antiquity who seem to consider it legitimate to retroject a 1460-year period into the Egyptian past. But no such Sothic period is ever mentioned by the Egyptians themselves. The Sothic theories of late writers such as Censorinus and Theon (or his annotator) are in no way a sufficiently strong base on which to erect the entire history of the ancient world. Indeed, unless we can identify Menophres, named by Theon, Censorinus' own statement will remain worthless with respect to the chronology of the New Kingdom.

[2] Tacitus, *The Annals*, trans. J. Jackson, VI, 28.
[3] Pliny, *Natural History*, X, 2.

Who Was Menophres?

Who was Menophres, whose name, according to Theon, was given to the Egyptian era? Theon did not write that Menophres was a king. He may have been a sage, or an astronomer who computed the period, or his name may have been given to the epoch for some other merit. These possibilities are not excluded as long as we have confidence in the accuracy of Theon's statement; if we lack such confidence the existence of Menophres must be doubted from the very beginning. In any event, nowhere in Egyptian sources can any mention of the era of Menophres be found.

A scholar in the last century expressed the opinion that Menophres stands for Men-Nofre, the Egyptian name for Memphis.[1] This explanation was in its time rejected,[2] but it has a definite appeal because the observation of Sirius by the priests of Memphis was regarded as valid for all Egypt, at least in Hellenistic times. The heliacal rise of Sirius is more than four days earlier in Thebes (Luxor, Karnak) than in Memphis (near Cairo), as every degree of north latitude means a later appearance of the southern star by approximately one day. From the mouth of the Nile at Alexandria to Syene (Aswan) there is a difference of 7°1'. When Sirius rose on the first day of Thot in Memphis, it had not yet been seen in Sais or Tanis in the Delta, and in Thebes it had already been seen for the fifth night, and for the seventh night in Syene. Then which of these days was regarded as the day of heliacal rising for calendar purposes? Olympiodorus,[3] a Greek scholar who lived in Egypt in the

[1] J. B. Biot, *Etudes sur l'astronomie indienne et sur l'astronomie chinoise* (Paris, 1862), pp. xxxvi–xxxix.

[2] Cf. Martin, *Mémoires, Académie des Inscriptions et Belles-Lettres*, 1 (1869), 275. In recent times D. B. Redford, *History and Chronology of the Eighteenth Dynasty of Egypt: Seven Studies* (Toronto, 1967), pp. 214–15, and other authorities whom he mentions have revived the view that Menophres stands for Memphis.

[3] A. J. Letronne, "Nouvelles recherches sur le calendrier des anciens égyptiens," *Mémoires, Académie des Inscriptions et Belles-Lettres*, XXIV, Pt. 2 (Paris, 1864); J. L. Ideler, *Meteorologia veterum Graecorum et Romanorum* (Berlin, 1832).

fifth century of the present era, solved this difficulty, unsolved by
the founder of the "Berlin School" of Egyptologists,[4] by explaining
that the date of the rising of the star at Memphis was accepted also
in Alexandria. Eduard Meyer, not aware of the statement in Olympiodorus, wondered what could have been the basis of Sirius dates
if the star makes its heliacal appearance on different dates at different latitudes in Egypt. He therefore thought that no real observation was the basis of Sothic dates and that they were placed in the
calendar on days calculated in advance. L. Borchardt, another of
the greats of the Egyptian astronomical chronology, also showed
his unawareness of the passage in Olympiodorus; he assumed that
Heliopolis' date was valid for all of Egypt.[5] The explanation of
Olympiodorus makes it rather probable that Menophres means
Men-Nofre, or Memphis.

But if Menophres is a city and not a person, then there is not a
single point left on which to erect a chronological system. As already stressed, in all the periods of Egyptian history with which we
deal in the present work—the time of the Hyksos, of the New Kingdom, the Late Kingdom, and down to Alexander the Great—there
is not one known Egyptian reference to reckoning by the years of a
Sothic period.

Even if Menophres was a king who lived at the beginning of an
era, and the era was a Sothic period, the difficulty of identifying
Menophres arises. In the dynastic lists of Manetho, as preserved by
Eusebius and Africanus, there are various kings with similar-
sounding names, but none by the name of Menophres. King Mer-
nere of the Sixth Dynasty, Mennofirre of the Hyksos,[6] Amenophtah
of the Eighteenth Dynasty, Ameneptas and Merneptah of the Nineteenth Dynasty (from the lists of Africanus and Eusebius), or again
Amenophes and Merrhes of the Eighteenth Dynasty of Manetho as
preserved by Josephus—all might be regarded as possible claimants
of the name of Menophres, though not all were historical persons,
or at least not all are known from the monuments of Egypt. The

---

[4] See E. Meyer, *Aegyptische Chronologie* (Berlin, 1904), pp. 17–18.
[5] Borchardt, *Quellen*, II, 13.
[6] *"Beaucoup plus convenable serait Mennofirre de quelques scarabées 'hyksos.'"* Weill, *Bases, méthodes et résultats de la chronologie égyptienne*, p. 11.

most likely candidate seemed to be Merneptah, the successor of Ramses II, and it was he who was often proposed as the Menophres of Theon. But on a consideration which is a *petitio principii*, it was ruled by the Berlin School of Egyptologists that it was impossible to place Merneptah in the year −1321, the beginning of the Sothic period, "because the earliest date when Ramses II [father of Merneptah] could come to the throne is about −1300" (Meyer).[7] Therefore, Seti, father of Ramses II, is identified with Menophres of Theon by Borchardt and his disciples.[8]

This method of construction is entirely without foundation. The chronology of Egypt has to be constructed by establishing the time of King Menophres with the help of Sothic reckoning. If it is actually known that "the earliest date Ramses II could have come to the throne is about −1300," and that therefore his successor could not have begun an era in −1321, why, then, the roundabout method of computing the delay of the star Sirius on a calendar short each year by a quarter of a day and identifying King Menophres? The chronology is apparently fixed without Menophres and the Sothic period.

Because the accession of Ramses II to the throne is ascribed to −1300, the year −1321 must have been either that of his father Sethos (Seti), whose other name was Menmaatre, or of Ramses II's grandfather, Ramses I-Menpehtire. It is clear that any choice must be arbitrary.[9] And yet Ramses I-Menpehtire is usually selected as King Menophres, possibly for the sole reason that his one-

---

[7] *"Wonach diese Periode bei Theon benannt ist, wissen wir nicht. Der Name Menophris oder Menophreus könnte ägyptisch Merenre sein, mit eingeschobenem Artikel (p) vor dem Gottesnamen. Könige dieses Namens kennen wir nur in der 6. Dynastie, an die hier nicht gedacht werden kann; dagegen gibt es im 14. Jahrhundert und überhaupt im Neuen Reich keinen Herrscher dieses Namens. Wenn man also einen Königsnamen und nicht etwa einen Privatmann, z. B. einen Astronomen, darin suchen will, bleibt nichts übrig, als den Namen zu korrigieren—man hat sehr oft Me(r)neptah, den Sohn Ramses' II darin gesucht. Aber es ist gänzlich unmöglich, diesen ins Jahr 1321 zu setzen, da Ramses II. frühestens erst gegen 1300 auf den Thron gekommen sein kann."* Meyer, *Aegyptische Chronologie*, pp. 29–30.

[8] Borchardt, *Quellen*, II, 17.

[9] *"Man könnte auch etwa an Menpehtire, den Vornamen Ramses' I, oder selbst an Menmaatre, den Vornamen Sethos' I, denken. Damit wird aber der Willkür das Thor geöffnet."* Meyer, *Aegyptische Chronologie*, p. 30.

year reign is regarded as the beginning of the Nineteenth Dynasty.[10] But it is not superfluous to remark that in Manetho's lists of the kings of the Nineteenth Dynasty, in the versions of Africanus and Eusebius alike, there is no mention of Ramses I-Menpehtire; the dynasty begins with Sethos (Seti). If Theon used some version of Manetho and not the monuments of Egypt—which appears to be the case—then the identification of Menophres with the missing Ramses-Menpehtire can be made only at the cost of additional great strain.

Placing Ramses I in the year −1321, before any support for this was found in the statements of Censorinus and Theon, was entirely unwarranted. After Ramses I was thus identified as Menophres the reigning years of the kings of the Nineteenth Dynasty were calculated from −1321. On the other hand, the new-moon festivals of the Eighteenth Dynasty were computed, and the reigning years of the kings of this dynasty were found, by arithmetical addition. After the Eighteenth and Nineteenth Dynasties, the great dynasties of the New Kingdom, were assigned to their respective centuries by this method, the histories of other peoples were adjusted accordingly.

The historical structure was erected on these assumptions: (1) that there had been an era of Menophres; (2) that this era coincided with a Sothic period; (3) that this Sothic period began in −1321; (4) that Menophres was a king who lived at the beginning of this epoch. In addition to all these assumptions and surmises it was maintained (5) that Menophres was Ramses I, because the beginning of the reign of Ramses II was *a priori* (and without any sufficient reason) placed at −1300.

The chronology of world history constructed on these hypotheses does not seem so stable and secure as was thought; it looks more like an aggregation of many unconnected things each unstable by itself, piled precariously one upon the other.

[10] See Hall, "Egyptian Chronology," *Cambridge Ancient History* (1st ed.), I, 170.

Astronomical Incertitudes of Astronomical Chronology

A chain of logical argument is no stronger than its weakest link. In the chain of arguments on which hangs the chronological system of Egypt a few links are missing entirely. There is no need to proceed with further arguments on the fallacy of a chronology based on the reckoning of the era of Menophres and the Sothic period. We could therefore close the case. The obligation to show why the "astronomical foundations" of historiography are arbitrary and inaccurate has already been fulfilled, and it is not necessary to expose further errors in them.

We shall dwell on this theme a little longer only for the purpose of contributing positively to an understanding of the Egyptian calendar. However, in the course of the discussion, more of the fundamental baselessness of the astronomical-chronological reckoning will come to light. The astronomical foundations of the Sothic reckoning are also insecure.

First, there are a few perplexing items to consider. We gave credence to Censorinus' statement as to the date of Sothis rising heliacally on the first of the month Thot in +139 ("in the year of the second consulship of the Emperor Antonius Pius and Brutius Praesens"); certain support for this date was found in the calendar date of the rising of Sothis in the year of the Canopus Decree.[1]

But if one Great Year ended and another began in +139, the event must have occurred in the lifetime of Claudius Ptolemy, actually in the mid-period of the prolific writing (+127 to +151) of this greatest astronomer of antiquity. Claudius Ptolemy was a resident of Alexandria. Nowhere in his writings is the event ever mentioned; neither did he display an awareness of a Sothic computation though he dealt in great detail with astronomical and calendar matters of his own age and of preceding centuries, even studying the Babylonian records of the eclipses eight hundred years before his time.

[1] Cf. Säve-Söderbergh, op. cit., p. 37.

Living in Alexandria and occupying himself with these matters, how could he remain unaware of or silent about the advent of the new Great Year in Egypt in his lifetime?

In this connection it is also worth while to consider the retrograde astronomical calculations of the heliacal risings of Sirius in the sky of Egypt. In the beginning of the present century such calculations were performed by Percy Davis. In the year +139, according to his examination, there was no heliacal rising of Sirius on the first of Thot in Egypt despite Censorinus' statement: on that date Sirius rose approximately one hour before sunrise and was therefore high in the southern sky before dawn. Equally, on the three dates assumed to inaugurate three preceding Sothic periods, Davis found, Sirius rose about an hour before sunrise. If this calculation is correct, these four dates do not represent days of the heliacal rising of Sirius in the sky of Egypt.

The feast of Sothis, therefore, "must refer to some celestial phenomenon other than a heliacal rising." "Did it merely refer to the appearance [not heliacal] of Sirius in the nocturnal sky? If so, an entirely fresh set of calculations would be necessary, and it is doubtful whether any data sufficiently precise for the foundation of a chronological system could be drawn from it."[2]

The chronology of Egypt was not revised. The Egyptologists felt that by that time no change could be undertaken: the structure of the historical building was already completely rigid or, as Breasted put it, "mathematically certain."[3]

The very identification of Spdt (Sothis) with Sirius was also questioned. Duncan Macnaughton in an extensive work endeavored to prove that Spdt was the star Spica of the southern constellation Virgo and not Sirius.[4] Chances, however, are remote that any re-identification of the star Spdt, in the face of the explicit statement

[2] G. Legge, in Recueil de travaux relatifs à la philologie et l'archéologie égyptiennes et assyriennes, XXXI, La Mission Française du Caire (Paris, 1909), 106–12. Legge's conclusions were based on calculations made by Percy Davis. It should be noted, however, that the calculations made by Davis may be wrong. Perhaps he used Thot 1 of the Alexandrian calendar (August 30, 139) instead of Thot 1 of the Egyptian calendar (July 20, 139).

[3] Breasted, A History of Egypt (2nd ed.), p. 22.

[4] D. Macnaughton, A Scheme of Egyptian Chronology (London, 1932).

of Censorinus, would find acceptance in the scholarly world. Therefore, this question is slightly mischievous: Is it possible that by Spdt the star Canopus was meant? Sirius is the most brilliant among the fixed stars, Canopus is the second most brilliant star, thus brighter than any other star except Sirius.[5] Canopus is positioned south from Sirius, almost on a straight line drawn from it to the South Celestial Pole and closer to it; it is never seen from the Northern Hemisphere north of the latitude of Norfolk, Virginia; it is never seen at Palermo, Sicily, though probably it can be seen from the volcano Etna for a few nights of the year. In Egypt its appearance for a limited time each year is very spectacular. The fact that the decree fixing the New Year (first of Thot) on the annual heliacal rise of Spdt was proclaimed by the conclave of priests assembled at the town of Canopus (the Greek name of Per-gute in Egyptian) seems to offer support for such an identification. Canopus was the legendary pilot of Menelaus, brother of Agamemnon, leader of the Greeks at Troy; according to the legend, Canopus died in Egypt and the town of his death on the westernmost (Canopic) branch of the Delta (now filled with sand) was called after him and so also the star. Is it not more likely that the Greeks called the city after the star? Could it be that the place was called Canopus by the Greeks because of the decree composed there, dealing with the star Canopus? However, Herodotus earlier named one of the branches of the Delta Canobic.

I spelled out this thought for whatever it's worth. I will, however, stand behind a new interpretation of the Canopus Decree: as we shall soon find out, the decree speaks not only of the star Spdt, presumably Sirius, but also of the star Isis—and very mistakenly the scholarly world assumed that both names refer to the same star.

The Canopus Decree was composed by a sycophantic group of priests and called for adding a new festival to the glory of the king Ptolemy III Euergetes and his queen, Berenice, "the beneficial gods." The five epagomenal days at the end of the year were already

[5] Actually, Canopus is much larger and more brilliant than Sirius but it is over 300 light-years away whereas Sirius is but 8.8 light-years from us.

festivals to honor the Ptolemaic pharaohs; the conclave decreed that every fourth year a sixth epagomenal day should be added in all eternity to honor Ptolemy Euergetes and his queen.

The Greek, demotic, and hieroglyphic texts of the decree differ rather widely from one another. It was argued that the Greek text is the original and, again, that the original is the demotic script. Because of inconsistencies among the versions, it appears also that the scribes translating the text from the original, whatever it was, were not too well aware of the meaning of the text where it dealt with astronomical matters, and they certainly permitted themselves much freedom.

Another point demanding emphasis is the fact that though the text speaks of emendation of the calendar by introducing an additional day every four years, nowhere in any of the three versions is a reference found to 1460 (or 1461) years or to any Sothic period. Actually, the decree mentions a time when the year consisted of 360 days only and the reform when five days were added to the year. As I already pointed out, this by itself destroys all basis for computing the beginnings of Sothic periods in the second millennium or in the earlier millennia before the present era, a computation based on Censorinus but not on the Canopus Decree, which preceded the Latin writer by almost five centuries. But even Censorinus, following the discussion of the Sothic period, wrote about a calendar calculation based on 2484 years that separate one cataclysm from another.

Chapter III

VENUS

Venus

IF THE LENGTH of the year was accurately known in the second and third millennia, the deliberate neglect of a quarter of a day each year and the loss of twenty-five days in a century would have been a deliberate disregard of the degree of exactness attained by the Egyptian priests. Why should the Egyptians have perpetuated such an error through centuries and millennia if they recognized it?

The scholar who asked this question (M. Knapp)[1] supposed that the Sothic period pertained to Venus rather than to Sirius. Sirius is the most brilliant star, Venus is a still more splendid planet.

Venus, like Sirius, is invisible during a part of the year. But the periodic invisibility of Venus is not the result of the seasonal shift of the Northern Hemisphere out of sight of the stars in the south, as in the case of Sirius or Canopus. It occurs because Venus, revolving in a plane at only a slight angle to the plane of the earth's orbit, disappears behind the sun for about two months and six days, being eclipsed by the sun for this period.

When east of the sun, Venus is the evening star; when west of the sun, it is the morning star. Venus revolves around the sun in 224.7 terrestrial days. However, observed from the earth, which revolves on a larger orbit and at lower speed in the same direction, Venus returns to cross the line drawn from the sun to the earth

---

[1] M. Knapp, *Pentagramma Veneris* (Basel, 1934), p. 22. At the time of the publication of his book, Knapp was on the staff of the Astronomy Department of the University of Basel.

once in about 584 days.[2] This is called the synodical year of Venus.

Eight terrestrial years approximate five synodical years of Venus, the difference being approximately one day in four years. Five synodical revolutions of Venus equal 2919.6 days[3]; eight years of 365 days equal 2920 days, and eight years of 365¼ days equal 2922 days.

Claudius Ptolemy, in his *Almagest,* indicated that this sort of calculation was known in his time, one century before Censorinus and two centuries before Theon. He wrote that "eight Egyptian years without a sensible error, equal five circlings of Venus."[4] The small difference between five synodical years of Venus and eight years of 365 days was, according to Knapp, disregarded by the Egyptians for simplification.

In *Isagoge* of Geminus it is said expressly that the festival of Isis goes around the seasons in 1460 years.[5]

We can elaborate this thesis further and prove that Venus played the decisive role in the Egyptian calendar in the period following the seventh century.

Geminus' source was Eratosthenes, who lived in the third century before the present era and was employed by King Ptolemy III Euergetes in his library in Alexandria. In the Canopus Decree, edited under the same king, it is said that the feast of the star of Isis and other feasts go around the seasons, and in order that the calendar may correspond to the order of nature the year should follow the star Sothis. The difference between the calendar of Isis and that of Sothis is eliminated if one day is added to every four years of Isis, the calendar and the feasts becoming regulated by the year of the fixed stars.

Confusion on the part of the interpreters of this decree and of the Sothic period arose because the star of Isis and the star Sothis

[2] Although the mean synodical year of Venus is 584 days long, the length of single synodical years may vary by a few days, depending on the relative positions of the earth and Venus.

[3] Until recently it was counted at 2919.6097 days. More recently, from radar measurements, it is found to be 2919.57 days.

[4] Claudius Ptolemy, *Almagest,* Tenth Book, Fourth Chapter.

[5] Geminus, *Isagoge,* Chap. 8.

were supposed to have been one and the same—both Sirius. But
the star of Isis is Venus—Pliny says that Isis is the planet Venus[6]—
and the Canopus Decree may speak of two different stars. The
Greek text of the decree[7] says that "a general festival and procession shall be celebrated each year . . . on the day whereon the
star of Isis rises, which, according to the holy books, is regarded as
the New Year . . . but if it fall out that the rising of the star shall,
in the course of four years, change to another day, the festival and
procession shall not be changed," and it should be held on the same
day as in the year of the decree. The calendar should follow "the
present settlement (or, constitution) of the world" so "that it may
not happen that some of the popular festivals which ought to be
held in the winter come to be celebrated in the summer, [owing to]
the Star . . . changing one day in the course of four years, and that
festivals which are now kept in the summer come to be celebrated
in the winter in times to come, even as has formerly happened."
It was ordered that an additional first day be added every four years
to the original three hundred and sixty days and to the five days
that had been added to the year at some earlier date.

The accepted interpretation of the decree considers that both
the star of Isis and the star Sothis designate Sirius; the question was
not even raised as to whether Sothis and Isis, mentioned in the decree, are two stars. However, Budge himself, when translating the
Greek text, realized that the reference must be to two different
heavenly bodies, and consequently assumed that the sun must be
mentioned.

Besides, a little reflection would tell us that the date of the heliacal rising of the fixed star Sirius would move slowly around the
calendar of 365 days, *advancing* on it a day every four years but
not around the seasons, occurring always at the same time in the
summer. The heliacal rising of the planet Venus moves around the
seasons, around the natural year of spring, summer, fall, and winter,

---

[6] Pliny, *Natural History*, II, 37.

[7] Quoted from the translation by Budge, *The Decrees of Memphis and
Canopus*, Vol. III, *The Decree of Canopus* (London, 1904). Cf. W. Spieg-
elberg, *Der demotische Text der Priesterdekrete von Kanopus und Memphis*
(*Rosettana*) (Heidelberg, 1922), pp. 70–76, 89.

and around a calendar of 365¼ days, being *retarded* by almost two days every eight years or one day in four years. Thus the name of the star of Isis, explained by Pliny as the planet Venus, and the statement that its heliacal rising goes *around the seasons* leave no room for doubt that the Greek version of the decree speaks of Venus and its relation to the star Sothis.

The demotic text, however, speaks of Sothis and then refers to the star that "delayeth a whole day every four years," but then speaks of the fact that "festivals which are celebrated in Egypt and which ought to be celebrated in the winter, come to be celebrated in the summer, the luminary [i.e. the star] changing his place by one day in every four years. . . ."[8]

The decree was intended to free the calendar from observations of the time of the rising of Venus by introducing a leap year every four years. The New Year (on the first of Thot) was connected with Venus but the "Opening of the Year" with Sothis, and two separate terms were used, *tpy rnpt* and *wp rnpt*.

The festival of the Opening of the Year traveled around the calendar, but the festival of the New Year wandered around the seasons. The intent of the conclave was to have the New Year festival made to coincide with the festival of the Opening of the Year. What sense would it have made to celebrate the heliacal rising of the star Sirius 1457 times in 1461 years on days that were not the days of its heliacal rising and only once for four consecutive years in this long span of time on the proper day? Would we call a day in August or December the vernal equinox?

The reform of Ptolemy Euergetes and the priests of Canopus did not take root. The reason for this is explained in a scholium of Germanicus.[9] This annotator said that the king of Egypt (in the time of the Ptolemaic pharaohs) used to swear in the temple of Isis to keep the year 365 days long and not to introduce intercalated months or days that would interrupt the revolution of the festivals. This, too, is more readily understood if the promise of the kings was intended to allow the calendar to follow the festival of the

---

[8] Quoted from the translation by S. Sharpe, *The Decree of Canopus in Hieroglyphics and Greek* (London, 1904). Cf. Spiegelberg, op. cit., p. 71.
[9] Germanicus' translation of Aratus' *Phaenomena*, ed. Buhle, p. 71.

planet in the temple erected in its honor. Why should the star Sirius be offended by a reform that would make the holiday of the rising of the star coincide with its actual rising?

As has been stated before, the reform intended by Ptolemy Euergetes was introduced by Julius Caesar, who, two centuries later, established a calendar with an intercalary day every four years. This calendar was enforced in Alexandria by Augustus and probably inspired Censorinus, more than two centuries after Augustus, to write that a mistake of a quarter of a day in a year accumulates to a whole year in 1461 years (of 365 days), and to add that in his time an era of this duration, related to Sirius, was observed in Egypt. The Egyptians outside Alexandria continued to celebrate the heliacal rising of Venus, to keep the New Year on that day, to have a year of 365 days, and to allow the holidays to move slowly around the seasons. Claudius Ptolemy wrote the very illuminating words quoted above, that eight Egyptian years, "without perceptible error," equal five circlings (synodical years) of Venus. However, since there is a difference of about 0.4 of a day between these two periods, the question may be raised, why at some longer interval of time the difference should not become obvious and make the Venus year and that of 365 days part by one day, and after another score of years, by another day? It could well be that Venus' synodical period in earlier times differed by less than 0.1 day from its value today if Venus was still in the process of reducing the ellipticity of its orbit to one nearly circular. The fact is that the same equation of the synodical period of Venus to eight times 365 or 2920 days was not limited to the Egyptian time reckoning.

The Synodical Period of Venus
and the Festivals

For centuries observations of the day of the heliacal rising of Venus or Ishtar were carried out by the Babylonians,[1] the Mayas,[2]

---

[1] See S. Langdon and J. K. Fotheringham, *The Venus Tablets of Ammizaduga* (London, 1928), for bibliographical data on these tablets.

[2] "They kept records of the days when the Morning Star appeared [heliacally

and the Incas[3] in hemispheres separated by oceans; records were made and kept, some of which are extant. It is well known that the Mayas also observed a Venus calendar, and it is strange that Egyptologists paid no attention to the fact that "the Mayas reckoned the Venus years in groups of five, making 2920 days equal to 8 years of 365 days."[4] Neither did the students of the calendar of the Mayas draw any conclusion from the Egyptian calendar.

The Mayas, more than a thousand years before the discovery of America, also knew the exact length of the solar or tropical year.[5] Nevertheless, they did not discard the Venus calendar but continued to observe it after America was discovered. This fact parallels what we found in the double calendric system of the Egyptians in the time of the Ptolemaic Dynasty.

The Venus calendar shows a close coincidence with the year of 365 days at intervals of eight years. The eight-year period could easily be divided in half, each half composed of two and a half synodic periods of Venus, the inferior conjunction and the middle of the superior conjunction being the dividing points. Accordingly the Venus year in Egypt was equal to four years of 365 days.

Thus it was that Horapollo spoke of an Egyptian year that was as long as four years.[6] This statement has ever since seemed very strange to the commentators, who used to assert that there is no such natural period. But here is the explanation.

Ancient and modern authors alike who wondered at Horapollo's

rose] and set with such accuracy that they never made an error," wrote Ramón y Zamora, who, in the sixteenth century, studied the beliefs and traditions of the Mayas. See E. Seler, *Gesammelte Abhandlungen zur amerikanischen Sprach- und Altertumskunde* (Berlin, 1902), I, 624.

[3] E. Nordenskiöld, *The Secret of the Peruvian Quipus* (Göteborg, 1925), Pt. II, p. 35.

[4] J. E. Thompson, *A Correlation of the Mayan and European Calendars*, publications of the Field Museum of Natural History, Anthropological Series, Vol. XVII (Chicago, 1927); C. Ricci, *Las Pictografías de las Grutas Cordobesas y su interpretación astronómico-religiosa* (Buenos Aires, 1930), p. 22.

[5] See notes of W. Gates to his translation of *Yucatan before and after the Conquest* by Diego de Landa (Baltimore, 1937), p. 59, and Gates, *The Dresden Codex*, Maya Society Publications, No. 2 (1932).

[6] "A year among the Egyptians consists of four years." *Horapollo*, II, lxxxix. See J. G. Wilkinson in G. Rawlinson, *The History of Herodotus* (London, 1858–60), II, 285.

statement too easily forgot that in Greece also the great year, or
the year of the Olympiad, was equal to four years. The feast of
Olympia had been observed since the eighth century before the
present era; at first, it is assumed, it returned every eight years,[7]
and later every four years. At Delphi three ancient festivals—the
Stepteria, the Herois, and the Charila—continued to be held octen-
nially until later times. The Daphnephoria, a festival of Thebes in
Greece, was also celebrated every eight years. The Pythia, a festival
recurring every eight years, was changed in the sixth century to
a four-year festival. The Panathenaic processions at the Parthenon
in Athens were held every four years.

The historians who deal with this problem of eight- and four-
year festivals cannot find an explanation for these periods and ask:
Why should a festival return once in eight years or four years if
nothing in the agricultural life of peoples is tied up with these periods?

In Mexico, too, according to an early authority, Bernardino de
Sahagun, "every eight years these natives celebrated a feast which
they called Atamalqualiztli."[8] Among American Indians festivities
connected with the heliacal rising of Venus have continued down
to our own times, and their description indicates that many rites
observed among the Mayas celebrating the heliacal appearance of
Venus have survived unchanged.[9]

The eight-, later the four-, year period of the festivals had the
same origin in Mexico, in Greece, and in Egypt. They were related
to a synodical year of Venus, called also "the queen of heaven."[10]

[7] "An interval of eight years was inconveniently long. Hence we may suppose the practice arose of celebrating not only the beginning but the middle
of the period, just as the beginning and the middle of the month had their
special observances. . . . The change took place at Olympia at least as early
as 776 B.C." E. N. Gardiner, *Olympia* (Oxford, 1925), p. 71. See also L. R.
Farnell, *The Cults of the Greek States* (Oxford, 1896–1909), IV, 293, and
J. G. Frazer, *The Dying God* (London, 1911), p. 78.

[8] Fray Bernardino de Sahagun, *A History of Ancient Mexico*, I, trans. F. R.
Bandelier (Nashville, 1932), Appendix to Book II, "Account of the Festival
Celebrated Every Eight Years."

[9] R. Linton, *The Sacrifice to the Morning Star by the Skidi Pawnee*, from
unpublished notes by G. A. Dorsey, Field Museum of Natural History Department of Anthropology (Chicago, 1922).

[10] Jeremiah 44:18.

The Egyptian calendar of 365 days was tied to Venus so that every eighth year the heliacal rising of that planet fell on the first day of the month Thot: it was the New Year. The shifting of the heliacal rising of Venus after eight years by approximately two days in relation to the seasons can be observed at simultaneous heliacal risings or settings of the planet and of any southern fixed star. In order to compare the heliacal rising or setting of Venus with the rising or setting of the fixed stars, the brightest among them, Sirius, was chosen. There are symbolic allusions in Egyptian drawings to their functioning as a team,[11] and the Canopus Decree refers expressly to the relative motion of the star of Isis with respect to the star Sothis.

The confusion of Venus with Sirius renders obsolete the astronomical computations made for Egyptian chronology. If this is not enough—and enough it is—then the calendar reforms made in the middle of the second millennium and in the eighth to seventh centuries of the first millennium before the present era stand as strong obstacles to any attempt to use Sothic reckoning or anything like it as a chronological pathfinder.

But should the reader turn to *Worlds in Collision* he will find an abundance of evidence for sudden and violent changes in the order of nature. Sundials of Egyptian antiquity do not show proper time in the latitudes in which they were found; water clocks are not functional either, though intact; the Babylonian and Egyptian inscriptions alike refer to a time when the longest day in the year was three times as long as the shortest day, a ratio which changed in various periods; the North Celestial Pole was once in the Great Bear, but since the eighth century the North Celestial Pole has been in the Little Bear—the change was sudden; the vernal and autumnal equinoxes were transferred once by 30.4 days and on another occasion by 9 days; the orientation of the temples in Greece, in Palestine (Shechem), in Egypt, and the Sudan was altered; the length of

---

[11] W. Max Müller, *Egyptian Mythology* (Boston, 1918), p. 56: "Sothis-Sirius was early identified with Hathor or Isis. . . . A noteworthy representation also shows her in association with (or rather in opposition to) Horus as the morning star, and thus in a strange relation . . . which we cannot yet explain from the texts."

the month repeatedly changed, as did the number of days in the year (the Palermo Stone refers to a year of 320 days during the Old Kingdom),[12] as well as the length of the day; the calendars were again and again reformed and the beginning of the year was transferred in most civilizations of antiquity, always following great global upheavals.

In the face of all this and the cumulative evidence of sudden natural changes as presented in *Earth in Upheaval*, what structural strength is there in the edifice of astronomical chronology founded on the assumption that none of the natural elements changed in the least since the earliest time? But purposely I undertook to probe the validity of the Sothic period chronology without recourse to the arguments rooted in my other books.

"Three Pillars" of World History

The "astronomical chronology" is a framework of the scientific structure of Egyptian history and, consequently, of the history of the ancient world. Within this frame the dynasties of Manetho were placed along the centuries; the historical pharaohs were conjectured into Manetho's scheme. Ramses I of the Nineteenth Dynasty, whom Manetho does not mention, was identified as Menophres of Theon; the era of Menophres of Theon was identified as the Sothic period of Censorinus; the date, 139 of the present era, was taken as the end of that period and −1321 was fixed as the year of Ramses I; the time of the kings of the Eighteenth and Nineteenth Dynasties was computed by means of vague calculations of moon festivals.

The specialists in astronomical chronology made their calculations and announced their expert results. The specialists in pottery took the results of the specialists in Sothic computation as a firm base on which to build. Specialists in the history of art, the history of religion, philology, and history in general followed. Difficulties were swept away and the findings of the specialists corroborate one another, and so they have scientific proof that their systems are

[12] L. Borchardt, *Quellen*, II, 33, note.

constructed with precision and are well fortified on all sides. The readers of cuneiform borrow dates from the readers of hieroglyphics; the Bible exegetes from the archaeologists; the historians from all of them. Thus there came into existence an elaborate, entrenched system that bears very little resemblance to the real past.

The Sothic scheme of ancient chronology is rooted in a fallacy; Menophres is unknown, if he is anyone at all; Manetho's list of dynasties is a bewildering maze. Yet the chronology of Egypt is erected upon these three "pillars" and the history of the world is built on this chronology.

INDEX